The hidden script

By the same author
Romanticism and Ideology: Studies in English Writing 1765–1830
(with Jonathan Cook and David Aers)

The hidden script
Writing and the unconscious

David Punter

ROUTLEDGE & KEGAN PAUL
London, Boston, Melbourne and Henley

First published in 1985
by Routledge & Kegan Paul plc

14 Leicester Square, London WC2H 7PH, England

9 Park Street, Boston, Mass. 02108, USA

464 St Kilda Road, Melbourne,
Victoria 3004, Australia and

Broadway House, Newtown Road,
Henley-on-Thames, Oxon RG9 1EN, England

Set in Ehrhardt, 10 on 12 pt
by Inforum Ltd, Portsmouth
and printed in Great Britain
by Thetford Press

Library of Congress Cataloging in Publication Data

Punter, David.

The hidden script.
Includes index.
1. English literature—20th century—History and
criticism.   2. American fiction—20th century—History
and criticism.   3. Literature and society.   I. Title.
PR471.P8 1985   820'.9'0091   84–15929

British Library CIP data available

ISBN 0–7100–9951–7

For Jenny

Contents

Acknowledgments *ix*
Introduction: fantasies and the future *1*

Section A: Narratives and the unconscious
1   J.G. Ballard: alone among the murder machines *9*
2   Angela Carter: supersessions of the masculine *28*
3   Doris Lessing: moving through space and time *43*
4   Beryl Bainbridge: the new psychopathia *59*
5   Kurt Vonnegut: the cheerfully demented *78*

Section B: Practice and theory
6   Fears of surveillance/strategies for the future *97*
     Fahrenheit 451 *100*
     The Sirens of Titan *102*
     'Morris in Chains' *105*
     'The Balloon' *107*
     Sovereignty and surveillance *110*
7   The politics of fear *113*

Section C: Trajectories through language and culture
8   W.S. Graham: constructing a white space *131*
9   Some cultural materials *154*
     Tommy *154*
     J.R.R. Tolkien and the legendary *157*
     The Englishness of Philip Larkin *161*
     'Dallas': modes of social identification *164*
     The naming of cigarette brands *167*
     Memorials to death *170*

Notes *175*
Index *188*

Acknowledgments

I would like to thank the following people with whom I have worked, during the last two years, in ways which – although they may not have known it – have contributed to this book:

Dr. Susan Bassnett (University of Warwick); Prof. John Broadbent (University of East Anglia); Dr Robert Clark (University of East Anglia); Anne Cluysenaar (Sheffield City Polytechnic); Prof. Ralph Cohen (University of Virginia); Dr Diana Collecott (University of Durham); Jon Cook (University of East Anglia); Dr Diane DeBell (Bell School of Languages); Dr Thomas Elsasser (University of East Anglia); Dr Colin Evans (University College, Cardiff); Dr Penny Florence; Tony Gash (University of East Anglia); Dr Su Kappeler (King's College, Cambridge); Jill Lewis (Hampshire College, Massachusetts); Barry Palmer (Grubb Institute of Behavioural Studies); Alix Pirani; Gordon Read (Devon County Probation Service); Jenny Roberts; Dr Mary Russo (Hampshire College); Lorna Sage (University of East Anglia); Dr Roger Sales (University of East Anglia); Dr Bernard Sharratt (University of Kent); Dr Allan Smith (University of East Anglia); Lorna Smith (University of East Anglia); Sun Jian (Fudan University, Shanghai); Joss West-Burnham (University of East Anglia); Prof. Bruce Wilson (St Mary's College of Maryland).

Parts of this book have been previously published elsewhere and I gratefully acknowledge editors and publishers for the following: parts of chapter 2 published in *Critique*; parts of chapter 8 published in the *Malahaut Review*; parts of chapters 1 and 6 given as a paper at the conference *Confronting the Crisis* and subsequently published in the book of the same name by the University of Essex, 1984, eds Francis Barker *et al.*

Introduction:
Fantasies and the future

Scene: the future, only a few years hence. There has been some
nuclear 'accident', and Britain has become a sinisterly nasty place.
Women have lost their freedom, and are frightened to go out alone;
the black population has been confined to the Pallisades – dangerous
territory for white visitors; education is too expensive for ordinary
people and government propaganda is beamed through cheap 'vid-
dies'; travel is almost impossible, but there are trains still, carrying
forced black labour to the nuclear stations. Rape is a commonplace;
fear and hate rule.[1]

As the year 2000 approaches, scenarios for the future abound; they are
present within what we conventionally refer to as the 'literary', but they
also provide some of the basic structures for televisual discourse, for
advertising, for the everyday formation of the image. It is one of my basic
assumptions in this book that these shapings of the future have a
relationship to unconscious wishes; never, of course, a simple relationship, whereby the wish is directly incarnated in the work, but rather one
which is fraught with reversals, duplicities, coverings, all the marks of a
difficult transition into consciousness.

It seemed to me when I began to write what follows that it might
nonetheless be the specific task of the literary critic to address the
'literary' in isolation; but I found myself revising this stance as it came to
seem increasingly arbitrary to break off this fragment of the social text
from other fragments in which it is embedded. It seems to me that the
literary phenomenon which we refer to as postmodernism, and which is
frequently assumed to have to do with fragmentation within the literary
itself, in fact emerges from a different constellation:[2] in Thomas
Pynchon's projections of chance and prediction, in John Barth's re-
assembly of the shards of myth, and in the work of most of the writers
who figure here, the effort seems to be more to do with a search for new

1

ways of bringing writing into alignment with forces at work in other discourses, and once again it therefore becomes apparent that we cannot seek the interpretation of literature in literary terms alone.

Thus the shape of the book. I have begun from the recent work (defined largely as the work written during the 1970s) of five writers whom I consider to be major, judging them against a criterion of discourse within and upon the unconscious. I have therefore, in Section A of the book, myself adopted a particular holistic fiction; I have supposed, perhaps within brackets, that we can make a kind of narrative sense of an individual author's career, and that we can arrange the images in an author's texts in a developmental way. Among these writers, four (J.G. Ballard, Angela Carter, Doris Lessing and Kurt Vonnegut) deal explicitly in the future, although often hedged with the implicit irony contained within the above quotation: these worlds may be in the future, but often only just, and their lineaments are simultaneously the contours of a rapidly evolving present. The fifth, Beryl Bainbridge, sets her texts resolutely in the present, and in an apparently more naturalistic mode; but, I shall contend, we can see similar materials welling up in this discourse of deprivation and family entrapment as in the futurists, and can produce a valuable counterpoint by setting her works in this other context.

It would then have been perfectly possible to move on through a series of other writers (Pynchon, Barth, Donald Barthelme, John Hawkes); but such a method generates its own significant problems, ones of which we have become particularly aware in the decade following the philosophical and psychoanalytic work of Derrida and Lacan. Centrally, these problems have to do with the fiction of wholeness: with the idea that common individual authorship somehow guarantees a coherence.[3] It seems to me that there is a general epistemological doubt about this procedure, insofar as it appears to derive from a specific wish for order which may itself be set alongside other unconscious wishes and brought to self-consciousness and self-criticism; but even more to the point, there is a doubt about it which is specific to the contemporary.

For it is a minor theme of this book that recent developments in literary theory (which now almost always mean developments in fields perceived as adjacent to literary theory which then proceed to inform a criticism which has its own doubts about the homogeneity and self-containment of its own disciplinary nature) have not taken place in isolation from literary practice: that many of the structures emergent in the theory are present also in the practice, and that we stand to gain by perceiving their interrelations.[4] The principal example, and one to which I shall return time and time again, is of change in our perception of the nature of the subject: here, I would contend, theoretical argument can be seen precisely as a refraction parallel to what actually happens to subjective coherence in the works of the authors under discussion.

And both of these refractions need themselves to be referred to changes at the level of the social formation. It is not, of course, simply a matter of claiming that, in some contentual way, theory and writing 'represent' historical development; but rather that the *forms* of historical development and technological change permeate all areas of the social text, and that this general text can only be interpreted in the light of wider changes in the actual situation of the subject in the West, and in the light of the social and political unconscious which is indissolubly though contradictorily wedded to these changes.

I have therefore moved, in Section B, to a pair of attempts to render this set of cross-connexions more visible. In Chapter 6 I suggest that, in particular, the work of Foucault can be seen as parallel to the more obviously imaginative work of the writers of fiction; and in Chapter 7 I suggest that it is possible to relate the fears being repeatedly expressed in culture (here particularly film) to the political constellation within which writer/director and reader/audience operate. For the coherence of authorial involvement, I have tried to substitute a coherence of unconscious structure: insofar as the unconscious is structured like a language, then it cannot be a language at the personal whim of a writer or director, but must be one which operates as a set of rules, a grammar, across a range of cultural forms and manifestations.

In Section C, I have therefore begun by trying to take a specific authorial instance – the poet W.S. Graham – and to read his work as the history of a series of encounters with language; thus as a specific trajectory through recent reinterpretations of the role and power of the sign. But here again, of course, there is a search for coherence, for stability and origins. And, it needs to be said in parenthesis, it is of course *not* the consequence of post-Lacanian psychoanalytic theory that we can simply, by an effort of will or technique, discard this search; only that we can attempt anew, at all stages, to subject the search to an investigation of unconscious wishes, can try to raise to the surface the governing principles of critical investigation and set them too alongside the other manifestations of a social text which is riddled with doubts about teleology and the validity of global constructs and hypotheses.

Later in the third section, in what is rather arbitrarily labelled Chapter 9, I have attempted to move a little beyond earlier procedures, by assembling some varied cultural materials and trying to probe them without subjecting them to prior hypothesising about overall shape. During these later parts, I have on occasion abandoned the focus of the earlier part of the book on the 1970s, because again this neat decadisation seems to be a principle which needs to be subjected to interrogation; although the 1970s remain, if you like, the temporary endpoint of enquiry.

I am aware of a paradox here: namely, that the attempt to relativise theory, to regard it as itself obedient to unconscious dictates, would in the end land us in a world of silence (and, indeed, in several of the fictions this seems to be precisely the underlying fear).[5] And so, on the one hand, I have found myself appropriating elements of theory (particularly, I would say, of Foucault and Barthes) while later trying to fit those elements themselves into a roughly psychoanalytic framework. But I have, on the other hand, not of course found it possible to move beyond or past theory altogether (and the wish to do so would itself be interpretable as, for instance, an example of a familiar contemporary anxiety about authority) and there is quite a bit of unreconstructed Freud around in my interpretations. There is also a set of assumptions about the political and about the nature and psychological structure of capitalism in the third quarter of the twentieth century, assumptions which deconstructionists would no doubt deplore as idealisation and 'semantisation'.[6]

I have myself, however, no experiential doubts about the epistemological status of labour and sexuality; and the attempt to wish away primal differentiations seems to me precisely the subtext of Derridean 'différance', seen as a wish to substitute for the possibility of social progress (now deeply bracketed in the West) a struggle at the purer level of language. And this then enters into its own circularities at the extreme point of post-structuralism, where there is a wishing away of solidity which produces a blank and empty landscape inhabited only by the shadowy forms of relations, a scaffolding for a building which is actually being destroyed (deconstructed).[7] I can appreciate this desire towards negation, particularly on the part of an intellectual stratum which peers towards its own supersession and the wind-down of educational provision; but the fact that we may no longer be called upon to occupy a place in the world does not (fortunately) mean that the world will go away or that the overall functions of criticism will be rendered pointless. It is, I would say, an evasion of the difficulties of this continuing task to collapse ourselves and our discourse into the apparently overriding dictates of the object, an evasion of the problems which arise when we are confronted with a paradigm in which we must inescapably reckon the experimenter into the structure of the experiment itself.

I could say, then, that in what follows I have tried to set in play the unconscious, the future and the relations between theory and practice; but such play will, of course, have only a provisional status. I have also tried to take on, to an extent, the problem of pleasure. For it is not the case that the ideological fictions which surround us rule us by force; insofar as they offer us subject-positions, they also offer us precise pleasures (substitute gratifications), as the advertising operatives know very well. I have tried to enter into this pleasure of the text while treating it frequently as a cover-story for darker wishes; it is the dialectic which is essential, the sequence and ordering of ways in which we are persuaded of the possibility of tolerable accommodations within a world where the intolerable has become part of the substance of our daily living.

Section A:
Narratives and the unconscious

1 *J. G. Ballard:*
Alone among the murder machines

At the heart of J. G. Ballard's fictions, there are, alongside each other, a strong, almost obsequious adherence to narrative and an equally strong erasure of character; and it is from this clash that much of his extra-ordinary world is born. In one form or another, this is the structural origin of much science fiction, and usually also responsible for its major weaknesses; but in Ballard, it is raised to an entirely new level of self-consciousness. Where character is concerned, Ballard is one of the few writers who can be sensibly termed post-structuralist: the long tradition of enclosed and unitary subjectivity comes to mean less and less to him as he explores the ways in which person is increasingly controlled by landscape and machine, increasingly becomes a point of intersection for overloaded scripts and processes which have effectively concealed their distant origins in human agency. It is as though, as we gaze at individuals, we undergo a visual slippage: the web on which they are suspended shimmers into view, and we are driven to refocus our attention, to notice how, at apparently different points of the web, similar intersections occur, character repeats itself, so that our notion of uniqueness becomes an illusion born of ignorance and we are reduced to the nodes through which pass specific channellings of energy, caught like marionettes, blown by the 'wind from nowhere'.[1]

Thus Ballard's landscapes are dried out, sapless, 'thirstlands': the parching heat and enervation suffered are the symbolic reflections of a yearning for a fullness of subjectivity which has been transcended by mechanism and the massive systems of information and data which order decisions and supplant choice. Often we are invited to collude in a fiction that these are regions of the future, but there is barely any separating distance, and a mass of local detail in fact forces on the reader the knowledge that the 'difference' is not a projection into the future but merely a slight relocation of perception, wherein the monstrosity of our environment might at any moment spring into focus. At any moment, the simplicity of plot structure is liable to be invaded or temporarily replaced by slabs of these other, dehumanised discourses: technological information, projections of nuclear destruction, ritual celebrations of culture heroes and heroines. It is as though the individual hangs on to a discourse which he or she can own only with enormous difficulty, often in the end failing entirely to do so: the pressure of these other discourses is too great, the areas of language already colonised by the public media too developed to allow for more than the slightest insertion of a discourse of individual desire. Even our deepest wishes owe little to anything we might recognise as instinct; instead, they are the surfacing effect of multiple implantations at the base of the brain, the gesturings produced by automatic programming while crews of scientists look on to observe the extent of our power to delude ourselves into believing in free will.

Far from joying in the omnipotence of language, Ballard nevertheless celebrates its power in his ironic portrayals of the individual scrabbling for purchase on the rock-screes of words which surround us, hem us in, limit our potential for individual brutality by setting up systems in which that brutality itself becomes a curious object for inspection. As in any system of determinism, there is simultaneously a marvelling in the capacity for self-destruction and a casual forgiveness, for after all, we know not what we do. It is not that there is no possibility for further evolution; it is precisely evolution to which we are condemned, but as we move forward we leave behind most of what we had imagined to be cherishable, and only with great difficulty do we acquiesce in the formation of new goals, new objectives, which appear to be laid down by forces greater than and outside ourselves. Everywhere we have implanted icons – photographs of dead film stars, records of murderous and murdered presidents – supposing that, in the cultural flux, they can be discarded when the time is ripe. But they have a greater material presence and force than we had dreamed; indeed, it is the icons themselves which seep into our dream-time, which provide the points of reference against which our action takes place, and refuse conveniently to slide away into the sand-dunes when we try to elbow them aside. We fill the stage with inscribed backcloths, enormous cartoons, objectified repositories of desire, and then spend our time wondering how it is that this stage machinery continues to form an apparatus which increasingly circumscribes the stage itself, increasingly dictates the forms of discourse and activity in which we can engage.

Even the name, the guarantee of individuation, breaks down and becomes interchangeable: each time the balance of force shifts, the texture of social reportage alters, so we too change, become continually and pointlessly reincarnated as the sum of a slightly different set of programmed responses.[2] Within the Dalek, the modicum of the fleshly which has appeared to provide its driving force and which has supposed in turn that the gain is protection, defence against environmental hostility, atrophies and has to fit itself into the tiny spaces left in the interstices of the masses of moving metal. The flesh is always about to be damaged: nuclear warfare, the technology of resources, the apparently simpler technologies of supermarket and motel all multiply to crowd the space, producing an increasing repertoire of sharp edges which threaten us with decapitation, castration, mutilation. There is nausea in these texts, the sickness born of a dizzying fear that while we are keeping our eye on the skies for the next 'rain' of fallout or bacteriological chaos, the bulldozers will have moved in and flattened our house, our town, burst the bubble in which we move and thrown us out into the dead lands at the moment when we thought we were most safely hidden.

Here, on this 'terminal beach', the moment of pleasure, of leisure and holiday which our machines have achieved for us, will inevitably turn into a moment of terror as we look back to see that what we left behind has changed shape. It becomes dangerous to move at all, in case we step on the half-buried switch which will set the machines going, machines which may have been laid to trap us in the remote past or which may have been planted as failsafe devices against the end of the world. We may survive Armageddon, but not for long: we have already seeded the earth with those subtler forms of destruction which will continue implacably to operate even though they are controlled by complexes of power which are themselves long since dead. Under the technology, we can discern the shape of the psyche envisaged as a mined beach, and may suspect a dreadful truth: that the lurking engines of destruction which keep us pinned down are in fact devices which we planted ourselves, to ward off strangers, to preserve our self from the encroachment of the Other, but which may now explode at the move of a finger. Thus as we make over our own individual development to an increasing concern with defensive procedures (as we hold our selves intact against the threat of de-individuation) we simultaneously create a psychic terrain which is uninhabitable even by us. We have carefully covered these anti-invasion devices in the sand of conformity, but we never thought to make a map, assuming that our technological servants would do that for us; now, if there is a map, deep in the bowels of the Pentagon or locked in the hardware of the military strategists, the computers will not disgorge it; we dread the fate we planned for our enemies, but below that we have a burgeoning suspicion that a different war is going on, that it is the machines themselves which have ownership of these devices, and that it is we, fragile and fearful, who have been programmed to lay traps for ourselves.

The beach is itself also a 'drowned world', and on and just below its even surface we are always liable to stumble over the protruding forms of a cityscape, the peaks of a skyline now buried beneath the desert, beneath the coming drought. We tread amid the ruins of empire, among the detritus of a civilisation which became top-heavy and broke through the crust of the world (broke it literally apart in the search for resources, which is also the effort to avoid being starved of love). Sometimes it is as though, if we could trace the half-hidden patterns in the sand, we could resurrect that power in a purer form; but below this, we suspect that it is too late, that all we might be able to achieve is an evasion of being sucked down ourselves into the suffocating sand, a survival in order to dance aimlessly, inscribing over the decaying manuscript of the West a 'requiescat' of futility and kicking a little more sand over the ambiguous face of Ozymandias.[3]

Within the interlocking technologies which form the geometry of our lives, our heroic identity is reduced to the meaningless letter 'A', which can be disassembled and reassembled in forms beyond our control: from Travis, Talbot, Maitland, Laing, to the names which are not even wholly our own (Blake, Wayne). Coupling with another individual, discursively or sexually, is no longer possible: we can impregnate the universe or nothing, because every act we undertake is in helpless series with other discharges of energy, every gesture is replicated down the line of mirrors, grains of sand fused into halls of glass. Thus we can only tremble on the brink of consummation: to undertake an act would be to risk the possibility of an unpredictable set of repercussions, as an atom fired in the fission machine brings down on our heads a rain of deathly particles, the shards of the personalities we ceaselessly break down as we fight for breathing space, our own fragmented selves and the tortured residues of others. Better, then, to empty out our dreams into the sand, for fear that they might, despite our wishes, move the universe and begin the terminal series of earthquakes.

The world of *The Atrocity Exhibition* (1970) is an architecture of death, amid which the reader is induced to seek the traces of a longed-for medication.[4] The central figure, nameless and discontinuous, travels along the hidden wires which hold up these brittle images – Marilyn Monroe, John F. Kennedy, Jayne Mansfield – while his course is plotted and the scientists try to image a future, try to catch and graph the glowing lines which mark the trajectory of the unanchored self. The old significations have drained away, and now the monuments of civilisation stand as vast hieroglyphs from which we try to deduce the shape of a set of purposes which evade revelation.

> *A History of Nothing.* Narrative elements: a week of hunting the flyovers, the exploration of countless apartments. With stove and sleeping-bag, they camped like explorers on the sitting room floors, Talbert refused to touch the furniture or kitchen utensils. 'They're exhibits, Karen – *this* conception will be immaculate'. Later they raced around the city, examining a dozen architectures. Talbert pushed her against walls and parapets, draped her along balustrades. In the rear seat the textbooks of erotica formed an encyclopaedia of postures – blueprints for her own imminent marriage with a seventh-floor balcony unit of the Hilton Hotel.
>
> Amatory elements: nil. The act of love became a vector in an applied geometry. She could barely touch his shoulders without galvanizing him into an apoplexy of activity. Some scanning device in his brain had lost a bolt. Later, in the dashboard locker she found a set of maps of the Pripet Marshes, a contour photogram of an armpit, and a hundred publicity stills of the screen actress.[5]

The search is for the node, the intersection of flesh and metal, which will carry meaning and will thus release pent-up desire, will permit a 'chimerisation' to begin the reabsorption of the machines back into our souls. All these manifestations of shape are encoded: somewhere, there will be a posture, an act of love, a full word which will crack the code and release the flood of meanings stored up in the anatomies of the city.[6] It is as though, having inserted ourselves so early into language, we are now powerless to use it; all we can do is turn the machine off for a while, experimentally, while we hunt. Deep in our unconscious, we have lost the power of image-making and have settled instead for a modelling of the impulse on the publicly available images of death and desire; as we act, all we do is approximate ourselves to one element or another of a pre-established dictionary.

Thus as we act, we accompany ourselves continually with retailed narratives, but those narratives are not our own: we are, from time to time, Western hero, corrupt politician, suicide – or we occupy other positions in those narratives of power. As we come to see that, come to see ourselves as suspended between sources of cultural energy, so the narratives themselves deconstruct, and we are spun outwards in fragments, centrifugally. As on a Wall of Death, we stop the machine at our peril, but if we can manage it successfully we find we have before and around us a stilled gallery of images, each refracting back to us some part of our painfully constructed story.[7] But as we move among them, searching, we experience only exile: dropped from the tension and the conflict, fallen from the moving wheel, we see only grotesques, signs which, when we perceived them relationally, appeared at least to offer a coherent picture, however horrific, but which now resolutely refuse inscription. We are lost in the night-time fairground, but all the while, through the gates, the experimenters are watching us, charting our paths, checking to see whether a flex of the arm, an inclination of the head against a tawdry background, will be the sign for the music to begin again, for the horses to leap and for the illusion of the organic to be once again formed.

The wish is to stop the world before its own centrifugal power spins us out of existence, flattens us into unnoticeable specks against the gigantic images of cultural self-destruction, but in *The Atrocity Exhibition* there is a curious doubling-back of that wish; it is not that we will begin the task of dismantling the fairground, or even find the hidden exit, for once it has stopped revolving we find that we too have ceased, and that our task is now to collect our selves again into human shape. Exposure becomes a multiple metaphor:[8] there is the exposure, the dizzying sickness which we suffer on the radioactive beach, the movie of the world stopped down to a succession of still shots, alongside the hope that, when the photographs the scientists are taking of our scramblings are developed, one of them may in fact show that vital/fatal conjunction, the matching of body and environment, the individual exposure which will in turn unlock the gate to a more human-shaped world, in which we will no longer be exposed to the wind which dries our bones and renders us transparent, jelly-fish through which the world reproduces itself visually and materially despite our cries of pain.

But to talk of that hope is to falsify Ballard's tone, for there is little hope at stake: this temporary ending, the freezing of the world, while it may seem at least to allow the establishment of a laboratory for productive experimentation, in fact merely serves to prefigure a more final freezing. Even by endeavouring to read the book of technology, we are playing the wider game and acclimatising to the changes of weather and temperature which symbolise the victory of the death instinct. Possibly there is a kind of survival at stake, but only through dissolution, through abandoning ourselves to the play of energy which criss-crosses us and mocks our unitary delusions. The only way in which we can continue to exist is by accepting our dissolved fate, by approximating ourselves increasingly to the stories Mother Culture tells us, and the only feelings which can gain plenitude are those which have already been experienced, as we vicariously join the martyrs of power in their deathspeeding limousines and feel that tug of millions of tiny hands on flesh which accompanies public existence and which also signifies the fate of the individual in a world characterised by overpopulation and resource starvation.

In *Concrete Island* (1974), the fate of the subject is expressed in an equally vivid metaphoric structure, and the problem of the adjustment of individual needs is foregrounded.

> Near the intersection of three giant motorways a speeding Jaguar has a tyre blow-out. As a result Maitland, the driver, finds himself completely marooned on a patch of wasteland, an island in a sea of hostile tarmac and high-speed metal. Here he must learn to survive with minimal resources, fighting for them with the island's other human denizens . . . [9]

Here the illusion of global knowledge is exploded, as is the illusion that we can recover the buried secrets of our origins: the ego is hemmed in irresistibly by a desolate pubic triangle. Maitland has to convert the rusted exhaust-pipes and tangled metal into use-value, but this happens only dreamily: in fact, nothing on the island is really any use, for the subject has ceased to be able to think of any uses to which things might be put. There is no possible knowledge, so in the end the experience of constant and surrounding surveillance, the imagistic equivalent of the internalised icons of the media, is itself converted into comfort: the endlessly speeding cars at least guarantee an end to striving, a closure of the task of discovery.[10]

As well as this new-found physical confidence, Maitland noticed a mood of quiet exultation coming over him. He lay calmly in the doorway of his pavilion, realizing that he was truly alone on the island. He would stay there until he could escape by his own efforts. Maitland tore away the remains of his ragged shirt, and lay bare-chested in the warm air, the bright sunlight picking out the sticks of his ribs. In some ways the task he had set himself was meaningless. Already he felt no real need to leave the island, and this alone confirmed that he had established his dominion over it.[11]

'Pavilioned in splendour', the ego can now abandon its shaping task: the only shape that matters is already given, and the investigations of the scientists cannot improve or alter it, any more than we can escape it; its edges cannot be changed. At the end, a police car goes by, searching, but Maitland is no longer interested: he 'thought of Catherine and his son. He would be seeing them soon. When he had eaten it would be time to rest, and to plan his escape from the island.'[12] But we know that this stage of preparation will be perpetual, an endless recitation of move-ment and progress that no longer has any grasp on the real.

Out there in the dark and the wild, Maitland does not grow savage, for he experiences no real opposition, only a continuous adjustment and scaling down of his needs. He presages a wider decline: if he is to see his wife and son, it will be when they, and through them the rest of the species, 'join' him in parallel isolations, realise their places on the web, retreat into the spaces left for them in the all-powerful lines of commu-nication. These lines have already frozen into the shapes of speed, the patterns left by moving headlights. It no longer matters to Maitland who or what is inside the cars: the species has divided for him into those who merely inhabit their machines, and those for whom machinery has become rubbish, a set of hieroglyphs which cannot be deciphered.

He gave up, unable to decipher his own writing. The grass swayed reassuringly, beckoning this fever-racked scarecrow into its interior. The blades swirled around him, opening a dozen pathways, each of which would carry him to some paradisial arbour. Knowing that unless he reached the shelter of the Jaguar he would not survive the night, Maitland set his course for the breaker's yard, but after a few minutes he followed the grass passively as it wove its spiral patterns around him.[13]

In this future, the grass provides a continuous production and erasure of meaning, a maze which really requires no interpreting effort since its patterns do not endure. There is a mirroring of 'joining and parting lines':[14] the unassailable fixity of the motorways and the incomprehensible motion of the grass.

As readers, we experience first a frustration at the apparent sparseness of Maitland's attempts at escape, his difference from Crusoe; we are then brought to realise, as he is, that what bounds the deserted space is not fact but wish, that the island provides the perfect setting in which to evade competitive demands and to share in a different kind of struggle, a struggle of adjustment. The power of escape becomes seen instead as a threatened return to the powerlessness of societal membership; only here at the still point can the subject still convince himself that he is experiencing real diversity, conjure unreal Others from the shadows, form the waving shapes into satisfactory adjuvants to the narrative of the heroic self. There is nothing further to be known by gazing outwards, for all the cars are the same: like sub-atomic particles, even their existence can be inferred only from the continuous tensed pattern they describe. Instead, we are brought to gaze in, into the 'arbours', although it is not that Maitland has any faith in an ability to make this dross and refuse into the habitable environment of earlier economic fantasies. He becomes instead the advance guard of passivity, and runs out of words (ceases to conjure meanings or addressees).

The concrete island thus symbolises a renunciation of the impulse towards the ideal society, and replaces it with a wish for abdication, yet in that act of abdication the self reasserts a useless sovereignty, apparently free from technological compulsion but free also from any location in discourse. Stuffed back into the womb, Maitland represents an end to differentiation, and thus himself comes to mirror the identical passing cars; a Genet of the machine, he weaves a texture for the world out of himself, covers the walls of his prison with images, yet these images are not of opposition and escape but of capitulation. His happiness comes to consist not in setting himself against the universal condition, but in seeing the universal condition contained in miniature within himself.[15]

Concrete Island and *High-Rise* (1975) both have an open connexion with cultural cliché: *Robinson Crusoe* and the disaster movie, the myth of solitude and the fantasy of survival. Encoded are two types of aspiration: the escape and the long slow climb, and the certainty that both only return you to the still point from which you began (the womb from which you emerged). What is not given is a bounding line, a conventional apparatus of values which would enable the reader to determine success or failure: 'the Eye altering alters all',[16] and what is reached is an accommodation, of a type still open to readerly interpretation. The endings represent two points of entry into systematic delusion, two ways of beginning to satisfy needs, but needs which have themselves been shaped through the narratives: the story-lines *are* the reduction and adjustment of needs, a twinned recognition also of the inappropriateness of masculine aspiration in worlds where the strength of the subject is demonstrably superseded.

In the dying high-rise block, the ego performs repetitive actions in the name of a sliding scale of goals. Life is a board-game, a bored game; the rules are set arbitrarily, the pointless circles of Ludo and the climbing and falling of Snakes and Ladders. Laing learns by a process of continuous forgetting, as a fantasy of leadership is tested in a world where there is nothing to lead except the barely living bodies of others who are also preoccupied with crawling from the wreckage. The reader is encouraged, largely stylistically, to readopt the conventions of childhood fantasy, where hostile worlds prove finally manipulable by the heroic individual: what is then studied is the price to be exacted, the failure of feeling when action is the only goal to be coveted and the failure of action when the world decides to drop its fiction of malleability. The paragraphs build up, here as in the earlier texts, by a kind of 'bricolage', hard-edged and terse, paralleling the construction of the motorways, of the buildings: thus the ego constructs itself from the very materials of its surroundings, and becomes incapable of escape. In the process of comforting ourselves against hostility, we take on the contours of that hostility: like Maitland, Laing is a sufferer under an inhumane system, but he is also the past and potential constructor of that system, a masculine power-broker who would still be building the wasteland if given the chance.

Thus Ballard exacts a kind of revenge, and condemns the technical operator to a lifetime of experiencing what he has created, reminded occasionally by those whom he has excluded from his systems (women, the derelict) of the double-bind: a representative of the captors is himself taken captive. In the reading experience, we thus find ourselves disquietingly capturing our 'selves', peering through the mirror at the all-powerful ego wriggling with despair and chained to the symbols of economic, social and military dominance. There is little attempt at real suspense, for little is necessary: the central narrative rule is a simple inversion, and incident flows from that inversion. The model is the television serial, or even situation comedy: a formula repeated, where in the end our satisfaction is mechanically geared in to the vindication of expectation, regardless of wider implications. Neither, however, a comedy nor a tragedy, *High-Rise* dwells in a world where adventure has shed its moral load; those characters who attempt to remember a concept of moral order become curious specimens for the memory to play over, and in the end Laing is 'sorry that Royal had died, as he owed the architect a debt of gratitude for having helped to design the high-rise and make all this possible. It was strange that Royal had felt any guilt before his death.'[17]

Somewhere, it seems, someone must carry the weight of acting out the end of the world and of the race: Laing thus welcomes others to 'their new world' of desolation and brutalisation,[18] for he has already effected a transition, and all that is left is the waiting, until the others catch up and recognise that the electricity has permanently failed. There will always be plenty of 'material' around, although its quality will inevitably diminish: the fear is not that the world might disappear, but that it might, through surfeit and repetition, cease to evoke an interested response. The holocaust is less likely than a kind of seizing-up, the parts becoming frozen into an ironic metal grimace. There can be no vandalism here, for there is nothing to protect; there is instead the strange purity which is a cover-story for undifferentiation, a kind of reverse ecology in which all things are connected to each other through their unuseability. *Concrete Island* and *High-Rise* are thus not cosmic fictions of entropy, which remain an American 'province', like interstellar space as a sub-department of the military/industrial complex; they are instead insistently surburban, the fiction of a (British) society which has already, through the abortive 'special relationship', abandoned its right to protest, and whose only role now can be as the less than conscious harbinger of the terminal tedium of the over-consuming West.[19]

In terms of gender, it seems that women may be farther along the road towards acceptance than men, for they end up incorporating the totally ambiguous sign. Eleanor and Alice may be dependent on Laing; but it could equally be that 'it was the two women who were in charge, and that they despised him totally.'[20] For sexual curiosity, Laing substitutes this curiosity of interpretation, but there is no doubt that the women are hermetically sealed, and that whatever secret they have come to embody (the 'feminine' as to do with generation and change, an understanding of the covert psychological purposes of power), there is now no key. Lying back and probably thinking of England, they demonstrate enigma.

Superficially, Ballard's masterpiece to date, *The Unlimited Dream Company* (1979), marks a break with the bleak contours of these dying worlds; the emphasis is on the possibilities for rejuvenation, on spinning out the theme of the flight to the stars through the body of Blake. William Blake figures as pretext, and many of the narrative devices appear to be verbal transcriptions of the habitual features of Blake's painting and engraving – the multitude of souls floating through liquid air, the transmutation of the material London suburb in all its detail into the stuff of dream, the investment of energy in the environment read as a state of continuous priapism, the consequent energising of the earth by a succession of metaphysical divisions and copulations. Where, however, this myth of the man become god reveals its connexion with the sand-floods of earlier Ballard is in the insistence on consumerist violence, engorgement, as a necessary precondition for rebirth: Blake (the hero) needs to absorb entire worlds, abandon children to wander forever through the 'dark meadows', the forests and landscapes of his own body in order to achieve the transcendence he needs,[21] and in any case this transcendence can take place only in Shepperton, where the line between material and fantasy is already eroded, where the omnipresent film studios demonstrate the filmic qualities of a life lived under conditions of surveillance.

It is as though Blake, with his Pied Piper delusions and early psychopathic tendencies, has been thinned beyond hope by his surroundings, and again it is only by stopping the world that he can reachieve a sense of wholeness. Stuck after his fatal crash in a realm where the boundaries expand like elastic and continually bounce him back to the still centre, he is thereby paradoxically enabled to convert the raw material of suburban life – the contents of the supermarkets and used car lots, the equivalent contents of the fantasies of housewives and executives – into energy, and thus he finds a place for himself in the systems of exchange, his dream of manpowered flight literally acted out in his absorption of souls and conversion of them into the force which will lift him ever higher off the ground. He tests different models for this carnivorous increase, from vampirism to the more beneficent versions which finally lift an entire population towards the sun; but behind them lies again the sense of nausea, vertigo, as though the sparseness and thirst which are the conditions of living in the meshes of capitalism here engender a massive megalomania as the only solution to the constant threat of atrophy – of the body, of the moral sense, of the future. In Blake's 'risings', sexual and aerodynamic, we detect the lineaments of a loop through time, as though the path directly forward into the future is blocked by excess of matter, an unbearable weight of deaths, and it is only by lifting ourselves past these blockages, at whatever cost, that we can reachieve a uniqueness, although it is one which can only be fulfilled in the conditions of the clinic – the actual clinic where the geriatrics sit and wait, Shepperton *as* a clinic and forcing-house.[22]

Confronted like his namesake with the unbearable constrictions of linear history, Blake becomes a dealer in radiance: at times he is able to bestow on the world the halo of a new vision in which every creature, every point of growth glows with a purer and more intense light,[23] but in doing this he is also enacting a version of market gardening, developing as in a laboratory the resources he needs in a world where there is no other available fuel. As he rises into the sky, so the demonic birds he has summoned lose their grip on the air and fall in feathered bundles into the streets, now newly converted into jungle paths. And within this complexly worked series of risings and fallings, we can also see a shadowy picture of the family. Like the earlier Blake's Seven Eyes of God,[24] there are seven (Blake's seven) characters (or character fragments) who remain, through much of the text, comparatively impervious to the development and demonstration of Blake's miraculous powers, and Ballard is explicit about their roles: father, mother, brother in Wingate, Mrs St Cloud, Stark; the tabooed sister who is also the only possible future mate (but to be 'taken' only on the wing, in dream) in Miriam; and the bonded group of three crippled children. Blake is the alchemical eighth, the figure just beyond the mystery:[25] in him, the oppositions of the generations and the boundaries between the sexes, the races, the species are blurred and fused as he impregnates each order in turn of the created world, yet these separated seven remain to remind him of those boundaries, remain the carriers of the structure of roles from which he seeks escape. As he struggles to overcome the division within the psyche engendered by role, so he appears to achieve victory over each of the seven in turn, but each victory is ambiguous: it is as though, by the end, it is after all they who have all along known the plot, who have in fact themselves conjured Blake from the river-bed, through a combination of 'Father' Wingate's amateur archaeology, his phallic probing of the deeps, and Mrs St Cloud's watchfulness, her receptiveness to the vision. The possibility is that, representing between them the forces of religion, domesticity, tradition, they have set a trap, and baited it with Stark and Miriam, sibling rivalry and the unattainable mate, and Blake has been dragged from the skies by the patterns they have woven. Each time he awakes from a dream (dreams which do, in fact, change the world) he nonetheless finds them all waiting, in the same places, a still tableau on the riverside lawn, and each of his attempts to remould Shepperton is simultaneously a question about how to thread his way through these static figures, to find a path between the frozen images of past conditioning.

Thus we are confronted again with a puzzle about agency; as in all of Ballard's worlds, there is an ever-multiplying complexity of available interpretations of the sources of power. All the rest of the world is 'unlimited' for Blake: he can impose on it his will, but for these seven he is still locked in position. Symbolically, the crippled children have a grave always ready for him, in case he should tire; they know they will succeed him when the power of his fantasies breaks under the strain, when his wings buckle and, like the raptor with whom he constantly compares himself, he finds there is no sustenance left after his depredations. Blake crashes through the roof of the tower of Wingate's church (breaks the father's phallic power) and the church is made over to him; but in it he undergoes a symbolic crucifixion, is framed for a purgatorial period within the shards of stained glass, becomes merely the barely moving enactment of Wingate's own desire for supersession.

What makes *The Unlimited Dream Company* a dizzying, heady text is Ballard's abandonment of himself and us in the midst of Blake's dreams, in a world where bright nature has returned but, just offstage, we can simultaneously hear the slitherings of that other, dark nature which will inevitably emerge into view.

> The air was bright with flowers and children. Without realising it, Shepperton had become a festival town. As I strode past the open-air swimming-pool I could see that the entire population was out in the streets. A noisy holiday spirit rose from thousands of voices. Sunflowers and garish tropical plants with fleshy fruits had sprung up in the well-tended gardens like vulgar but happy invaders of an over-formal resort. Creepers hung from the neon sills above the shop-fronts, trailed lazy blooms among the discount offers and

bargain slogans. Extraordinary birds crowded the sky. Macaws and scarlet ibis watched from the roof of the multi-storey car-park, and a trio of flamingos inspected the cars outside the automobile showroom, eager for these burnished vehicles to join the vivid day.[26]

But this world of surfaces and perceptual joying is not to be sustained without the sickening crunch of bone on bone as Blake ingests the lives of those who have become thus objectified; as he struggles to avoid the gaze of his 'family', so his own gazing turns into violence and exploitation and the process of sacrifice begins.

Soon after dawn, as I sat in the rear seat of the limousine, I found a twelve-year-old girl peering down at me through the window. Somehow she had made her way through the labyrinth of the car-park, up the canted floors crowded with brambles and bougainvilia [sic].

'Blake, can I fly . . . ?'

Ignoring the waiting sun, which I left to get on with the task of feeding the forest, I opened the door and beckoned the girl towards me. From her nervous hand I took her brother's model aircraft and placed it on the seat. Reassuringly, I helped her into the car beside me and made a small, sweet breakfast of her.[27]

The choice the text offers is stark (Stark is the other choice offered by the text, with his succession of attempts to bring the vision down to earth, by shooting it, or by dredging the remains of Blake's abandoned body from the sunken cockpit): to avoid the objectification which perennially threatens the individual, at the hands of family and a deformed society, Blake transforms himself, on our behalf, into the limitless eye, and reveals the demands according to which the limitless 'I' must function: taking the population of Shepperton into the skies, he simultaneously exports them, and is himself left on the beach, in a world evacuated of competition but also of 'company'. Yet Ballard does not resolve the issue, and the final vision of company parallels that at the end of the Ur-Blake's *Jerusalem*:

On all sides an immense panoply of living creatures was rising into the air. A cloud of silver fish rose from the river, an inverted waterfall of speckled forms. Above the park the timid deer ascended in a tremulous herd. Voles and squirrels, snakes and lizards, a myriad insects were sailing upwards. We merged together for the last time, feeling ourselves dissolve into this aerial fleet. Taking them all into me, I chimerised myself, a multiple of all these creatures passing through the gateway of my body to the realm above. Concourses of chimeric beings poured from my head. I felt myself dissolve within these assembling and separating forms, beating together with a single pulse, the infinitely chambered heart of the great bird of which we were all part.[28]

The dialectic is thus between emptiness and plenitude, and is predicated, again, on the impossibility of unitary subjectivity: Blake can either scatter himself through the universe, quivering drops of semen on each leaf, in each throat, or gather himself into the dark and enclosed form of the dead pilot, waiting below the surface of the river. In *Hello America* (1981), the same dialectic operates and again Ballard pushes the populousness of the world inside (by depopulating the North American continent) to make a space where dreams may develop and demonstrate the play of the instincts; not, that is, the instincts as given to us by Freud, but the instincts as they really are, shaped, warped and instructed by generations of accepted societal and familial violence. (John) Wayne travels an empty America (hope wanes) until he meets the only person who can exist amid the legacy of fantasy which still populates the abandoned swimming-pools, the decaying freeways, the nightmare of a jungle Las Vegas: a reincarnation of Charles Manson, escapee from a European asylum, a creature born of the putrescence of technology:

A metallic blue light, as if in some hospital intensive care unit, shone down on the marble-skinned body of a middle-aged man lying on a surgical couch in front of a battery of television screens. He was naked except for the towel round his waist, and held an aerosol inhaler in one hand, a remote-control TV unit in the other. The blue light trembled against his white skin, and gave it a look of engorged, unhealthy activity, that of trapped venous blood struggling to return to an over-active heart. His eyes were fixed on the tiers of screens, as if his real existence resided in this ionised flow of flickering images rather than in his own restless musculature.[29]

America has died, victim of resource greed, but its body lives on in this incarnated death-wish, which wants more than anything else finally to enact the nuclear doom which has been averted by the breakdown of fuel supplies. Surrounded, at the end, by the apparatus of a war control room superimposed on a gambling casino, Manson brings his own Titan down on his head, the self-defeating phallus tracing its inevitable self-destructive arc.

The text enacts the vengeance of an endlessly war-torn Europe, for too long at the mercy of distant warmongers, as Wayne and his various companions investigate the secret places of this body of death, the United States at last in its true disunited state, and draw back the jungle to reveal the coronary malfunction at the root of an insane and over-sanitary patriotism. In this future, the presidency is there for the asking, while the presidents themselves figure as a motley gang of semi-efficient robots, endlessly mouthing the platitudes and enacting the mannerisms which were their only claim to fame. Manson uses the still surviving detritus of technology, the 'limitless computerised tooling facilities'[30] abandoned in the flight from America, to build himself a new body, of weaponry and laser illusions:

> Behind him [Wayne] heard the sinister clatter of the two robot gunships, these blank angels which Manson moved around the sky. They came down from the night and hung fifty feet above him as he strode along the centre of the Strip, gatlings pointed at his back, camera zooms in their empty cockpits straining to catch Wayne's profile. Manson had named each of them now. Across the nose of the first gunship was stencilled *Hate*, between the gatlings of the second, *Love*. Wayne stared up at them, tempted to seize their landing rails and pull them from the sky. *Love* and *Hate*, the knuckle tattoos on the fists of the psychopath.[31]

Each member of the landing party brings to America a set of fantasies to be tested in an apparently empty land, but what they find is that, in the very geography and ecology of the country, the old dreams still hold sway, and the militaristic shaping of desire retains its strength even when there is nothing to fight for. The myth of moving further West results merely in another encounter with imperialism, prefigured and shadowed by Manson's vast laser projections of the images of America, Monroe, the cowboy actors, Mickey Mouse, hollow icons of power which continue to threaten even when their substance has drained away.

There is thus no new world available, only a renewed struggle with ghosts, with the hauntings of a past which we have tried to forget. There are two things Wayne does not know: the identity of his own father, and the significance of Manson's adopted name. The suggestion is that these two forgettings have become elided: that Wayne enacts a striving to forget the past, to wipe out the terror of a bloody origin, yet it is the very enactment of that striving, the long haul across America, which returns him to the presence of trauma. Thinking he is moving away, he in fact moves back and circles closer and closer to the seed of decay. At last, a choice becomes available to him: to accept the vice-presidency under Manson, or to help Manson's erstwhile colleague Fleming (figure for a science professing its ignorance of politics) with a plan for escape. Fleming may be Wayne's actual father; but Wayne, almost under Manson's spell, initially decides that Fleming's glass gliders provide no real hope. Yet again, nothing is resolved: on Manson's death, the gliders do indeed fly, and Wayne with them, but here there is a further removal to fantasy, a further reticulation of the will to escape which has already more than once proved an illusion. There is, then, no America, no inflexible signified, only an interplay of signifiers, but this has nothing to do with a hope that we might be able to impose meaning: the play has already started, and our problem is about how we might insert ourselves into it, how we might begin a new meaning when the old ones still animate the twitching body of an intolerable state.

Ballard's texts present us with a gallery of images of the male ego as hero, but in order to demonstrate the forms of the clash between limitless aspiration and the material limits which a phallomorphic culture has already engrained deeply into the sand and stone. The image of Mount Rushmore recurs, the dead faces of power looking out over the desert which they have created. The masculine is a drying force in these texts, constantly associated with thirst and the agonising irritation of airless membranes,[32] but there is no salvation to be expected from the female: time after time, the expected consummation does not occur, until in *Hello America* we never even begin to suppose that Wayne, his mind filled with Western movies and the skyline of Washington, will move beyond a Boys' Own world. Land and sea are held in a fatal reciprocity: it is the alteration of the oceanic flow which has contributed to America's condition, and although Wayne has fantasies of breaching the Bering Dam and re-establishing a humane climate, these fantasies are drawn into Manson's web and contaminated, and the possibility of irrigation becomes itself mechanical, another stony outcrop of a man-made world.

The intense and fevered sexuality of *The Unlimited Dream Company* is incapable of differentiation, and ultimately onanistic: Blake moves towards a condition of continuous ejaculation, and thus dispenses with a specific sexuality which might draw him back into the nets of maturation. The white lab-coats of Miriam St Cloud and of the doctors in *The Atrocity Exhibition* are an ironic refraction of gender distancing: sex is either a guarantee of individual aggrandisement, or a minor surgical operation, as though, since sex is implicated in the systems of reproduction, it can only contribute to the perpetuation of a world from which the movement of the electrons has been stripped, a world of condensed matter and heavy water, where human fusion has been already replaced by nuclear fusion. Blake bombards the world in a sequence of attempts to remake its structure, but the energy thus released cannot move out of Shepperton, cannot spread but can only evaporate upwards or be sucked down into the river.

Thus the unlubricated style, the piling of paragraphs, the refusal of inward inspection become themselves parodic equivalents for the deathly masculinisation of the planet. As readers, we are constantly pulled into the hermeneutic code,[33] constantly placed as followers of a detective story or a Western fable, while at the same time we are haunted by all that is absent from this thinned version of narrative, a version of narrative which can nonetheless even encompass and shape within itself the fantasies on whose wings we might otherwise suppose a possibility of escape. We are sealed into the open-air prison of a terminal economic order,[34] locked into the speeding car alongside a grim-faced autopilot in whose features we eventually recognise our own; as we struggle to unlock the passenger door (to remember the point from which the journey started) we share in the sweating panic of those whom we knock aside or drive over, and eventually abandon ourselves to the delusion that, somehow, we might at least finish the journey safely, while renouncing any control over this all-commanding fusion of car and road, weapon and computerised track.

2 *Angela Carter:* Supersessions of the masculine

Angela Carter has now been charting the unconscious processes of Western society for a number of years, principally in her series of novels but latterly also in the form of a kind of psychoanalytic journalism and in *The Sadeian Woman* (1979), a major history and interpretation of sexuality and its acculturation.[1] What is important is to identify a principal shift of attention in this body of texts which occurred in the 1970s, through an examination of two of her novels, *The Infernal Desire Machines of Doctor Hoffman* (1972) and *The Passion of New Eve* (1977). That change can be expressed in plain terms, although these do not do justice to the convolutions of the psyche which structure the two texts. Both novels, and indeed all Carter's work, are to do with the unconscious and its shapes, and thus to do with sexuality, and in *Doctor Hoffman* this concern reaches a peak in the interplay of Freud and Reich which forms the underpinning of the text. But that peak is also a point of division, and what is new in *New Eve* is that the issue of sexuality is linked in a new way to the different issue of gender; that is to say, *New Eve* speaks – and, indeed, helps to form – a language in which it is impossible to conjugate the pure term 'sexuality', for the questions of ownership, agency and power which surround our use of language have been made manifest, and now there is 'male sexuality' and 'female sexuality', without an assumed bridge. The intensity of focus on hermaphroditism is present in both texts, but to different purpose: in *Doctor Hoffman*, hermaphrodites are merely the object of the gaze, the Platonic linked double to be worshipped and admired; in *New Eve*, the structures of hermaphroditism operate within the perceiving subject itself, so that the gaze is dislocated at source.[2] And the dislocation of the gaze entails also a primary dislocation of plot: it is significant that *Doctor Hoffman* is intensely reliant on literary models, from the picaresque pretensions of the hero (in some of his phases) to the conventionality of the love-plot in which he is enmeshed. *New Eve*, of course, is not without models; but the relation between plot and character is more twisted, if only because of the further depths to which Carter has taken her exploration of the construction of the subject.

For both novels are dramatisations of the constructed subject, and they relate to each other precisely along the lines of the development of recent theoretical debate about such construction, and specifically about the exact point at which gender enters as a structuring principle.[3] 'You could effectively evolve a persona from your predicament, if you tried',[4] Desiderio is admonished in *Doctor Hoffman* at one point, although Carter does not here go in for easy answers. Indeed, the 'answers' with which she presents us are exceedingly difficult, rather in the manner of the metaphysical speculations of Flann O'Brien:[5] and thus the question of the reality status – or, perhaps, varying reality statuses – of the 'phantoms' which Hoffman unleashes on the city remains to the end a matter for conjecture. That conjecture is simultaneously a metaphysical one, about the concept of the symbol; what we might term a semiotic one, about the relation between the sign and its referent; and a sociosexual one, for it raises the questions of the ontological location of desire and of the arbitrariness of change.

Imagistically, the 'question of reality' – and to give it this formulation is already to underestimate the powerful web of ironies through which Carter mediates this metaphysicalisation of the political – is represented in terms of opacity and transparency, vision and shadow. A key term, cropping up throughout Desiderio's wanderings like a talisman but never subjected to the indignity of abstract 'explanation', is 'persistence of vision', which carries two different but related meanings. First, it is this ambiguous persistence, manifested chiefly in the emaciated and academic shape of the Doctor himself, which achieves the alchemical transmutation of desire into material manifestation and thus threatens those limits of the conceivable which Desiderio ends up by defending. But second, it is persistence of vision which maintains our illusion of continuity in the world, which moulds our discrete presents into a coherent narrative. It is the proprietor of the peep-show, which perhaps causes these transformational phenomena, who points out that there is 'no hidden unity';[6] thus, that his demonstrations of carnality and violence become coherent and intelligible only through a 'persistent' trick of the eye and psyche, through a refraction of the perennial Oedipal search for origins.[7] Sexual energy is the key to the manifestation of desire; but to subdue this perpetual slow explosion to the logistics of orgasm and climax is to submit ourselves to a teleology which merely demonstrates our obsessional inability to escape from the family which gave us birth. The ultimate acrobats of desire, down in the technological hub of the Doctor's replacement universe, embody postponement, or perhaps a hidden fear of premature ejaculation; certainly it is premature ejaculation which occurs in terms of the narrative itself, as Desiderio knows: both in that, within the mutual fiction of the later course of the world which Desiderio weaves around himself and the reader, we are supposed already to know the outcome of the story through history books, and also, more concretely, in that he gives us the conclusion of the story ahead of its 'natural' place, and himself bemoans the fact: 'but there I go again – running ahead of myself! See, I have ruined all the suspense. I have quite spoiled my climax.'[8]

The Doctor's system, for system it is (the unconscious here is very deliberately structured like a language), operates on the basis of continuing possibility, and it is this which strikes the hard resistant material of the universe in the shape of the Minister of Determination and his Kafkaesque police force. The early stages of the conflict, of which Desiderio, the 'desired one', is going to become the solution, involve the Minister's attempts to prevent the Doctor's illusions from swamping the real by the use of various technological devices, none of which prove particularly effective in a world where objects may change their names, shapes and functions from moment to moment. One of these weapons requires for its efficacy the construction of a model of the Doctor's 'unreality atom', which turns out to be bristling with 'projections';[9] but these projections, of course, are not literal bumps but the material form of the psychological projections which colour and shape our apprehension of the Other. The universe Carter portrays, however, cannot be simply predicated on the limitless power of these projections as far as the individual is concerned, for here ignorant projections clash by night; that is, projections ignorant of their own and others' origin, so that a battle of psychic power is enacted reminiscent, especially in the shape of the vampire Count, of the psychological power-struggles which lie at the root of sword-and-sorcery fiction.

Besides, since the projections teem from the unconscious, they can be *known* neither in their aetiology (the lost box of 'samples') nor in their manifestation; and we remain uncertain, in particular, about the nature of Desiderio's own unconscious. He is at once an allegorical figure for the object of desire, and thus undergoes transmutation with each book of the novel; and a representation of a historically specific type of alienated consciousness, which means that despite these transmutations he possesses a residual consistency felt as boredom and disaffection. It is precisely the survival of this root of tedium which provides him with the vacant strength to quash the Doctor's schemes, and at this level we can read the text as a series of figures for the defeat of the political aspirations of the 1960s, and in particular of the father-figures of liberation, Reich and Marcuse.[10]

But we can nonetheless plot the shapes of desire as the text envisages them by entering the kaleidoscope of what Desiderio variously becomes, even if he pulls back from the brink of immersion in these internal fictions and, indeed, never fully understands his own role in them. There is the faithful operative given a heroic mission; the visitant lover whose congress with the enervated Mary Anne precipitates her death; the compliant member of family which he becomes on the boat of the River People; the peep-show proprietor's nephew who, in a world of transitory freaks, possesses 'the unique allure of the norm';[11] the half-willing companion of the 'erotic traveller'; the again heroic killer of the black chieftain of cannibals; and, of course, over all the potential lover of the elusive Albertina. But the structure which is woven from these tales remains ambivalent. It might be that the Boys' Own quality of Desiderio's incarnations reflects a paucity of imagination, perhaps specifically of male imagination, on Desiderio's part; or it might equally well be that in these largely adjuvant shapes is reflected a specific historical role for the 'British' consciousness within international conflict, that the unconscious of the text, split as it is between New World and Old, has an even more precise bearing on cultural attitudes than would appear from the examination of Desiderio's attenuated psyche.[12]

It is only with the River People that he claims to feel 'at home', and this feeling is made the site for an appalling summary of familial claustrophobia. His putative child-bride appears at first to carry everywhere with her a doll, but this is next revealed to be a fish in doll's clothing, symbol indeed for desire and for the phallus but neatly bound up in conventional wrappings, slippery and to be toyed with as Desiderio is himself toyed with by her family. But this representation of captured 'difference' finally yields its secret, and is replaced in turn by a knife, the knife which will effect the real desire which the family has invested in Desiderio and will ensure that his knowledge, severed and offered with the hunks of his meat, will pass for ever safely back to the family and ensure a closed circle of deprivation and incest. From the doll to the fish to the knife, we move from pure representation through the shadowy realm of the symbolic into the ghastly manifestation of the real. It is the ambiguous realm of the fish which Doctor Hoffman's enemies suppose him, Nemo-like, to inhabit, although in the end it seems doubtful that this is the correct interpretation. Albertina, his daughter, describes the Minister's assaults on her father's efforts, and in particular that functionary's decision to 'keep a strict control of his actualities by adjusting their names to agree with them perfectly':

> So, you understand, that no shadow would fall between the word and the thing described. For the Minister hypothesised my father worked in that shadowy land between the thinkable and the thing thought of, and, if he destroyed this difference, he would destroy my father.[13]

The Minister employs a team of logical positivists to embark on this great work of classification, on the construction of a philosophy of identity, and, indeed, through the agency of Desiderio he is in the end successful and the forces of order inflict another crushing defeat on the uprising of the imagination; but then Desiderio is the 'new youth', has himself been formed by the Minister's society, by the society of apparent institutional order and totalitarian conformism. How, then, could it be otherwise? To Desiderio, even the form of the Doctor himself, which we may presume to be as malleable for the perceiving subject as that of his daughter, appears only as another grey-suited seeker after power, and Desiderio's cynicism brooks no culmination but a restoration of the 'absence' which bred him.

Doctor Hoffman, then, attempts a subversion of narrative, on the grounds that narrative is itself ideological in form, even before we begin to consider its content; in other words, that narrative attempts to bind together and naturalise the disunited subject and that this attempt is made at the service of specific societal interests. But this places us, of course, again in the hall of mirrors: 'Desiderio', the desired *one*, is also anagrammatically ambivalent: the name contains the 'desired I', but also the 'desired O', and this encapsulates the problems of subjectivity which the text explores. Desiderio reverses the tradition of the search, or rather he displays the ambivalence of that search. Alongside the seeking for self lies always the hunt for the zero, for the still point, the thanatic impulse which requires him to set all things at nought and thus to represent the 'limits' of consciousness in their most extreme form, as a closing in and closing down. What gives him privilege is his apparent lack of interest in the unification of the self; but this is associated throughout with a negation of value, and thus the final consummation with Albertina is turned almost accidentally into a series of deaths as Desiderio makes real the point of resistance which brings all the efforts of fantasy to emerge into the world down to dust.

The parallel between the operations of the psyche in its ambivalent dealings with unity and the operations of language is made apparent throughout. For instance, the ship on which Desiderio, Lafleur/ Albertina and the Count sail from South America begins to suffer from slippages in consistency; although, because of the strength of the Count's will, it appears to be an early nineteenth-century vessel, the captain nevertheless has a radio. But Lafleur refers to these slippages as 'puns',[14] which refers us in turn to an expanded Freudian notion of parapraxis, whereby it is through these apparently unaccountable and accidental knots in time and space that we can glimpse the almost mechanical workings of consciousness and language as they go about their business of providing us with the necessary ground of consistency on which we can formulate our illusions of the integrated self.[15] The parallel image is, again as in Flann O'Brien, the bicycle, the only means of transport which requires a continuous operation of will and thus the only one on which we can be sure of not falling prey to the Doctor's manipulations of the Real.[16] But it is, again, this inflexible will which is called into question in the shape of Desiderio, because it is his fate to will away pleasure for fear of the damage it might do to him and to others.

And the bicycle, again, connects with the view of social organisation in the text, which is characteristically double. The Minister sees his society, and the city, as a neat and harmonious web of interlocking institutions; the Doctor, on the other hand, states that he has chosen the city as the site of his ambiguous liberationism precisely because of the weakness of those institutions, because of their hollowness. Presumably these manifestations of 'advanced' society, like the more advanced forms of transport, suffer precisely because they do not require a continuous effort of will to keep them going, but thrive precisely on will-lessness, on the force of a custom whose origins have long been obscured. Thus again we come up against the ambiguity of the politics of the 1960s; is it that the apparent strength of conservatism has a real basis, in the forms of desire of a nation or of a sub-group within it, or is it a sham, will the walls crumble at the distant sound of surfacing desire? The Count himself shrinks and diminishes when his desires are thwarted, and the world he has imagined and thus brought into being consequently falls apart; but it is he who had 'lived on closer terms with his own unconscious than we',[17] and this is at least the guarantee of a temporary success in manifesting desire in the world around. What is also significant is that the Count may be seen in Carter's fiction as the last figure in connexion with whom this gift of living 'close' to the unconscious can be asserted in a way free from the ultimate divisions of gender, the last figure so far in Carter's writings who escapes or transcends the gender distinction which she will now come to see as the major structuring principle in the organisation of subjectivity.

The Passion of New Eve is dedicated to America, and as the novel unfolds the meaning of this inscription becomes clearer.

> It [New York] was . . . an alchemical city. It was chaos, dissolution, nigredo, night. Built on a grid like the harmonious cities of the Chinese Empire, planned, like those cities, in strict accord with the dictates of a doctrine of reason, the streets had been given numbers and not names out of a respect for pure function, had been designed in clean, abstract lines, discrete blocks, geometric intersections, to avoid just those vile repositories of the past, sewers of history, that poison the lives of European cities.[18]

New York has, of course, become precisely such a vile repository by the time Evelyn arrives there, although it could be said that the bizarre shapes of resistance which are haunting this city are less the relics of the past than the prefigurations of the future. But the point is nonetheless that there is a contradiction here, made actual in the decaying carcass of the city, between the neat lines of the skeleton and the grotesque abundance of flesh, between the grids of the streets and of electricity and the prowling lines on which the muggers, prostitutes, lunatics, criss-cross those grids. It is not that one kind of order is disappearing below another: rather, that a moment is being recorded at which one fear gives way to another. That which is dying, encumbered by the weight of historicity, is itself a fantasy: if New York were projected along these lines, the product would be a vision of total order, total organisation, Brave New World. What is happening is that such a fate is beginning to fade from consciousness and is being replaced with its darker twin, the evolution into chaos. From this conflict of fantasies spring the shapes of the landscapes through which Evelyn, and later Eve, passes; but also at root, of course, what is being represented is a conflict between the genders, although of a highly complex form and at such a level of psychoanalytic self-consciousness that its lines remain difficult to grasp.

Carter herself gives various explanations, through Leilah and other characters, of the internal connexions between different levels and stages of the narrative; in particular, what is emphasised is a struggle between symbolisation and the forces of history, so that in the depths of the book we can see a political battle between symbolic action (writing, the formation of the new self, the representation of Woman within women) and historical action, guns blazing – although there is no question as to the materiality of both of these modes. Thus Eve herself becomes passé in the very moment of her new inception: while the finer points of the nature of the 'new woman' are being explored by the technicians of Beulah, the world is collapsing and we are confronted with the fearful necessities enjoined by a power vacuum. And here, we sense a problem: for the autodestruction of phallomorphic power is clearly not going to produce a situation in which new forms can simply flower in the desert. On the contrary, the women are doing military training with nuclear hand-weapons (!) just as the blacks are sealing themselves into the armed fortress of Harlem, and although Leilah/ Lilith's commando group are distinguished from the others by the fact that they wear no uniforms, in all other respects they adhere to the new conformities of guerilla warfare.

Which brings us directly to the symbolic heart of *Passion of New Eve*, which has to do with mirroring.[19] We can list a number of crucial instances, crucial interchanges across the silvered boundary. Leilah's existence as whore is predicated on an everyday refraction of herself into the perceived Other, in which shape she figures male fantasies as she arrays herself in the form of the totally fleshly; her self slides away in a haze of narcotics and she reimplants herself nightly before the mirror, soulless, a self-creation of painted nipples and exotic furs. As Evelyn speeds away from her, having reduced her to the plight of grief which will provide the narrative dynamic for the rest of the book, he senses that by his contact with her he too has locked himself into Wonderland; although the fullness of this realisation is long in coming. 'I felt that I was in a great hurry but I did not know I was speeding towards the very enigma I had left behind – the dark room, the mirror, the woman'.[20]

Later, Leilah redoubles herself: the existence which is predicated on the mirror is stripped and reincarnated in the form of Sophia, Evelyn's guardian through his time of transformation and rebirth.

> This girl had been my captress; I recognised the face she had revealed when she unmasked herself to drink from her water bottle, but now she wore civvies, a vest or tee-shirt with, silk-screened on the front, a design based on the motif of the broken phallus that had greeted me upon my arrival at the town, and a skimpy pair of blue denim shorts. She looked, however, entirely and comprehensively clothed, even though so much of her skin was showing; she looked like a woman who has never seen a mirror in all her life, not once exposed herself to those looking glasses that betray women into nakedness.[21]

Evelyn's brief attempts to convert Sophia into an object of male fantasy are entirely unsuccessful, and his bafflement serves to prefigure the moment when, transformed by the obsidian scalpel of Mother, he/she looks into the mirror for the first time and experiences the vertiginous doubleness which, it is implied, is parallel to the feminine impasse: 'when I looked in the mirror, I saw Eve; I did not see myself. I saw a young woman who, though she was I, I could in no way acknowledge as myself, for this one was only a lyrical arrangement of curved lines.'[22] What, it seems, the new Eve does is experience, on behalf of the world, the wrench and dislocation which is at the heart of woman's relationship with herself in a world riddled with masculine power-structures: inner self forced apart from the subject of self-presentation, an awareness of hollowness, a disbelief that this self-on-view can be taken as a full representation of the person alongside the bitter knowledge that it will be, that at every point the woman is locked into the metaphysical insult of the masculine gaze.

At this point, of course, the structure of doubleness becomes too complex for narrative; we are not seriously invited, for instance, to explore the cohabitation of Eve's masculine and feminine selves within a female body, for instead we are to be offered the symbolic parallelism between Eve and Tristessa. The narrative of the mirror turns, for a time, into the narrative of glass, Tristessa's glass house (to which people come to throw stones) and her glass sculptures, shapes wrought from tears which achieve materiality by being dropped into the deep and scummy pool of the unconscious.[23] When the mirror reappears, it is in the caves which are the womb of Mother, to which Eve is (almost) finally returned.

> There was a mirror propped against the rugged wall, a fine mirror in a curly, gilt frame; but the glass was broken, cracked right across many times so it reflected nothing, was a bewilderment of splinters and I could not see myself nor any portion of myself in it.[24]

Eve, perhaps, has achieved freedom, although not through any particular actions of her own; it is rather as though, having proved useful in the incarnation of an idea, she may now be allowed to recede from the processes of history. In this respect she is rather like those Old Testament figures who, having had their all spent in one act of supernatural service to God – at God's own direction, and not their own – are permitted to shortcircuit the processes of life and death and to retire exhausted and, we may perhaps hypothesise, still only half-comprehending. From her part in the continuous cycle of the desert – it is the sand of the desert which is turned into glass, and the glass which is silvered into the mirror, in a process of alchemy which is constantly underlined, in Baroslav's production of gold, even in Zero's belief in sympathetic magic – Eve is allowed out to that other sand, to the far beach where there is the doubled blindness of Mother's caves and of the old woman with her vodka bottles, and where the absolute ocean forbids further development.

But the analysis of symbolism, of course, is inadequate in the absence of an analysis of narrative stance, and it is here that we sense the refractions of the mirror operating between reader and text. My own experience of the reading relations of the text, as a male reader, is bizarre, and makes me doubt – as it is designed to – the gendered structure of narrative. In one respect, the critique of male intellect is clear enough. Zero hates Tristessa – or, perhaps, he hates the sibilant (Sibylline) 'name-of-Tristessa', as a bulwark against which, we may assume, he has resigned all naming, attempted to become the absolute zero, refused the lures of language – because she has destroyed his potency; and thus he accuses her of homosexuality:

> I think Zero must have picked up some distorted rumour about Beulah, unless there was some other women's commune in the desert he might have heard of and speculated about; he fed his paranoia on rumours until his head was full of strange notions that cross-fertilised one another and ingeniously produced reams of

fresh, false, self-contradictory but passionately believed
information. He no longer needed news of the world, since he
manufactured it himself to his own designs.[25]

I take it that this is a definition of the male psyche; not, presumably, a
description of an eternal state of affairs, but a precise historical com-
ment on the condition of paranoid suspicion to which the masculine has
brought itself in a world where the feared rebirth of the feminine may be
about to recur. It is the logical consequence of the historical systems of
masculine competitive individualism, the bitter fruit of centuries of
monadic metaphysics; out there in the desert, something real may be
about to occur, a rough beast is indeed moving its (her) slow thighs, and
Zero's response is to inoculate himself against female power by arranging around him a set of living symbols of female subjugation and then to
construct his alternative, fantasised world in the hope that thus the
forces of change can be repulsed.

But the harder question about narration, about the ways in which the
sexes narrate the world, is both closer to the reader and simultaneously
harder to grasp, because it has to do with the mirror through which we
view the text. As a male reader, I find myself the victim of illusions.
Although I am aware that Carter is a woman, and although that extra-
textual consciousness is incarnated within the text in her obvious
proximity to Leilah/Lilith, I nonetheless find that the first-person narrative of Evelyn/Eve appears to me throughout, no matter what the overt
sex of the new Messiah at the time, as a masculine narrative. When
Evelyn becomes Eve, my experience is of viewing a masquerade; I read
Eve still through the male consciousness (Evelyn's) of what he has
become. It is as though Evelyn forms a barrier, a thin film which
stretches between 'Carter' and Eve at all points; and thus I too am forced
to tread that line, to respond as a male to the residual male in Eve.
Perhaps this is a recourse against humiliation, a refusal of the childed
quality of masculinity which is postulated both in Evelyn's encounter
with Mother and also, earlier on, in his fear when he is returned to the
artificial womb of Beulah:

> I was utterly helpless, in a strange land, in the strangest of places –
> buried deep in a blind room seamless as an egg deep in a nameless
> desert a long way from home. I broke down and I think I must have
> called for my mother because, when I did so, there was an explosion
> of soft, ironic laughter from the concealed loudspeakers so I knew

that, however silent they were, they were always listening to me. At that, my shame became too much to bear and I buried my tear-stained face in my cold bed. Oh, that low, bubbling laughter! 'Cry baby. Cry baby.' No humiliation like a child's humiliation.[26]

And yet, of course, the real humiliation is not quite that; rather, it is the re-emergence of the child at the inappropriate moment, the discovery that this solitude does not excite the enactment of male myths of heroism but is, instead, insupportable.

One of the many unlikely cities on which Marco Polo reports to Kubla Khan in Italo Calvino's *Invisible Cities* (1972) is called Thekla, and it is perhaps worth recording the whole of the account he gives:

> Those who arrive at Thekla can see little of the city, beyond the plank fences, the sackcloth screens, the scaffolding, the metal armatures, the wooden catwalks hanging from ropes or supported by saw-horses, the ladders, the trestles. If you ask, 'Why is Thekla's construction taking such a long time?' the inhabitants continue hoisting sacks, lowering leaded strings, moving long brushes up and down, as they answer, 'So that its destruction cannot begin'. And if asked whether they fear that, once the scaffolding is removed, the city may begin to crumble and fall to pieces, they add hastily, in a whisper, 'Not only the city'.
>
> If, dissatisfied with the answer, someone puts his eye to a crack in a fence, he sees cranes pulling up other cranes, scaffolding that embraces other scaffolding, beams that prop up other beams. 'What meaning does your construction have?' he asks. 'What is the aim of a city under construction unless it is a city? Where is the plan you are following, the blueprint?'
>
> 'We will show it to you as soon as the working day is over; we cannot interrupt our work now', they answer.
>
> Work stops at sunset. Darkness falls over the building site. The sky is filled with stars. 'There is the blueprint', they say.[27]

The 'blueprint' of Beulah, Carter tells us, is also 'a state of mind': 'in Beulah, myth is a made thing, not a found thing'.[28] Thus there is constant questioning of the limits of the 'natural'; Blake used the term Beulah for his land of restfulness, stasis, a retreat from the hard labour of political and interpersonal progress, relapse into the pleasures of the flesh and the delights of wordless music. Carter ignores this, or rather on occasions she savagely parodies it; what she takes up from the Blakean myth is the connotation of Beulah as the land where extremes meet, and here what is at stake are the extremes of technology and magic. Mother is a surgeon and a prophetess; she wields a ritual scalpel but she wields also a hypodermic syringe. Magic, says Evelyn, there masquerades as surgery, but this is by no means the last word; rather, it is the voice of a man who cannot believe that the script of magical matriarchy has also a material validity in the real world, cannot believe that efficacy and power can be conjoined with incantation and rite.[29] Zero's one-eyed view is much the same:

> . . . Tristessa, Witch, bitch and Typhoid Mary of sterility. She'd blasted his seed because he was masculinity incarnate, you see. Utilising various cabbalistic devices, Tristessa had magicked away his reproductive capacity via the medium of the cinema screen.[30]

And it is here, of course, that the cinema and the star system become the most potent and ambivalent images of the union of technology and charisma. What is at stake in the hovering presence of Tristessa is the shaping of fluidity: as she drops her glass sculptures into the pool and sees them harden on the instant into the frozen forms of pain, so she/he, a living person, is dropped into the alchemical medium of the screen, which corresponds to the mirror as prerecorded tape to the blank cassette, and frozen into the perpetual form of female suffering, his 'natural' sex, the referent, irrelevant in the system of significations of which he/she has become the lynchpin, hidden under the weight of desire.

To this name-of-Tristessa, Zero counterposes the interdictions of the Father, and foremost among them is the prohibition of speech.[31] This is coupled with his intense fear of female homosexuality to produce a world where, on his isolated ranch, all the lines of power and communication pass through his own body, and thereby acquire the imprint of his own mutilation. His control is only partially effective: it leaves, again, the trace of the double image, the whispering in the shadows, just as the attempt of the children's crusade, the 'Moral Majority', to practise self-control as a prelude to reactionary power leaves them whimpering in the night, for mother. As a representation of the still point, the urge towards control and stasis, Zero is obviously endowed with a good deal more specificity than Desiderio had been in *Doctor Hoffman*: the struggle of Eros and Thanatos, recognised already in the earlier text to be shaped by specific histories, is now shaped also and predominantly by the societal processes of gendering.

And it is this area which Carter goes on to explore in greater detail in *The Sadeian Woman*, a text which takes to an extreme point the problems of the manifestation of desire encountered in *Doctor Hoffman*. As an empirical history, or indeed as a history with traces of the empirical, the stance of *Sadeian Woman* appears at first reading tangential to the feminism which it ostensibly espouses; but what is really at stake is not so much a history as a reading of the sign and of the processes of sign-formation. For *Sadeian Woman* is a history of representations, but with the added implicit claim that that is all the history there is: we do not have access to a neutral world of 'facts', but are ourselves the constructs of desire, but particularly of those desires which are allowed approbation and material confirmation because they serve the interests of the social formation. It is pointless to say in response to *Sadeian Woman*, as has been said, that the claim that women are 'impregnated' with a will to submission leads into a stance of political defeatism;[32] according to Carter there is no eventual, Platonic essence of femininity which is done disservice by this claim, for the concept and stereotype of femininity is itself constructed within the overarching web of ideological forces which shape the substance of subjectivity.[33] It is not even a question of collusion, for collusion implies choice; rather, we are required to move into a world where the symbols and signboards are our total environment, behind them lying nothing but vacuity, or perhaps the nameless, shapeless essence of sexuality which Doctor Hoffman seeks to free in the form of nebulous time.

But if there is no world beyond the hoardings, this does not mean that no activity is possible, for we remain face-to-face with the work of interpretation, forced up against it at every point: for if the process of signification is built on the interlocking of projections and introjections, all the questions about our relation to the stereotypes remain open, as do the questions about the picture of society which we can form from our investigations of the semiotic milieu.[34] For, as in Ballard, nothing here is accidental: the least curve of a thigh, the faintest hint of proffered pleasure, on the cinema screen or on the tube-train advertisement, constitute the geometry of the social formation and can be read as such. Therefore each and every action, and especially each manifestation of sexuality, becomes instantaneously inserted into a code, becomes a fragment of text to be read. The endpoint of this self-consciousness, of this ceaseless plotting of event onto the structure of language, is the pronunciation of sex as impossible, and this motif is reiterated throughout Carter's fiction: from the rape of *Love* (1971) and the momentary encounter with the idiot boy in the earlier *Heroes and Villains* (1969), to the evasion of consummation in *Doctor Hoffman* and the lifeless mating of Eve and Tristessa in *New Eve*, the sexual act can be figured only as instant emission, an eruption of desire so small and so unsatisfactory that it serves only to confirm the boundary between the genders and the incompatibility of desires.

Eve's new body, equipped with an instantly pleasured clitoris but racked with unassuaged desire (for unity within the self, for unification with another) is the symbol for this promise which cannot be satisfied; and although *New Eve* and *Sadeian Woman* loftily, and even on occasion gloatingly, ironise this state of deferral, the suspicion remains that all ejaculation is premature, and that this truth applies also to narrative itself, insofar as the urge towards climax and ending is to be read only as the displaced version of an urge to return to the womb and obliterate self-differentiation. Insofar as we do not and cannot fulfil this urge, all else remains provisional, and to imagine that it could be otherwise is to immerse ourselves in fantasy – just, again, as this immersion in fantasy remains the only route open to the writer who wishes to avoid the ideologically collusive techniques of realism. Through fictions, our interpretations of the social codes may be enhanced; but only in the direction of isolation, rejection, an accommodation with death as the circle within which provisional actions take place.

The notion of an alternative accommodation, between the genders, is no longer on the 'agenda', and it is here that Sade, present throughout Carter's work, provides the bounding line, for in his life and works are figured a resolution which relies on a double movement: the adoption of the outward forms of violence and organisation which typify society, accompanied by a withdrawal of the inward to a still point from which all is ironised, and everybody looks much the same.[35] The divided self which has been produced in women cannot be reunified; but it can be turned into a weapon and a sanctuary, worn on the sleeve as the simultaneous mark of threat and rejection, of the conjoined liberation and despair which are signified by the broken phallus which, in *New Eve*, gapes backward to reveal the unslakeable womb beneath the skin.

3 *Doris Lessing:*
Moving through space and time

I do not intend here to attempt any kind of summary of the many and various strengths and achievements which make Doris Lessing one of the West's most significant writers; for more than one generation of women, at least, she has been demonstrably the most apt chronicler of social attitude and change.[1] *The Golden Notebook* (1962) stands out as one of the few attempts in English twentieth-century writing to get to grips with ideas directly in their personal dimension; decidedly not, that is, as filtered through the eccentricities of an individual consciousness but in their moving historical context, which is precisely where ideas actually assault us. Marxism and Freudianism figure here, as in other of Lessing's writings, neither as disem-bodies of thought to be come to terms with ratiocinatively, nor as backgrounds of idea which can be ironised through the romantic supremacy of the creative urge – neither, as it were, in an Eliotic nor in a Joycean mode – but as real elements in a lived web of relationships with an extraordinary historical depth. And historical depth here has little to do with an obsessive regard for the past: on the contrary, Lessing's skill is to robe the present in historicity, to convey to us the simultaneity of the ordinary and the momentous which is the true aspect under which history presents itself to us as we, inevitably, live it; or at least, as we would live it if we were able to emerge, to the extent that Lessing is able to emerge, from behind the shields and defences which we put up against the cold winds. And, of course, it is precisely in Marxism and Freudianism that we have historically experienced the divesting of those defences; in their multiple and complicated attacks on protectivism that we have been invited to find, as men and women trying to live against a felt background of alienations, some clues which will lead us, in our hesitant following of the thread in the carpet, below the bland and apparently encompassing assertions of liberalism.

And it is apparent from Lessing's writing that such liberalism, far from proffering us unheard-of freedoms, is intricately bound up with a last-ditch defence of the patriarchy; apparent, that is, not because Lessing offers it as her opinion that such might be the case, but because the structures of feeling in her work make it clear that it is indeed oversimple to regard the systems of determinism as themselves authoritarian. What the insights of Marxism and psychoanalysis offer, in Lessing's earlier texts, is precisely the possibility of a wider liberation, in the shape of a de-naturalisation of male supremacy which is, presumably, the essential prior stage to any possible exercise of freedom, between the sexes as in other, less important loci. It has been suggested before that Freud, among his other ambiguous achievements, undermined the tragic mode in that Oedipus – the essence of plot – becomes rewritten as a premoral account of life; it is therefore hardly surprising that Lessing's writing is sometimes weak on plot, because plot only begins to occur in the uncleansed wound which opens between fiction and autobiography. It would be foolish – and patently untrue – to suggest that Lessing is not wounded, that her writings heal the unhealable; nevertheless, the drive to avoid the benevolent but damaging incision is patent, as is the attribution of that dreadful surgical skill to the hegemony of an evasive male intelligentsia, bent on avoiding its own overwhelming fears. One of the other consequences of this stance, for Lessing, is that her books occupy a curious temporal space: her intentness on the present, evident above all in the painful ageing of the narrative voice, renders closure impossible, and at the 'end' of so many of them we are left spinning on towards the void, occupying lines into the future that many of us, and particularly men, would prefer not to have to imagine.

Four of her most recent fictions – *Memoirs of a Survivor* (1974) and the linked trilogy *Shikasta* (1979), *The Marriages between Zones Three, Four and Five* (1980) and *The Sirian Experiments* (1981), elements in the unfinished sequence *Canopus in Argos: Archives*[2] – take us unrelentingly in pursuit of this elusive future. In doing so, they move us increasingly on to a terrain where few assumptions are possible, and where specific differences in the present condition are propounded and worked through to increasingly difficult conclusions. It is of course true that in the process much of the paraphernalia which we have come to know as realism is left behind, and it would clearly be convenient to label the residue as fantasy; but this would be a misnomer insofar as it suggests that our imaginings of the future are inessential constructs tacked on to our experience. In fact, as Lessing knows, our concepts of the future are no such thing, but form the groundwork of present action: it is only in the light of our projections of the future that current thought and action take place, and only those systems which propound futures are likely to be capable of rendering that thought and action effective. This is not, of course, necessarily a proposal for revolution; on the contrary, it might merely amount to a proposal for resistance to antidevelopmental pressures. Nonetheless, the future exists for us prior to the present in important ways: without our imaginings, we have no impulse towards one load of hay rather than another, and since clearly we rarely actually find ourselves in that parodically stoic position, it must be the case that we find within ourselves from time to time sufficient reserves of imagining to render choice possible. It is, on the contrary, Beckett's immobile Murphy who is the rare and perverse phenomenon, perverse to the point where we recognise him as an excessively 'literary' figure.[3]

'Attitudes towards authority, towards Them and They, were increasingly contradictory, and we all believed that we were living in a peculiarly anarchistic community. Of course not. Everywhere was the same',[4] says the narrator of *Memoirs of a Survivor* near the beginning of her record, underlining the theme of authority which centres the text at the same time as stressing the proximity of present and future in this unspecified time. The experience of reading the text is vertiginous in that, since no time is specified, events and situations which sometimes begin by seeming to us to be conditioned by a currently unimaginable wind-down in services and social relations will continually reveal themselves as functions of what is, after all, actually going on. Never, of course, here: the derelict and violent landscape is not quite the one we inhabit, but it is the one of which we receive constant media glimpses, in Derry, Beirut, Glasgow. So the question becomes one of our own trust in authority, in the 'official account', and more particularly one of that peculiarly late-twentieth-century configuration whereby theoretical disavowel of the truth of that account can nonetheless continually fail to act as the propulsive fuel towards a greater degree of understanding.

In this respect no doubt Lessing is as much a victim as her readers, and we experience this particularly in her apparent espousal of a mystical way of seeing manifested in the 'world beyond the wall'. Yet there is a lack of arrogance in the narrative assertions about the relations between the world beyond the wall and the world this side of it which nonetheless continues to resist closure. Many possibilities are aired. It may be that that second world offers us a truth not otherwise available. It may be that it offers us the unconscious base, the base of desire and destruction, which promotes particular manifestations in the more familiar sphere – although if so, a question arises about whose this unconscious is, whether transpersonal or personal, whether rooted in the narrator or in her mysterious charge Emily. It may equally well be that it offers us a terrifying view of the ineradicable past – the familial past which has accustomed us to fear and scorn – and that, after all, our only hope in relation to it should be for escape.

Certainly it is the second world which throws up the resonant images: the egg which turns into an egg of iron,[5] the drifting leaves which endless sweeping (and weeping) leaves untouched, the various manifestations of travel between different 'levels'. There is some sense in which this is underpinning for the scenes of urban violence and generational aliena-tion, quasi-parental envy and fear of energy, the dialectic of civilisation and barbarism, which are played out, as on a film, before the narrator's commonplace apartment window. But the relationship is always ambi-valent. On the one hand, we are invited to ask of Emily, 'how could this heavy, dreaming, erratic child, so absorbed in herself, in fantasy, in the past, survive what we would all have to survive?'[6] But on the other, we know that she 'found the materials for her dreams in the rubbish heaps of our old civilisation'.[7] What is true is that the world beyond the wall is one from which there is no escape: whether we come to be able to recognise it or not, whether we acquire the gift of passing through the tawdry patterned wallpaper,[8] nonetheless that world will continue, as it always has done, to shadow our present and to unveil for us ambiguous hieroglyphs which we may choose to interpret as guides to present behaviour. It would be beyond the nature of that world to force itself on us as an insistent companion, as it would be beyond the nature of Emily's extraordinary pet Hugo to declare himself a dog, a cat, or a benighted and waiting human; yet in the face of that world we cannot avoid a question, a question which has to do with our responsibility for our present actions, and thus with the kinds of authority we are prepared or not prepared to accept. What if, indeed, we accept officialdom's abdica-tion, and with it, clearly, the abdication of that 'official' part of our own psyche on which we have so heavily relied? Are we then prepared to stomach the automatic authority of the 'Underground gang',[9] the children of violence and survival, or must we find some stopping-place, some residual faith in the autonomy of the softer emotions, some belief that Emily, within her trappings of insecure maturity, remains a child and that we have a better idea of what to do with children than our predecessors (and parents) did? 'We sit in the ruins of this variety of intelligence',[10] that is, of the variety of intelligence which has set up machines and systems which we can no longer operate; but what are we going to find to supplant those systems, at what point can we arrest the death impulse if we reject our hope in the conventional ordering mechanisms of society and psyche?

It is we who make the barbarians: so Lessing assures us time and time again. We are even shown in detail how we need to make them, how we need, through the agencies of social welfare and discriminatory education, to make the families she collectively refers to as the 'Ryans', need to make them so that we can have some external housing for the impulses towards communitarian anarchy which would otherwise tear apart the comfortable abodes which we place (and wallpaper) around our vulnerability. The patterns go back through the past: our need to make Ryans has been historically concomitant with our anal desire to purify our own children, and thus we have given birth to the cruel polarities of dirt and cleanliness, poverty and officialdom, abandon and overwrapping.[11] We need to make somebody small: our own children, who may never recover from our incessant reserving of size and authority to ourselves, and also pitied neighbours, who have been unable or unwilling to internalise the overspecified demands of maturity.

And it is perhaps thus also we who make the holocaust, who eventually choose to consume the entire unsatisfactory world as a natural follow-on to the consumerist excesses of imperialism. But here there is an ambiguity, which persists through Lessing's more recent work. For behind the scene of human action there is, clearly, another scene, materialised in *Shikasta* and its sequels as a larger galactic empire, with its own internal conflicts which are played out on a decaying Earth. So in a sense we are not responsible for our actions; and among the consequences of this is that the holocaust itself can be exonerated as a necessary purging. In *Shikasta* this is fitted into a vast panorama of reinterpreted historical and mythical stories, documenting the ceaseless interventions of others into the planet's affairs. The imagery consistently used is of bloodsucking, of the leaching away of life and energy by evil forces or by more present 'vampires'; and behind this we sense a fear of a population spread too thickly, one where individual action has largely ceased to be perceptible, and a consequent need for 'slimming down'.

And it is at this point that we can see the ways in which the unconscious structure of *Shikasta* indeed taps the roots in the Imaginary of

Europe's response to decline. The wish is to create a community, but a community of superbeings, and it is of no consequence that in the course of this painful and often catastrophic evolution the masses must go to the wall. The earth is cluttered up, so the argument goes: it has become impossible to discern the real lines of force (ley-lines, the arrangements of standing stones, meaningful cities); although there is still a modicum of communal feeling around, it is spread too thinly across the peoples of the world. It is therefore no accident that large parts of *Shikasta* select the Chinese as the enemy: a mass society is inherently impossible, a contradiction in terms. What we need instead is a slimmed-down workforce, able to take new stock of the world's resources; a myth of new beginnings, and one which we can trace now in the highly functional myths of the reactionary governments of the West.

This, of course, is not to condemn Lessing's politics; but rather to adumbrate the way in which the openness of these texts to everyday unconscious process reveals for us the unpalatable desires of a class and a region which is facing the collapse of a strongly held set of beliefs. We are again, as in *Memoirs of a Survivor*, bound hand and foot by our upbringing, by the endless reproduction of petty cruelty and by the exigencies of fitting ourselves uncomfortably into a world too small to hold us; because of this, we have become unable to recognise real authority where it still exists – in the visions of the asylum, in the extra one or two percent of vision which, for its bearer, makes conventional perception redundant. It would be easy to trace in this the trauma of the writer in an age of democracy and scarce resources, a new seeking for a vision of socially significant 'poesy' and a fear of a still-coming mass society for which the book may itself be redundant. For the new leaders whom Lessing portrays, the incarnations on Earth of galactic messengers, are the real possessors of authority whom we must heed; but they demonstrate that authority in a peculiar way. And here there is a contradiction in the text: on the one hand, the native official class is constantly derided because it has lost purchase on real events and has retreated into an ivory-tower world of words; on the other hand, George Sherban and his accomplices and acolytes, whose task is planetary renewal, function also through words, through endless talk. There is a discourse of impotence and a discourse of power. The former is charac-terised by argument, the primacy of individual concerns and opinions, the latter by innate acceptance, a level of unspoken sharing which lies behind and accompanies the word.

There are several crucial scenes of this type in *Shikasta*. One occurs when the principal messenger comes to Earth to speak to the Giants, who are the decayed remnant of the race originally placed here to help the Natives towards a rapid and healthy development. Originally, then, a benign people who are the bearers of the 'full word', they are gathered together in a 'transmitting chamber'[12] which is meant to amplify the togetherness of their deliberations; in fact, because they have already been corrupted, the meeting breaks down in petty argument and bickering. There is a myth here of the ideal group, the group of ten, so perfectly – and numerically – in tune that words become so replete as to be unnecessary. This occurs again when Sherban's brother attends a meeting to consider planetary problems, and at one point a level of communication is reached which enables individuals to sit in silence and understand; but this group focus is shattered by a representative of evil. These situations can be centred on another image, of the individual 'bound and gagged' while an 'inferior impersonator' speaks for him:[13] the disjunction between feeling and word is, in this text, the evidence of all that we lost when the breaking of the language in the Tower of Babel destroyed our group consciousness and armoured us in the encasing Selfhood.[14]

Johor the messenger, the spirit which is incarnated in Sherban, accounts for the all-encompassing nostalgia of a dying race in vivid terms, describing the fate of his fellow Canopean messengers amid the confusions of Earth's inhabitants:

> . . . it is only with the greatest of effort that we prevent ourselves
> from grasping at every sensation that seems to promise or guarantee
> a meaning, even usefulness – as these creatures do, who lacking the
> substance, chase after shadows, after anything that seems to remind
> them – for the memory is still there, somewhere deep in them, of
> Canopean truth. They look at the sun as if they want to pull it down
> to them, they linger under a moon which is much further away than
> I remember it – and they hunger, they yearn, holding up their arms
> to the sun, and wanting to bathe in moonrays or to drink them. The
> gleam of light on a tree, or on water, the brief heart-breaking beauty
> of their young, these things torture them, without knowing why, or
> they half know, and make songs and tales, always with the hunger
> behind, a hunger not one of them could define.[15]

Thus the hunger and thirst, the determinants of an unsatisfied and nostalgic culture, are in fact removed from the realm of psychoanalytic explanation, are severed from the initial childhood severance, and referred instead to literal memories of a time when life was longer, when the moon was closer, when the expectation of togetherness could be daily gratified. *Shikasta* incarnates a myth of the Fall with a frightening naturalism; and in doing so it offers us despair of any return except via the dubious path of submission to the unquestionable will of the benevolent galactic gods.

Thus our cities, for instance, actually drive us mad because they are out of cosmic alignment; our aspirations torment us because we have degenerated from the powerful races of the past. We are left with clutter and dictatorship, or that meeting-point of a cluttered dictatorship of the masses. We are the victims of an automatic process of fission which renders all politicking pointless and substitutive:

> . . . there was a recurrent phenomenon among young people: as they
> came to young adulthood and saw their immediate predecessors
> with the cold unliking eye that was the result of the breakdown of
> culture into barbarism, groups of them would suddenly, struck for
> the first time by 'truth', reject everything around them and seek in
> political ideology . . . solutions to their situation, always seen as
> new-minted with themselves. . . . Inside a cocoon of righteousness,
> for the essence of it was that they were in the right, these young
> people would live for weeks, months, even years. And then the
> group would subdivide. Exactly as a stem branches, lightning
> branches, cells divide.[16]

Thus a fascination with the dynamics of terrorism and the connexion with familial decay; again a focus on the all-important dialectic of age and youth, although to an even greater extent than in *Memoirs of a Survivor* the reliance on the young to rise to the occasion, even if only symbolically, threatens to upset the careful balances elsewhere achieved.

Turning from *Shikasta* to *The Marriages between Zones Three, Four and Five* is very much like experiencing one of those abrupt alterations of perception which Lessing is now so intent on describing. In place of the reports, illustrative materials, interplanetary messages, we have a long, drifting monologue. In place of the presumed vastnesses of a space empire, we have a geography of three zones none of which appears to be larger than an average English county. And in place of a narrative which

seems to exist primarily to effect new connexions between actual historical or mythical events, we have a fable set in realms which are clearly not
Earth, although the attempts to estrange them seem perfunctory. In this
change of mode and scale, we catch the attempt to produce a less
catastrophic concept of change: in realms which have, after all, not yet
evolved to a point where nuclear warfare might incarnate the destructive
urge, it might be possible for peoples, acting again under an unquestionable set of occasional edicts, to move together through the more gradua-
list imagery of marriage and slow accommodation. There is not a
prospect here of newness: rather, all the elements of a fluid world order
are present from the beginning, but located in different places: the task
of the imagination becomes to set this locked system in motion, to
permit flow across boundaries.

The crucial boundary is one of gender. In the long sequence of
engagements between Al Ith, queen of Zone Three, and Ben Ata,
warlord of the lower Zone Four, are spelled out in enormous detail the
incompatibilities of male and female desire and the processes of learning which might break through the non-alignment. It is clearly Ben Ata
who has most learning to do, learning about the possibilities of intimacy,
about the damaging effects of hierarchy, about the self-destructive
circularity of phallic domination and its habit of rendering its objects of
violence so abject that domination itself becomes a pointless and paltry
game. But there are also some crucial asymmetries elsewhere in this
simple structural dialectic. Zone Three signifies communality, proximity to the natural, a peaceful evolution whose problem is that it borders
on stagnation: at the beginning of the book reproduction itself is failing
as desire curls up comfortably and dies under the pressure of too much
delight. Zone Four signifies militarism, a land of heaviness and neatly
cut canals, sexuality patterned on rape. But also in Zone Four the sexes
have entered into a curious and sterile dialectic of their own, whereby
the women, forced into a position of exclusion, have evolved for themselves an underground movement whose object is to keep alive the
fragments of lost bliss, however shadowily they may be imagined and
however ritualised the ceremonies in which they have come to be represented; and the strength of this underground movement emerges in the
way the women child their men, acquiesce in the futile and hypocritical
wargames which keep the whole Zone in poverty and dereliction. In that
part of the text which carries most immediately obvious resonance with
current issues, these women, gratified and vindicated now that Al Ith

has brought certain news that Zone Three exists and holds out a hope of a more egalitarian life, mount an expedition of their own, but it is heavily indicated to be a mistake: the inhabitants of Zone Three are just as shocked by the appearance of these noisy and tasteless women as they earlier were by the armed male escort which arrived to take away their queen. Thus, presumably, essentialist feminism, whatever its function might be in the fallen world of Zone Four, the world of technology and economic degradation, will receive no credence in the world immediately above: the only path forward – or upward – is straight through the incompatibility of the sexes, through patient self-education and sub-mission to the inexorable will which has dictated the 'marriages' in the first place.

Much of the text has to do with the breaking of dependence, but ambiguously: dependence on the Other, and the grating claustrophobia which this produces, is to be rejected yet we are still adjured to give our allegiance to the higher will of the Protectors. At many points, the world of *Marriages* meshes with the worlds of Beckett's *Waiting for Godot* (1955) and Pinter's *Dumb Waiter* (1957): the principal characters wait for messages – at one point brought by a previously unknown and only half-glimpsed child, at others simply heard in inner space – and find themselves obeying them even when it seems that the effects will be disastrous.

Zone Four, Ben Ata's hapless kingdom, is flanked not only by Zone Three's William Morris-like beauties but also by Zone Five, also ruled over by a queen: and Ben Ata himself appears to become the channel through which the 'civilising' influences of Zone Three can be passed on further down the chain, and through which also some knowledge of the harshness of natural conditions can be passed up to impress itself on the stagnating minds of the higher orders. Where Zone Four is based on a farcical militarism which has no real wars to fight, Zone Five has wars which are real enough; there the cities are in thrall to nomad warriors whose queen is close to the warrior woman of films like Don Chaffey's *One Million Years BC* (1966).[17] In one sense, Ben Ata represents the central masculine block – his limbs are obsessively referred to as carved out of wood – which prevents flow and which must be shifted before a more mutual impregnation can take place; this shifting is accomplished by forcing him up against the contradictions in his own position. To Al Ith he is a barbarian, without finesse or thought; to Yahshi, queen of Zone Five, he is an organisation man, a repressed middle manager whose armed forces, of which he is so proud, have for long been a standing joke in the lower zone because of the absolute precision with which their manoeuvres can be predicted.

It is thus this doubleness of masculinity on which the text converges, strung between Al Ith's freedom of flow and Yahshi's random violence, between spirit and instinct. In bed with Al Ith, Ben Ata is a pleasureless slob; to Yahshi – but by this time he is already partially enlightened by his first 'marriage' – he represents an unaccountable sexual hesitation. Economically, the solutions suggested appear meagre and naturalising: Ben Ata sensibly reduces the size of his armies and turns the redundant soldiers over to land reclamation and urban renewal. There is no apocalypticism here: attempts to make a sudden leap into the future encounter a severe divine disapproval. Psychologically, the position is more ambiguous: the crucial figures, Ben Ata and Al Ith, suffer symbolically the fate of the unhoused individual, the figure who has seen too much and cannot escape the suffusion of longing, Al Ith isolated on the remarkable borders of the still higher Zone Two, the realm of flame and voices, while Ben Ata has to oscillate between the realms, his symbolic function partly taken over by his former chief of staff Jarnti, now retired from military service and endeavouring to find meaning in a life newly devoted to minor house repairs. Again, the question is one of authority:

> There are some who say that where there is rulership, there has to be criticism of this ribald kind, because no matter the level of the ruler, it is in the nature of the ruled to crave identification of the lowest sort. We say this is not so, and Zone Three proves it. To recognise and celebrate the ordinary, the day-to-day levels of an authority, is not to denigrate it. . . . Zone Four ballads, travelling upwards to us, found themselves transformed as they crossed the frontier. For one thing, there was no need of the inversions, the ambiguities, that are always bred by fear of an arbitrary authority.[18]

What, however, is the shape of a non-arbitrary authority, or one to which men and women can give free acquiescence? Lessing tells us, several times: 'we are the visible and evident aspects of a whole we all share, that we all go to form. Al Ith was, for most of her life, queen . . . the substance of Zone Three expressed itself in her in that shape . . . queen.'[19] Thus authority resides in the recognition that differentiation itself is a response to the life of a group, that the positions we may occupy are relative to the group as a whole, and in the consequent and unceasing effort to be reflexive about what we may as individuals be 'holding' for that group. In the very manifestations of our 'selves', we are through and through symbolic, and thus it is no paradox that 'to be brought up by women is to bring up a nation of soldiers',[20] for the overall economy of libido will reassert itself whatever our arrangements. 'Ben Ata's people's poverty bred monsters',[21] and those monsters are themselves precisely the form of unaccommodated need.

The Sirian Experiments returns us to cosmic perspectives, and seeks to insert into the pre-established dialectic of good and evil, Canopus and Shammat, benign necessity and unauthorised caprice, a third term in the shape of Sirius and its administrator Ambien II, a female dry as a leaf and tempered by millennia in the service of the Sirian Colonial Service. This third, mediating term is complex. Where Canopus runs an empire – and obviously by this time empire has become the central figure for Lessing's concerns, taking up and condensing the threads of her earlier African work – according to the principles of minimal intervention and species empathy, and Shammat according to violence and blood, Sirius holds to a different model. This empire's keynotes are administrative efficiency and carefully controlled experimentation, and Ambien's trajectory is from belief in the caring supremacy of this model, through Canopean tutelage to the beginnings of an understanding that even the most cautious of administrative decisions is fraught with danger if it is severed from real questionings about purpose. In the name of science, and for the assistance of other ruled species, Sirius uses the Southern half of Shikasta/Earth for a series of biosociological experiments, but without noting carefully enough their potential effects: at a key point in the text, Ambien is offered a vision of an evil South American empire where genetic engineering is built into the very social fabric, and comes to see this empire, with its amusing mutants and bloodthirsty experimental psychology as an image for her own practices, literally indeed as we are told that they have evolved precisely as a ritualised memory of all that has been done to them in the past by the visiting technicians of Sirius.

Ambien, the withered leaf, desiccated by service and duty, symbolises an uneasy colonial pragmatism, not only at the planetary level but also as a model for a certain kind of education which stops short of a consideration of ends. All is pieced together, to achieve a series of temporary stabilities, but meanwhile in the Sirian empire at large there is a growing awareness of what is disparagingly but hauntingly referred to as the 'existential situation', a creeping knowledge that a society which has produced a technology which can effectively end work has no defences left against the ensuing psychopathology. Invented tasks will not suffice; nor, indeed, will the drastic slimming down of Sirius' galactic populations save her from what becomes a necessary fragmentation of the group mind which has sustained this empire through the ages. Sirius, in many ways, represents current international practice: the automatic disbelief in the benevolent purposes of other powers; the consequent attempts to institute systems of total surveillance so that the unpredictable can be erased from the quasi-mathematical formulae which are used for control; the fits of impatience which mean that, once a certain level of technology is present, its use becomes increasingly impossible to avoid. In relation to Canopean method, the Sirian faults are of over-directiveness, and derive from a wish to bring other peoples, other planets, up to a level of development perceived as universally advisable – precisely the faults which, we are shown later, mutate into white dominance of the earthly globe and the erasure of the traces of other ways of thinking and behaving. Klorathy, on the other hand, the major representative of Canopus, operates through a cosmic version of non-directive counselling, arranging situations in which real needs can be felt and groups and societies can come at a reflexiveness about their own practices. Another of Canopus' agents reflects regretfully on the difference of the two systems, thinking about Ambien in particular:

> How it is possible that an Empire can be so large, so strong, so long-lasting; so energetic, so inventive, so skilled; how can it be so admirable in so many ways – and yet never have any inkling at all of the basic fact?[22]

The basic fact is expressed in various ways; essentially, it has to do with a version of totality, with the need to consider systems *as* systems, and thus with the necessity of avoiding arbitrary action. 'I think day and night about group minds and how they work',[23] writes Ambien near the end, when she has been thrust into the ambiguous and perhaps temporary exile which is the result of her attempts to bring Canopean tutelage home to her Sirian colleagues; and here she is speaking for Lessing, and for the whole of this massive fictional attempt to portray a world beyond the invented conceptions of individualism. Where Sirius fails to understand this systemic thinking, it does so precisely in the terms of that other master-text of imperialism and genetic engineering, Wells' *The*

Island of Doctor Moreau (1896), where an argument which might be cast in terms of basic purposes and needs is cast in the end merely in terms of relative pain and the quantity of interference which might be permissible.[24] The question of deviant individuals is only a perennial cover-story for the main question: 'may I . . . suggest', says the partially enlightened Ambien, writing of her own situation,

> another possibility for this deviant and so irritating individual? If he
> or she is not expelled, or does not expel herself, but remains,
> contemplating her position, then a certain train of thought is
> inevitable. She has been part of a group mind, thinking the same
> thoughts as her peers. But now her mind holds other ideas. *Of what
> whole is she now a part?*[25]

There is another way of putting this argument, and one which does not touch on the mystical. If a system exists through its allegiance to a specific task or set of tasks, then the breaking away of a fragment of that system, instead of being read as criminality or subversion, may instead be interpreted as evidence that this task or set of tasks is losing its hold at an unconscious level, that other forces are at work, that there is a discrepancy between perceived, proclaimed tasks and the actual unconscious processes which are at work in sustaining that system.

Accordingly, the role of Canopus is to figure a system which works by a continual process of reflection on task and unconscious process; Shammat, the violently self-aggrandising ego, attempts the total repression of such considerations; Sirius, pragmatically acting for a partial best, becomes the point of instability which will, in the end, arbitrate, even if unknowingly. But Sirius, and Ambien, are continually hampered because they are caught in a trailing skein of past guilts, historical espionage. Sirian government is clearly closely modelled on a kind of social democracy, or perhaps on the 'socialist' pragmatism of the Wilson years: lip-service to democracy abounds, while the actual rulers labour to conceal their own oligarchical tendencies. And to fuel false needs in a population from which knowledge of real needs is kept, there is a consequent dependence on a pointless expansionism:

> There is something in Sirian nature that demands, that flourishes,
> in situations of challenge, provided best by the takeover of a new
> planet, its problems, its regulations, its development. To *expand*, I
> maintain, if not normal for us (in the sense that it is *right*) is at least

the most agreeable condition. To monitor and police planets kept deliberately stable, and on a low level of energy generally, is *not* exhilarating, does not inspire and develop the members of the Service.[26]

With a text with this level of awareness of unconscious process, whose major concern indeed is with portraying the terms of the psychological struggle which underlies international relations, and which therefore holds within itself a powerful understanding of the political unconcious, there are barriers against moving further into its own depths. But certainly there is something hidden in the peculiar being that is Ambien, with her frailty, her thin pale hair, her dryness, her unquestioning longevity. Entering into her (symbolically: she has not, we are told, experienced physical relation although she is the mother of distant children) is to feel a set of contradictions: her existence challenges a protective urge, yet Sirius is neither weak nor strong. To represent the dilemmas of a cosmic Civil Service in female shape is to cut off several points of obvious narrator/reader attachment; and besides, it is not even clear in what Ambien's femaleness resides. Certainly not in sexuality, although there is a hovering fringe of desire in her successive attachments with Klorathy/Canopus and Tafta, representative of Shammat; yet her characteristics are never allowed textually to occlude our perception of her as female. Like a mirror image of Ben Ata in *Marriages*, she is the third term, the embodiment of a simultaneous, or alternating, will to learn and resistance against learning.

What is certainly significant is that in *Shikasta*, in *Marriages* and in *The Sirian Experiments*, a series of attempts is made to flesh out the puzzling dislocation of *Memoirs of a Survivor*, where the narrator, proceeding into the world beyond the wall, successively finds herself participating in two different orders of vision: one she refers to as the 'personal',[27] which consists largely in suffocating images of childhood and familial and generational constraint; in the other, which is not named but might most uncontentiously be referred to as the Imaginary, the experience is of freedom, of a succession of scenes in which the role of the self is not predestined but becomes a task to be decided upon in the light of the empty scene perceived. The concept of the personal and the individual as restriction and loss of vision is a consistent undertow to these texts; contrarily, the realm of the Imaginary becomes, not one where gender or other characteristics are lost, but one where it becomes up to the self to decide on how he or she will translate these characteristics into a relation with a whole.

There is no desire to transcend gender, or age; but there is instead an enormous urge to see these givens as meaningful only in the context of a relevant totality. We thus, Lessing tells us, interpret society and its unconscious not only by looking outward and filing our endless reports on the surrounding facts, but also, and more importantly, by looking inward and attempting to read what our own feelings, as determinate selves, as existent subjects, may be trying to tell us about the system of which we, however temporarily, form a part. The rest is rationalism, strategy, manipulation, acquiescence in the machine. The plight of Shikasta/Earth is caused by the fact that it is cut off from its own sources of energy; thus that the flexible passage between conscious and unconscious (symbolised, among other ways, in the risings and sinkings of Atlantis and the Central American isthmus) has been fortified as a boundary, between cultures, between races, between zones, but most significantly between the workings of the group mind, which are always and everywhere unconscious, and the petty accommodations of the individual ego.

4 *Beryl Bainbridge:*
The new psychopathia

Beryl Bainbridge has acted Krafft-Ebing in response to the self-aware
Freudianism of many of her fellow-writers; where Lessing, Carter,
Barth, have paraded analysis, she has presented herself during the
1970s as a meticulous chronicler of 'everyday' events, who would raise
an innocent eyebrow at any mention of psychosis, whether attached to
writer, character, reader or text.[1] The calamities she depicts are, so the
surrounding authorial fiction goes, conventionally implicit in our lives:
they are a mechanical consequence of our upbringing, and either they
will spring out, fully armed, at a later date; or, indeed, they have
happened already, and only a thin skin of self-protection prevents us
from remembering the terror of adolescence or of poverty. We do not
need psychological sophistication to see through to the depths: events
are hideously transparent, naturally manifesting the results of age-old
cultural trauma. Yet of course in her descriptive and guileless way she
forces us back to the schoolroom, back to early occupational experience:
did we not then, she asks, experience the fear of being alone, of being
unversed in the ways of our parents/employers? Were we too not
brought on to a scene where everybody else understood the conventions,
and then victimised for not possessing that unobtainable knowledge?

The question below that runs again in terms of gender, and has a
curiously symmetrical relation to the question Nabokov poses to his
audience. Where he asks whether we too shared, long ago, his experience of dividing the world (of young girls) into the 'knowing' and the
'unknowing' (and he is not so unsubtle as to be referring merely to carnal
knowledge), Bainbridge asks whether we shared in the more dire
experience of *being known* (as inferior, as junior, as incomplete); and
whether, if as readers and particularly as male readers we claim not to
remember such a time,[2] we are thereby collaborating in a great refusal,
a refusal of understanding which perpetuates hegemony and the
transmission of fear between the sexes. The central characters in

Bainbridge's fables of psychosis are mostly small, by nature or by nurt-ure:[3]: they experience, indeed, the undeniable fact that, through murder, rape or anger, they produce large effects in the world, but there is a gap between cause and effect, between desire and achievement; and is this not, runs the apparently supplementary but really more important ques-tion, something which has been specifically done to women? Are not these acts of moral and carnal outrage precisely the inverted reflection of what a masculine culture has visited upon women, and are not male desires in the end fulfillable only through violence, of one kind or another?

None of this is to deny that Bainbridge writes about victims; but when her victims turn, there is a gleefulness in the outcome, even with the young Hitler. All of this, all this grotesquerie and bloodshed, is after all only to be expected while you (the reader?) capitulate in subjecting others to inhumanity. Thus there is in Bainbridge a wish for rebellion, but no special interest in the rebel: the excitement is more pure than that, more focused on downfall and the upturning of a deadly world. The time for the Other, the inversion, to emerge is, of course, the traditional moment:[4] it is the moment of celebration, the bottle factory outing, the particular exemption granted in the form of injury time. It is at these moments, when we most hopefully imagine that some form of ritual is going to crown our efforts and achievements, that the voices of those whom we have suppressed in our facile forms of organisation, of those whom we have never prepared to understand the pleasures of our parties, will be raised; in a scream which, at first, we may mistake for participation, but which is eventually revealed as a cry of anguish and fury, the inarticulate sign for all that has been swept under the carpet in order to prepare the (primal) scene for a confirming ritual.[5]

During the 1970s, the furrow Bainbridge has ploughed has appeared a lonely one, in that she has consistently refused the displacements which have become conventional in the 'new fiction', the construction of a mythicised future or the return to a putatively explanatory past; she has also refused to parenthesise her fiction, to frame it within a satisfyingly self-conscious exploration of the writerly task. Her stories stand on their own, largely unweighted by a tacit compact between writer and reader: the signifier remains uncompromisingly rooted in the signified, resisting that increasingly convenient tendency towards play which could con-vince us that these traumas and psychoses are merely 'effects of the text'. If anything, they are the effects of Liverpool, as a sign for the anti-metropolitan, as the standing rebuff to the existing modes of economic and social organisation, as the continuous 'harbour' of a freer interplay between the material and the aesthetic, as, implicitly, the place where art is determined by the mere resources available and the imagination which seeks to soar over the Mersey is more or less severely punished. For every success which emerges from the North-West, Bainbridge suggests to us, there are a hundred enactments, not of failure, but of simply not breaking through: a hundred endeavours hurled against the wall of deprivation, which receive only the answer, 'Not here, dear', or, at least, 'Not *now*'. Bainbridge country is a land where the most bizarre of denizens may be found, but only on sufferance: anything can be entertained, but only a few transplants 'take', in either direction. Mostly, we will be condemned to tread the same gravelly roads, only as time goes on they will be all the more bitterly sprinkled with the detritus of hope.

The volumes are therefore slim, and motionless: they stack, like the early recordings of forgotten pop groups, redolent of spent sweetness, of untasted deadly nightshade, of ambitions carried through in thought only. The fact that, so often, the narrator comprehends a larger portion of the story than any one character does not serve as a guarantee of readerly wisdom, real or to be attained, but as a reminder of interpretations unmade, of understandings unreached, of all the moments we *could* have seized to construct patterns whigh might have continued to inform us. It is thus that childhood and adolescence are the essential terrain: for it is only back there, in the painful rememoration of the fear of parental absence, that we can be brought to admit to the continual defeat of expectation. If, Bainbridge says, these fables appear to resonate with present experience, that is by chance: it is too late to learn those lessons, and when the lessons were on offer we were usually looking out of the window. All that remains is a 'quiet life', a life in which those peremptory voices are content to remain silent, having weighed up their chances of audibility; yet it is also within those quiet lives that our secrets are held, every moment of collapse held sequestered in the continuing story of a locked family, an individual reduced to silence by the pressures of conflict. Each family, each place of work, stands as a silent monument to our past; each gesture we made is replicated at large in the frozen posture of some group locked into fear, incomprehension, worst of all guilt. Behind the net curtains, our own past survives; we can be brought, by the narrator, to see it, but the possibility of learning has probably been eclipsed, many years ago. These situations survive as hieroglyphs, encapsulated signs in the language of the unconscious, visible warnings on the road; but we give them little credit, and cannot predict the future moment when we too will see ourselves in the waxworks, will realise that our movement, our escape to the bright lights, has been illusory, that we too are being observed in our role as monitory sculptures, turned to permanent stone in the very moment of indignity.

In *Harriet Said . . .* (1972), the narrative plays delicately around the problem of signification: that is to say, the central characters are clearly enacting a script, but we are never certain whose, and thus the meaning of events remains in doubt. At a fairly obvious level, Harriet is the succubus, the ever-present whispering self who eggs the narrator on (harries her) to mate with her father (the Tsar) and kill her mother (Mrs Biggs – who is, just before her death, 'huge and menacing',[6] the frozen statue of adulthood before whom the narrator initially quails, but who has to be reduced to dust.)[7] Yet at every turn Harriet's plans are in fact undercut by the narrator's; this blank and terrible 'I' takes Harriet's words and injunctions and twists them to an unconscious but preformed plan of her own. Thus there is an inversion: Harriet becomes the blank slate on which the narrator inscribes the record of her own desires, the ambiguous authority who can be invoked to justify any practice. If the unconscious is indeed structured like a language, the narrator's ritual progress through puberty is depicted as a dramatised encounter with that language, and as a subjugation of it: Harriet ends up baffled and threatened by the power of the narrator (who is, of course, structurally the only agent who can confer meaning) to distort her comparatively puny imaginary crimes into a realised tale of sex and murder. Thus the narrator acts as a pure 'embodiment': she exists to give carnal form (and the form of carnage) to the promptings of the unconcious. She is thus herself empty (nameless); and the fear we experience as readers springs from our uncomfortable proximity to a superior shaping power (Bainbridge incarnated) before whose unseen plans we can manifest only a shudder. What *Harriet* says is significant only insofar as it provides the pretext for the narrator's interpretation: Harriet offers, for instance, the category of humiliation (the Tsar/father must be 'humbled'),[8] but it is the narrator who connects this empty signifier with the available contents of the unconscious, and carries the desire through to a dreadful completion before which the prompter can only stand aghast – for a moment, before she begins again to act her role and fabricate cover stories after the event. Yet for the narrator, it is vital to maintain the claim that Harriet is the true 'agent':

> How could I not understand her? I would have given all the power
> of my too imaginative mind and all the beauty of the fields and
> woods, not to understand her. And at last I gave in to Harriet, finally
> and without reservation. I wanted the Tsar to be humiliated, to
> cower sideways with his bird's head held stiffly in pain and fear, so
> that I might finish what I had begun, return to school forgetting the
> summer, and think only of the next holidays that might be as they
> had always been.[9]

What is thus enacted is the story of the girl-child's revenge against the
father (the real father is constructed as a caricature, compounded of
practical ineffectuality and swearing, absurdly laying claim to a power
which is actually wasted beyond recall), in its full duplicity: the narrator
constructs a false Other (the script of Harriet) in the name of which (in
the name of the sister) she is then freed to humble and mutilate the
masculine.[10] As well as an absent father, the text also presents us with an
actual absent sister (Frances); we are invited to suppose that the narrator
acts under an imperative to fill in those blanks in the familial text, even
though violence is the only sign under which they can come to have
meaning: only through death can life be affirmed.

The narrator is stout and imaginative, body-full and fantasy-full:
Harriet's dry and slender presence provides only a frame within which
this over-present femininity can perform a drama, *the* drama. And yet
there is no fullness in the narrator's response: the subjugation of the
male and mother-murder contain a meaning to which she (so we are
invited to suppose) has no conscious access. It is only by reference to the
mythical authority of Harriet that she can convey to us the significance of
her actions. Before this mirror (and filling the empty reflection with her
own wishes), she can experience fullness, but in so doing she renounces
the claim to interpretation: thus we are drawn into a circle of shared
naivety, and invited to examine the Others we erect as justifications, as
objective correlatives, for our crimes.[11]

> How often had Harriet recoiled from me, telling me I was ugly, that
> I must modify and govern the muscles of my face. It was not that my
> feelings illuminated and transformed me, as Harriet became
> transformed in diabolical anger or joy, it was more a dreadful
> eagerness and vulnerability that made my face like an open wound,
> with all the nerves exposed and raw.[12]

Thus Harriet provides the pretext on which the 'wound', the assumed castration, can be made manifest, and the Tsar can be 'un-manned'; we suspect that this 'ugliness' is the outward sign of something quite different, of the unmanageability of female trauma, something before which Harriet, like the Tsar, cowers. We are thus presented with a drama of female omnipotence: if, as Cixous claims, the feminine consciousness is plural, in part a defensive linking of many in the face of the demanding, phallic 'one',[13] then we should not be surprised if this plurality begins to act like a team of bent detectives, endlessly covering for each other in an unscripted spiral so that the excuses for crime are themselves multiplied as the alibi becomes totally secure. Like Macavity, the narrator was never there, and so the story of her own burgeoning sexuality and its links with violence is again buried. There is no growth possible in the text, only an increasing complexity of cover stories:

> At last I was allowed to go to bed. I lay in the dark wide-eyed. I had avoided real displeasure, I had been kissed, I had explained the broken window. They would never trace it to me, the more so as Harriet had been home early. I had lied very well and cried effortlessly; I would look white and ill in the morning. I thought of the beautiful night and my god-like strength in the church and I began to smile when I remembered the Tsar's banged nose under the lamp. Harriet could not have managed better.[14]

It is thus, Bainbridge suggests, that the girl-child grows to maturity: fragmenting, developing a spurious self-management, endlessly referring desire to a hypothesised Other (Harriet is the spurious plural, 'Woman'), and thus becoming, paradoxically, the means for enacting the necessary vengeance for the thousands of years of male domination.

The construction of the female superego, and its purposes (which are quite different from those of the male equivalent), are again the ground against which *The Dressmaker* (1973) takes its form, and here again we are given a story which we are invited to see through: coupled with female vengeance, we are invited to a view of female 'transparency', as the writer's own revenge for generations of pornographic scopophilia. The tiniest of devices is significant:

> Afterwards she went through into the little front room, the tape measure still dangling about her neck, and allowed herself a glass of port.[15]

In the 'allowance' to her self, a severance of the female subject already suggests that one part is going to be capable of anything; there is a ridding of scruple, a preparing for the feast, and this premonition is confirmed by the description of the fleshy young male American:

> A great healthy face, with two enquiring eyes, bright blue, and a mouth which when he spoke showed a long row of teeth, white and protruding. It was one of those Yanks. Jack was shocked. Till now he had never been that close. They were so privileged, so foreign; he had never dreamt to see one at close quarters in Nellie's kitchen, taking Rita and Marge, one on each arm and bouncing them out of the house.[16]

The masculinity evidenced here is expressed in consumerist metaphors: yet also this manifestation of flesh is to be consumed and discarded, the developed but useless teeth finally helpless against the deprivation which breeds a truer violence. For the overall sign of *The Dressmaker* is deprivation: as in *Harriet Said ...*, it is as though Bainbridge is chronicling the grotesque shapes which the passage to maturity may take if the main channel (and the coastal setting makes the metaphor apt) is no longer negotiable; the difficulty of transit through dried tributaries and across unmeasured sandbanks, which always carry the threat of permanent beaching, of a sudden and premature halt after which we can never again progress. Nellie and Marge between them, riven and full of friction as they are, incarnate a solid maturity before which Ira (the ambiguous name, anger with a feminine ending) cannot even begin. In any case, he is simply a refraction of 'Rita', but thus, of course, derives the complexity of the story: for the vengeance the aunts wreak is displaced, does not fall on the phallic (Chuck, the drill-bit) but on a junior manifestation of masculinity, and similarly Rita fades from the narrative as the aunts reassert a complementary hegemony.

This displacement is crucial, because Bainbridge is not trying to offer a simple reversal of norms, or to claim that the force of the feminine can somehow rejuvenate society: on the contrary, she is showing the destruction which has been visited on the female in order to convert it into a force for conservatism, and therefore the insurrection performed is not a real insurrection but rather one which re-enacts the dominance of the phallic. The dressmaker 'wins' her battle through her employment, by sticking pins in wax effigies, but also through a fake penetration in a more general sense, a penetration of the potential links between the other characters. Partly she is enabled to achieve this by the fact that the forces of masculinity are already really dead: in the triumvirate of Nellie, Marge and Rita the entire force of the family is contained, with Marge (a name-changer; she is also Margo, but she cannot 'go', she is stuck, familially and sexually, within rememoration)[17] as the substitute father, especially since she alone is presumed to have had previous sexual experience. Within that drama, what is predicted is that the line of communication which carries the sexual charge (father/daughter, but here Margo/Rita) falls within the control of the mother as the transmitter of inhibition: Nellie can sever that relationship at will, and thus reaffirm the future Rita-as-mother as the only possible shape for progression. It thus falls to Nellie, as the reincarnation of an unchangeable and frozen past, to lay down the tracks into the future; thus Rita is herself symbolically killed when Ira meets his (masculine) fate, but more significantly thus is depicted the fate of an entire culture, starved of meaning (in the shape of products for consumption, but also of the affections, sexual relations, feelings presented in the world) and thus trapped into a murderous resentment of change. The phallic sign which Ira represents, in however weakened and limp a form, cannot penetrate the tensed surface of this constructed and well-defended world, in which men have been reduced to Jack's role as absent provider; but meanwhile, within that hygienic bubble from which the male is excluded, significance has drained away and been replaced by a discourse of ritual.

It is in ways like this that Bainbridge, for all her surface naturalism, nonetheless provides us with a map of unconscious process: for her narratives are situated at those points where the covering operations are ceasing to be effective and the barbarous shapes of desire are poking through the torn fabric. The doubling of roles which lies at the root of *Harriet Said . . .* reappears in Brenda and Freda in *The Bottle Factory Outing* (1974), and accompanied, as in *The Dressmaker*, by a diminution of the phallic. Here the men are almost all Italians, illegal immigrant workers, hidden and cowering, often described as a group of children and largely unable to speak the language of power: Rossi's sexual desires extend only as far as rumpling Brenda's clothing to the accompaniment of a meaningless and evasive patter. In this world of masculine midgets, the abundant Freda draws into herself all the power of conveying signification: it is only through her suggestions, her ideas, her interpretation that the world has any meaning at all, and it is only she who retains a potential for change, although this potential becomes increasingly unreal. Not surprisingly, this gigantism is the prelude to humiliation and death: and when Freda dies, she too has to be hidden away, in a barrel, to show that the forces of weary containment have won another battle. Yet, in a sense, it is Brenda, thin and anxious, who has won a Pyrrhic victory: it is her emaciated version of femininity which proves the only one able to survive in a run-down and barely moving world. It is as though she projects all the hope and desire into Freda, thus pumping her up into an unstable shape which causes her death: symbolically, Brenda wonders whether it was Freda's horse-ride which caused the bruises found later on her body, speculating really on whether any manifestation of sexuality might be irrevocably linked with Thanatos. Thus Freda's death acts, for Brenda, as a redemption of an awful kind: she is confirmed in her knowledge that there is nothing to be done about fate. After the death, she has a dream, and when she wakes 'she didn't feel ill any more or cross':

> She had been in a cinema with Freda: Freda was wearing a trouser suit and one of those floppy hats with cloth flowers on the brim. She complained bitterly that she couldn't see the bloody screen. The men in the row behind said 'Sssh!' loudly and kicked the back of the seat. Brenda whispered she should take her hat off. 'Why should I?' said Freda; and Brenda remembered a little doggerel her mother had taught her, something about a little woman with a great big hat . . . went to the pictures and there she sat, Freda shrieked and recited rapidly . . . man behind couldn't see a bit . . . finally got tired of it. Somehow it made Brenda very happy that Freda too knew the little rhyme. She beamed in the darkness. She turned and kissed Freda on the cheek and woke instantly.[18]

What appears to cheer Brenda up is her recognition that Freda too, despite her ambitions, knows that underneath it all women are merely laughable, that the big hat is only a sham and below it lies fear and withdrawal. In this dream, Freda is an honorary man, trouser-suited and swearing, but this does not make her acceptable, it only renders her a target because she has dared to put her head above the parapet. She confuses the men, who cannot see past her; but this does her no good, for she herself cannot see either. By transgressing the stereotypes to which Brenda rigidly adheres, she turns into a kind of chimera and hence cannot survive. Brenda finds comfort in her mother's 'doggerel', as Rita is reduced to belief in the defeatist wisdom of Nellie: in Freda's trajectory through power to death, Brenda watches an enactment of what might happen if femininity were to cut itself loose from these apron-strings, and learns the lesson that it is better, in the end, not to have emerged into the world at all than to risk the violence visited on the admired.

What is appalling in *The Bottle Factory Outing* is the portrayal of low expectations: that nothing can be hoped for except the shoddy and the inappropriate, and thus the outing itself, hilarious though it is, is also sinister. Throughout it there is the fear that, really, even if we get the chance we shall not remember how to enjoy ourselves; and the concomitant fear that, in our flailing efforts to remember the nature of pleasure, we shall go too far and the 'games' will turn into mayhem and inarticulate rage. It is as though, for Brenda, all experience is bracketed: as though she is waiting, exhausted by past attempts to participate (her defunct marriage), for her mother to call her in for tea. At the end, she calls herself in, and regresses: the entire process of the story comes to seem as though it has itself been only an outing, an excursion into activity; the 'real life' which will be resumed by those who survive will be a life devoid of incident, in which Brenda can subside into a role of pure observer, those parts of herself which she has invested in Freda safely cut out, buried, forgotten.

Sweet William (1975) describes a similar trajectory: Ann is presented, in the shape of the ambiguous William, with a text which she makes a continuous series of attempts to read, in that she involves herself in an effort to bring her own life into an intelligible relation with the life of another. But as she reads this text, she becomes increasingly aware that such completeness of comprehension is not possible: that there are always further corners which cannot be explored, always unexplained absences and erasures.[19] As the book moves on, Bainbridge signifies the way in which understanding eludes Ann by talking increasingly over her head to the reader; thus we sense Ann slipping away, as only we, for example, divine the probable secret of William's relationship with Mrs Kershaw, or the reasons for his reported fight with Roddy. No matter how close Ann seeks to draw to this reincarnation of the father, there is always something in the way, some surviving element of his earlier life, some continuing manifestation of his previous wife or wives. Ann, of course, goes through a period of strong ambivalence towards Edna, the principal incarnation of William's past, sensing the appropriateness of Edna's 'theatrical' manner to William's way of life: it is only by considering action as though it were bracketed on a stage (William is a playwright) that we can bring ourselves to refrain from asking illicit questions. Where do the actors go at night? Do they even continue to exist? Or are they, in fact, merely two-dimensional, and must we settle for a version of living in which facts are reduced to whatever William wants to present as his current fiction?

The splitting of the female self which is a habitual theme in Bainbridge is present here too, in the relation between Ann and Pamela; and its contours are becoming clearer.[20] The nameless 'I' of *Harriet Said . . .*, Brenda in *The Bottle Factory Outing* and now Ann experience an impossibility of role: they cannot hold on to their ability to observe the world if they simultaneously have to be themselves observed objects, and so they slide into invisibility and project the contours which they seek to shed into their Others, Harriet, Freda, Pamela. It is as though the body itself is too much of a burden to bear, and must be exiled so that its shapes will not give away anything of the self's identity or gender; but whereas in *Harriet Said . . .* this process still permits of a terrible victory, and thus the disguise enables a real crime, by the time of *Sweet William* there is less to achieve, and disguise has become an unconscious device for its own sake. Where *Sweet William*, however, diverges more radically from the previous fictions is in its insistence on the role of the male in producing this projective self-mutilation: it is William's capacity for generating self-justifying fictions which reduces women to the actants of roles in a predetermined script. Thus also, by a reticulative process, it is male writers who have laid down the terms of female 'character':[21] and Bainbridge's response is to move towards dispensing with this concept of 'character' altogether, rendering her women progressively more emptied, so that, paradoxically, they shall not fall victim to the domineering habits of masculine interpretation. What is rejected is the familiar recourse to the portrayal of a 'rich inner life' as a substitute for thwarted action: these women do not have rich inner lives, or if they do they salvage them only at the expense of articulacy, because their words are not valued. William, we are invited to suppose, is at best a pretty poor playwright, a second-rate Pinter, yet even as that he is in a position to transmit within the social body: to the extent that he is given credibility, as playwright, director and philanderer, there is a concomitant societal refusal to credit the different accounts of women, and at the same time a blocking of the paths for communication within the feminine. William's need to separate his life into compartments is itself a reflection of fear,

fear that for women to talk *about* him rather than *through* him would be to produce him too as an object, and that this would sap his agential status in the world.

But for Alan, in *A Quiet Life* (1976), the choices available for the male are themselves limited by the ineradicable record of parental defeats and disasters.

> Most of the time he thought about Janet Leyland – the way she looked at him, what she said, a certain mannerism she had, of touching the lobe of her ear when she was unsure. He wasn't lovesick or anything like that. He wasn't off his food. It was more that he was engrossed in her acceptance of him – his ideas, his cleverness. She thought he knew a lot. He came from a household that regarded men as inferior; they were fed first and deferred to in matters of business, but they weren't respected.[22]

Yet this experience of subjugation does not lead to rebellion: for Alan, ingrained habit is far too deeply laid.

> He knew, somewhere at the back of his mind, that he could only hope to be an extension of his parents – he'd step a few paces further on, but not far. His progression was limited, as theirs had been. . . . He'd always be polite and watch his manners. Most likely he'd vote Conservative, in rebellion against his father.[23]

Thus rebellion is converted into political regression, and the lesson Alan learns has also to do with not taking risks, with adopting a discretion which will ensure that he does not, indeed, end up despised like his father; but there is a terrible price to be paid. His life is to be led in the same way as, in childhood, he moves nervously about the cluttered living-room stuffed with reminders of richer and better days. The wish is to vanish, to become part of the pattern in the over-ornate wallpaper; and now it is he who, in his 'wild' sister Madge, watches warily as adolescence shudders its emergence from the chrysalis. Claustrophobia can itself become a habit: Alan experiences no desire for the wide open spaces, but wants instead to turn himself into the ideal and non-frictive inhabitant of a space seen as inevitably closed.

The inversion of the oppressive interior and its burden of partially visible trauma is in the pinewoods, where Madge not only encounters more real experiences, but simultaneously covers them under a patina of lies. Seen like this, the question posed by the text is symmetrical with that posed in *Sweet William*: in a world where knowledge can never be complete because the story (the play) began before we arrived, how are we to make the necessary adjustment to an acceptable level of incomprehension? And worse than that, in a real or projected sibling situation, where the Other has somehow already adopted or grown into the admired role, the role of freedom, how are we to find another space to occupy without falling prey to the sneaking suspicion that all we have done, every shape with which we have wrestled in the process of self-formation, is not simply itself an inversion, a fitting into a space already unconsciously designed by our elders? This, certainly, is Alan's fear, and it recurs to him when he meets Madge again years later: 'immediately he felt disturbed. He hated reviving the past, the small details of time long since spent. Seeing her, he was powerless to push back the memories that came crowding into his mind.'[24] What, of course, he is also scared of is the possibility which was ever present to him as a child: that Madge, from her position across the boundary of the family, from her magical haven in the pinewoods, might in fact also have a story to tell, a story about *him*, which would invalidate the years of patient and painful self-suppression; the possibility that, in fact, the neurosis now so carefully grown over might have been there and evident all along and that Madge might have seen it more clearly than he had cared to see himself.

Thus to be watched, indeed to be seen at all, is to be humiliated: the net curtains, the unused parlours do not seem strange to Alan, because he shares with his parents a despairing assumption that what might otherwise be seen would not bear the light of day. His own watchfulness, initially of his parents and later of himself, can survive and continue to operate as a protective mechanism if he is himself out of the reach of harm or affect. At the end, coming back to his wife from the brief meeting with Madge which frames the earlier narrative of memory, 'turning his back on the house, in case his wife watched from the window, he let the flowers spill from his folded newspaper on to the pavement. Then', freed from any incriminating evidence and thus restored to his conception of untrammelled masculine strength, 'squaring his shoulders, he walked up the path'.[25]

In many ways, Edward in *Injury Time* (1977) shares Alan's situation, as a conformist whose tissue of habits papers over early cracks: but here there is something softer in the writing, some flicker of hope as Edward, forced towards a change of behaviour by his bizarre encounter with a gang of bank-robbers, has to attend again, if only momentarily, to voices he believed he had silenced. Here, for the first time, there is a fair match between the major subtexts: Edward and Binny, telling fragments of their own stories, have perceptions which at least connect with each other's, even if, time after time, the possibility for an actual sharing of these perceptions is lost, and shafts of light cross the gloom to no avail. This is structurally Bainbridge's most conventional narrative: a complex set of marital secrets, already on the point of blowing themselves apart, are thrown into full relief by the chance appearance of the criminals, and we are led to believe that, as usual, some kind of growth, if only into a deepened realisation of inadequacy, will occur – as indeed, to an extent, it does. But what is foregrounded is the essentially regressive content of this narrative structure. Edward's obsession is, like Alan's, with child-hood events, with a difficult matrix of public-school betrayal and paternal excommunication: what the eruption of violence achieves is a return to that world. Edward, Binny and the others are themselves plunged back into a realm where callow bids for leadership and adoles-cent resentments replace previous emotions; and in this they enter into a curiously mirrored relationship with the invading gang. Where the dramatic interest of previous Bainbridge texts, and the apparent interest of the first part of *Injury Time*, lay in a splitting and redoubling of individuals, here the interest shifts to the redoubled interaction between the two separate groups.[26] At some points where the various representa-tives of the bohemian and respectable middle classes are being held hostage by the workers, the two groups crosscut and intermingle; else-where, they hold themselves rigidly apart, fastidiously drinking their breakfast tea in the separate halves of Binny's kitchen/diner. The criminals, on the whole, are shocked: by Edward's infidelity, by the squalor of Binny's house. There is no change at stake for them; it is only the unstable syntheses of the initial appalling dinner party which might get remade, but in the end there is little felt impact across the groups, except perhaps for Edward himself: forced at one point to 'stand in' for Ginger, and purged by his repetition of an early cricketing incident, he becomes able to seize a moment of potential heroism, with – as we might by now predict – the proviso that it almost certainly entails his death.

But behind this drama lies another one, more marginalised, and more to do with youth and age than with gender relations. In the face of the toughness of their children, women like Binny and Alma are reduced to meditating on their own softness, and the relationship between Binny and Edward becomes a mutual consolation for ageing. Binny's elder daughter has acquired masculine disguise, army boots and overalls, although this is curiously parodied by the female disguise of one of the criminals, a disguise to which Edward proves completely unable to accommodate, continuing to treat him as a woman despite full evidence to the contrary. It is, indeed, as the title suggests, as though the time given to Edward and Binny for their faltering relationship does not really count: as though it is extra time, snatched from death, in which boundaries become unimportant, and the yearning is for the state of undifferentiation which age might bring. And this, in fact, is what is enacted, as under pressure the characters start to swap roles at regular intervals, and become immersed in a common predicament. The reader is soothed by suggestions of collectivity: but the price to be paid is a desexualising, as though we are supposed to share in a welcome abandonment of real concerns to the young, and to approximate ourselves to the image of Mrs Montague, over sixty yet still looking for a suitable hedge behind which to take her pleasures. Binny is made to feel young and old in dizzying succession, ending up in a grey area where nothing much matters any more, but where also, consequently, there is no need to accept the damaging descriptions offered by her children, by the criminals, by Mrs Montague: once again, there is a kind of invisibility to be achieved, and thus it is Binny, by virtue of her lack of determinate outline, who is the one chosen by the robbers to serve as a continuing hostage. Edward, with his suspect high profile and his suddenly found new reserves of energy, cannot survive: his final inducement of himself to take a risk is fatal, as, symbolically, the entire risk of the affair with Binny has been bracketed within the sign of an imminent heart attack. Bainbridge presents us, for once, with images of at least partial success in the acquiring of self-knowledge, but only by suggesting that the boundaries of the self are in any case pointless, that we may as well resign ourselves to the unpreventable invasion signified in the hostage process and in Binny's ambiguous rape.

Thus in *Injury Time*, the body is frail, softened by careless living and weakened by corrosive memories; we are in the constant whispering presence of imminent paralysis, shadowed for Binny by imminent menopause. There is a sense in which the main characters are already ghosts, although the arrival of the gang does not increase their reality: rather, it is as if two species of half-beings seek to inhabit the same space in the unconscious hope that, somewhere among the tangle of crossed wires, a spark might jump and a whole might be formed. It is mostly around Binny that these hopes are encouraged to coalesce, as though, perhaps because of her extensive motherhood, she might possess the alchemical skill necessary to convert waste material into gold, but her experiences with Edward and Ginger demonstrate bitterly for us that the hope of resurrection is a foolish one, and that nothing is about to be born of these sterile and furtive unions. The doubling of relationships passes down the line: from the public and ceremonial life of Edward and Helen (whom we never see, who is, perhaps, herself already an emptied shell), through the apparently more broadminded marriage of George and Muriel Simpson, which turns out to be a vicious fiction barely covering hatred and envy, through the relationship between Edward and Binny, which is finally forced to 'go public' by the intrusion, and on to the brief and 'ineffectual'[27] encounter between Binny and Ginger: at each point of intersection, we are invited to share a moment's hope that *here* at last there may be some form of life which has both shape and content, but it is never the case. The symbol with which we are left is the one offered to us in despair by Muriel: of the house prepared for union, where one partner never arrives.

If the secret of *Injury Time* is sterility (a lack of the materials for birth, but also a multiple sealing-off of incompatible areas of life), then *Young Adolf* (1978) offers us a monstrous birth which provides an ironic exit from the dilemma. Adolf Hitler, we know, at least went on to make a mark on the world; but equally, that 'mark' was to be a gigantic magnification of the marks inflicted on Adolf himself by his environment and upbringing. The text is riddled with the signs of displaced violence and birth trauma: most significantly in the extraordinary sequences which feature the appearance and disappearance of the hole in the wall of the third-floor room.[28] Time after time, the apparently solid surface of that wall shatters ('Old Shatterhand' is Adolf's 'alter ego') and Adolf, among others, is flung violently through it in a parody of birth, to find his account unbelieved. His trajectory, then, becomes bound up with the attempt to discern the secret of the appearing and vanishing point of entry into the world; and that act of continuing displacement underpins his sexual hatred. The problems of accounting for his origins are further symbolised in his role at the hotel where his brother Alois finds him a job: although here is a luxurious sign of the kind of world for which Adolf longs, he is condemned never to enter or leave it by the front entrance, his complicated circuits through side and rear doors becoming ever more bizarre as he becomes increasingly involved with criminal designs. Through these symbols, a world is established where all the principal doors and windows are blocked up, and Adolf – and the reader – has to creep furtively around the edges, often occupying spaces apparently actually within the walls: the wider implication is of a world twisted so far out of true by divisions of birth and class that we have to make our passage through it in secret and by night, and where the questions we might need to ask, in order to explain how we got to our present point, are always thwarted.

As with many of Bainbridge's previous fictions, there is a tissue of interlocking texts and plans, half-revealed, constantly conspiring to prevent achievement. It is not, indeed, that we are drawn to feel much sympathy with Adolf; but it is suggested that, after all, from this tangle of errors and deprivation nothing much better can be expected, unless it be the passivity of Bridget, who acquiesces, half helplessly and half resentfully, in manipulation and inarticulacy. Kephalus and Meyer try to 'save a few',[29] prevent one or two of the most deprived from falling directly victim to the presumed cruelty of the authorities, but not much real hope is attached to their activities: indeed, it may even be that their efforts are misplaced, a romantic charade which does not touch upon the roots of evil. Whatever location we seek to establish for ourselves as subjects, the very word 'subject' carries a fatal duplicity of meaning: our subjectivity involves also our continuing subjection, and we are left perennially listening through the wall for intimations of the real agency of the story in which we are acting a minor and subjugated part. It is this inevitable subjugation, Bainbridge suggests, which produces the hideous fantasies of domination which Adolf will go on to act out; this sense of rootlessness which will engender the fantasies of 'roots' which emerge into the world as racism and sexual violence; this knowledge of being battered which will make us in turn find people to batter. Alois and Bridget act as substitute parents for Adolf, but we know that this is merely a displacement: the real father exists only as a portrait on the wall, and as a nameless sign around which contradictory narratives are constructed; there is no path back to the truth.[30]

Taking the fictions as a series, we find ourselves in the presence of a detailed investigation of familial conditioning and of the baroque shapes for the self generated in a world where wholeness is not possible. The key process of splitting, from which later shapes derive, is between the acceptable and the rebellious, between the self as defined by an already present pattern and the self as a point of divergence from the familial norm. The problem is that neither choice actually leads away or forward: both enter us into an endless circuit where the only possible dialogue is with father or mother, the only reaction to the possibility of other relationships a terrified probing to see whether this stranger has the quasi-parental gift of seeing through the fictions we wish to present as our life story. The most feared figure is thus the sibling: because at the moment when we settled for an option, or claimed to have done so, he or she was there, observing, and might have a different account to give which would undo all the decades of self-suppressive work. And even if there was no real sibling, or not a significant one, the problem still remains: there is still the fear that our disguise is inadequate, that we have not sufficiently approximated ourselves to the shape we want, and that this will be glaringly obvious to the Other.

Thus, at all costs, we must not be *seen*: and it is, of course, at this point that the account of familial development (or lack of it) interlocks most importantly with the account of gender differentiation. For observation is also objectification, freezing the Other and turning it to stone; and principally, says Bainbridge, this is what men do to women, partly by regarding them as sexual objects and founding an entire culture on a violent pornography, but also by in a thousand other ways using the 'gaze' as an instrument of control.[31] Not, of course, that this does the men much good: by replacing real women with moving statues, they in fact create a world of monsters before which they can only cower. Thus the ambition towards control is shown as fundamentally circular; and while we are embedded in these self-defeating ways of dealing with the outer world, we also stand no chance of achieving control over ourselves.

Bainbridge's characters can rarely interpret each other's behaviour: they are too preoccupied with trying to fight clear of acknowledging the constraints on their own. And, certainly, there is no freer, better, less ritualised life available at those levels of society where we might expect to find the regulations less rigorously observed; on the contrary, 'down there' is where deprivation makes itself most clingingly felt, and where there is barely enough substance available to flesh out the form of the individual. The experience is of an overwhelming scarcity, either actual or imagined: and that scarcity is itself a reflection of a deprivation of love, of an endless competition to achieve the security of having at least one parent, for a time, all to ourselves. By splitting, perhaps we hope that we might double our chances: that we might become, on the one hand, the competent agent in the world who might expect to attract a father's approval, and on the other the figure of pathos who might hope for a reincarnation of a mother's love. In fact, the trick results in a locked solipsism, in which the only object on view is our self-as-agent; meanwhile we, as subjects with an inner life, are further starved of the resources for survival.

And thus, in the end, this fiction which apparently makes little concession to the modernist habit of self-consciousness produces a highly self-conscious reader: because we are made increasingly aware that, in gazing at the squirmings of these Others, we too are looking only at parts of ourselves, that all these enactments are ones in which we too have shared or will share, objective correlatives for the dilemmas of maturation. And further, we become uncomfortably aware that the readerly position is itself voyeuristic: that we are being treated to a banquet of secrets which we would rather not have known, are being beckoned into the empty and sheeted front parlour where every framed photograph tells a story of defeat. And thus of course, if this is possible, if we can be beckoned through the net curtains and shown the skeletons, what of our own secrets? Is it that we too in time will find ourselves listening dumbfounded to the *other* story, to the narrative about our self which we have refused to acknowledge, but which nonetheless remains, somewhere, to haunt us with the possibility that our self-development has been a massive artifice built on willed ignorance, and that our power of relating is built on half-subdued hatred and half-known fear?

5 *Kurt Vonnegut:*
The cheerfully demented

The uniqueness of Kurt Vonnegut's style has been summarised in many different ways.[1] One of the principal distinctions seems to me to be the continuous holding together of different poles: high technology and human eccentricity, the manipulative and repetitive languages of commerce and the faltering expression of love, intense patterning and emphatic inconsequentiality. Around Vonnegut's worlds there are closed circuits, perimeter walls, forged from material deprivation and metaphysical irony; but the problem is how to convince his characters of that when they persist in being unbowed by the handicaps which are shackled to their limbs. It is in the gap between constriction and transcendence that pity arises: in the gap, between the cell block and the outer wall of the prison, where freedom seems close but the high searchlights are always waiting to be snapped on. Blithely, Vonnegut has acquired a licence to pass political partisanship off as satirical neutrality: while it may indeed be that 'a plague on both your houses' becomes the message in relation to ideology, there is nevertheless no doubt that the sheer disgust inspired by late capitalism renders the other critical material pallid. We are not even at the point at which we may reasonably take a political decision; but the reason why is not immutable, but is that the decisions have been, and are being, taken for us according to a perfectly recognisable set of class interests.

To make sense of this world of withheld information, Vonnegut stretches the category of coincidence in a way which can no doubt be conveniently labelled post-modernist, in the sense that the blatant manipulation of plot becomes itself the key motif of the texts, and temporal and spatial simultaneity become the evidence of a continuing joke. 'This is a very great book by an American genius', we read (in Vonnegut's own words) on the back cover of *Palm Sunday* (1981),[2] knowing that one way of reading that is by speculating on what the condition of America might be if the nearest thing it can produce as the great American novel is a collection of autobiographical debris linked together by deadpan cracker-barrel philosophising. Vonnegut presents himself as the provider of those secret areas of information clutched to themselves by the political and military establishments; but what is revealed when that information is brought out into the light is mainly that it is very silly, that up there in the higher echelons the games that are played cluster around the refrains of old playground songs; not that this stops those refrains acting simultaneously as the verbal triggers for destruction, as the keys which turn the locks of the slaughterhouse.

Breakfast of Champions (1973), as befits its title, is a looping meditation on power. Dwayne Hoover possesses the obvious trappings, a Pontiac franchise, a chain of cheap eating-houses, and a bad case of paranoia. Kilgore Trout has none of these things, and engages in an attempt to present himself as an exemplar of failure, but by mistake goes on to win the Nobel prize for medicine. The narrator, sitting behind his mirror glasses in the cocktail bar of a Holiday Inn, knows he can manipulate his puppets, but never perfectly:

> Here was the thing about my control over the characters I created: I could only guide their movements approximately, since they were such big animals. There was inertia to overcome. It wasn't as though I was connected to them by steel wires. It was more as though I was connected to them by stale rubberbands.[3]

Thus when Dwayne's increasing anxieties break out in a series of violent attacks, the narrator cannot escape completely, but suffers a broken watch crystal and a broken toe: his control of time is incomplete, and he suffers identically with his characters from the frailty of the body.

The text builds towards this explosion, and it does it in the careful way of a controlled scientific experiment. Dwayne possesses one half of the volatile substance – the hollowness of materiality, a tendency towards solipsism, a doubt about the reality of the Other – while Trout possesses the other, a Skid Row experience and a surreal sense of his misplacement on the planet. The catalyst, of course, is the written word: one of Trout's widely ignored science fiction novels in which he has posited a world which contains only one human being, set down amid several billion robots. This confirms Dwayne's worst fears and simultaneously his highest hopes: it conveys meaning to him but at the inevitable cost of stripping it from everybody else, sanctions his aloneness but at the same time gives it purpose, since the purpose, according to Trout's novel, of

God's little experiment is to test his one and only created human being before letting him loose in the Garden of Eden. Thus people are machines, 'doomed to collide and collide and collide',[4] bouncing off each other without penetration, without a meeting of soft edges: they are the only possible inhabitants of a world of shining metal and automobiles, of interstate highways and identical hotel rooms. The image of this world without lubrication, without discursive sharing, is 'locomotor ataxia', the outcome of venereal disease which drains fluid from the vertebrae and locks the spine rigid. Such people, Vonnegut tells us – such *men* – appear to possess an extraordinary dignity as they wait, for instance, at a pedestrian crossing, upright and firmly staring, while inside they are struggling to transmit signals from their brains to their feet through what might as well be a thousand miles of intractable material and ineffective internal wiring. But the symbol itself represents a different constellation in the realm of the real: the machine-men who have been formed by slavery and its more modern correlatives, by means of which people are transformed into labouring machines, farming machines, and thus, inevitably, machines for sex and for offence and forgiveness.

Thus, like all Vonnegut's texts, *Breakfast of Champions* works by a series of estrangements. As readers, we are estranged from the planet by being treated as though we know nothing of human history, or of economic needs. We are simultaneously estranged from character, because character here is sublimated into type:

> It didn't matter much what Dwayne said. It hadn't mattered much for years. It didn't matter much what most people in Midland City said out loud, except when they were talking about money or structures or travel or machinery – or other measurable things. Every person had a clearly defined part to play – as a black person, a female high school drop-out, a Pontiac dealer, a gynecologist, a gas-conversion burner installer. If a person stopped living up to expectations, because of bad chemicals or one thing or another, everybody went on imagining that the person was living up to expectations anyway.[5]

So, of course, it takes a long time in this society to register the signs of madness, since they are pretty well indistinguishable from the kinds of behaviour designated as sane and successful; or, it takes a long time to realise that, down the locked spine, one of the smaller vertebrae has at last been crushed out of shape by the corkscrew creatures which are supplanting the nervous system.

This stripping of signification, the process whereby the real relationships between elements in a society or in a language are replaced by the frozen forms of conditioned behaviour, is accompanied by a set of puzzles about the connexions between signifier and signified. Trout hitches a ride in a truck, and notes that on its sides, in letters eight feet high, is the word 'Pyramid'. 'Why did he name his company "Pyramid"?', asked Trout. 'I mean – this thing can go a hundred miles an hour, if it has to. It's fast and useful and unornamental. It's as up-to-date as a rocket ship. I never saw anything that was less like a pyramid than this truck.'[6] When the truck driver answers that he supposes the owner liked the sound of the word, Trout is disquieted; but then, his whole experience has tended to show him that the connexion between word and object is the site of severance, and indeed he has enacted this in his own life and work, writing an endless series of novels and stories and sending them off into the blue without keeping copies. He knows only that some of them have occasionally been used as padding for pornographic magazines, ornamented with suitable graphics which have no connexion whatever with the text, and occasionally retitled. He encounters only one patron, and does not believe in him, and only one reader; and when, finally, a text of his takes effect in the world, it is only to produce a small maelstrom of minor injuries.

Trout's solipsism and the solipsism of the narrator form the entrance to another hall of mirrors, but mirrors here are renamed: for Trout they have long been 'leaks',[7] leaks from or into another world, or, indeed, leaks through which the unwelcome knowledge of the mirror-phase seeps into the world. Trout attempts to be purposeless, but cannot manage it; like the narrator, he is uncomfortably aware of bondage to family structure, of the search for father or mother, and although he wants to have no dealings with his magical creator, when he finds himself in his company he is left with only one demand, to have his stolen youth restored. But he screams this to a blind universe. Treated like a coming saviour by his only reader, he can react only by announcing that he is not exempt from constraint:

> 'Oh, Mr Trout', nice Milo went on, there in Trout's suite, 'teach us to sing and dance and laugh and cry. We've tried to survive so long on money and sex and envy and real estate and football and

basketball and automobiles and television and alcohol – on sawdust and broken glass!'[8]

But Trout brings nothing but 'desolation and desperation', and is, indeed, the originator of it. 'We are healthy only to the extent that our ideas are humane',[9] announces the narrator portentously, which means that it is the books themselves, the records of culture, which promote the decay of value. The narrator comes to understand 'how innocent and natural' it has been for Americans to 'behave so abominably, and with such abominable results: They were doing their best to live like people invented in story books. This was the reason Americans shot each other so often: It was a convenient literary device for ending short stories and books.'[10]

It is thus that the 'Pluto Gang' comes into being: Trout, attacked by a gang of muggers and asked by the police who they were although he never saw them, dismally points out that for all he knows they came from Pluto. This is picked up by the press, and before long a group of Puerto Rican youths decide to incarnate error as fact, much to the satisfaction of the social imagination: 'New Yorkers, who had so many nameless terrors, were easily taught to fear something seemingly specific – "the Pluto Gang".'[11] Thus the function of the writer comes to be precisely this: to offer concrete images around which anxieties may coalesce, or at least to pick up and incarnate the images which may be lying around unnoticed on the cutting-room floor.

In *Wampeters Foma and Granfalloons* (1975), which is a collection of reviews, speeches and other bits and pieces, there are plenty of these key images, and they are, of course, largely the ones we would by now expect. We can find the myth of primal longevity explored largely as it is by Lessing; we can also find, in the *Playboy* interview, Vonnegut's version of the Manson myth. He is asked to explain Manson's appeal:

> His willingness to be father. It's one of the weaknesses of our society that so few people are willing to be father, to be responsible, to be the organiser, to say what's to be done next. Very few people are up to this. So if somebody is willing to take charge, he is very likely to get followers – more than he knows what to do with. . . . I assume that Charles Manson projected not only a willingness to become father but to remain father and become grandfather and then great-grandfather.[12]

And this assessment dovetails with Vonnegut's major social imagery, which is to become the lynchpin of his later fictions: the imagery of the extended family. The views expressed are basically organicist: Vonnegut mourns the passing of the 'folk society', a social organism in which there was no distinction between neighbours and relatives; and he clearly thinks that a great deal of social and cultural activity can be explained as part of the rush to fill this vacuum. Thus, the truth about society is simply that it is intolerable: the question is whether Manson and the forces of brute power can offer more satisfying lies than the harbingers of beauty and peace. Vonnegut claims, again in the *Playboy* interview, that he wants a new imposition of quasi-familial fealty, if necessary by legislation; even though – or perhaps because – he recognises that this would entail the wind-down of the social services. It is impossible to project the image of a large-scale caring society: if there is to be care, then it can only be a function of the local community, and the rest is alienation and mistrust.

In many ways, the most fascinating essay in the book is the short piece on Hesse and his significance as social adviser. There is obviously a spark here: Vonnegut finds himself treated as an interpreter of and to youth, and Hesse shares that cult status. But as Vonnegut points out, the crucial question is what image of the self Hesse makes available:

> And I say again: What my daughters and sons are responding to in
> *Steppenwolf* is the homesickness of the author. I do not mock
> homesickness as a silly affliction that is soon outgrown. I never
> outgrew it and neither did my father and neither did Hesse. I miss
> my Mommy and Daddy, and I always will – because they were so
> nice to me. Now and then, I would like to be a child again.[13]

Hesse's novels, then, are models of the narrative of the ego; what has happened historically is a loop whereby the middle-European home-sickness of Hesse's generation has reconnected to the generational rejections of the 1960s and 1970s. But again, what Vonnegut is here diagnosing is nothing less than the plight of America. Hesse's heroes are useful to us as garb at those moments when, perhaps, we walk into a bar in a strange town; or when, sitting at the controls of a machine we only dimly know how to handle, we suspect that there is some gap between instrument and purpose. And these are precisely the stuff of modern American experience: pointless travel, failure of societal integration, the ambivalence of the prosthetic relationship. In the absence of effective or organic parent/child relationships, we re-invent them in distorted forms: rather than treating with them, taking the work of a life as the proper transformation of a relationship with our parents into a wider stock of forms of love, we set up the family as a rigid pattern because only thus can we escape our feelings of loss; but of course, by the very act of doing so we underline our perpetual disappointment with the relationships which are available. For Vonnegut, writing is one way of effecting transformation, dissipating the transference:[14]

> One thing writing *Breakfast* did for me was to bring right to the surface my anger with my parents for not being happier than they were. . . . I'm damned if I'll pass their useless sadness on to my children if I can possibly help it.[15]

Thus the writer engages in symbolic action, by means of which persistent structures in the social fabric may be loosened, although there is a considerable time lag. Vonnegut subscribes to the 'canary-in-the-coalmine' theory of art:[16] in other words, when things get bad writers chirp and keel over. As he also points out, during the Vietnam war most American writers did precisely that, and nobody appeared to take much notice; but then, says Vonnegut, the effect won't be felt yet; the important thing is that the minds of the young have been benevolently 'poisoned'. The main form of this symbolic action seems to be the surfacing and expiation of guilt, a guilt which is connected with the homesickness. Americans can never go home any more, in two senses: they cannot return to that middle Europe which, for Hesse and for Vonnegut, represents origins, and they also cannot find the quality of home in the United States, for their claim to the land is built on a web of lies and fraud. There are, of course, the Indians: sitting, during a political convention, absolutely still, because the least gesture they might make would be immediately reinterpreted by the white media in the form of caricature. But there is also 'the terror and guilt and hatred white people feel for the descendants of victims of an unbelievable crime we committed not long ago – human slavery'.[17]

Here, perhaps, we are near the root of Vonnegut's own appeal to the young. For his style is one which seeks to take account of the problems caused by these primal lies and severances: it is improvisatory, disconnected, it is as though the narrative structures themselves are temporary, provisional, and as though the ideas are moment-by-moment responses to desperation, not to be erected in a coherent system. On this shifting sand, the style appears to say, nothing lasting can be built; and anything that can be built at all must be in a constant state of change, we must always be looking over our own shoulders for the signs of decay and replacement. Thus, of course, the persistent device of adding 'And so on' to the ends of paragraphs, to signify that there is so much more randomness to the world than can be expressed on the neat page. Thus, more significantly, the echolalia which sporadically grips Vonnegut and his characters:[18] it is the sound of the void, of the endless space in which the voice rings and hears its own doubt about an audience. As in *Breakfast of Champions*, perhaps there is nobody real out there at all, perhaps we are only spinning out of our entrails a various and illusory monologue; just as at the societal level, there are doubts as to whether it is really possible for America to hear the voices of dissent, reproof, reminder, or whether to pay attention to them would provoke the feared trauma and make us realise that homesickness is not a subjectivistic affliction but the pale reflection of a deeper and more profoundly troubling rootlessness.

The authorial gesture of these collected pieces is to do with an attempt to save before collapse; before we fall into the pit which awaits us, Vonnegut would like to provide us with a safety-net of fictions, and is willing to press eclectically into service whatever sufficiently harmless lies he can find. Under the present conditions, he believes man will always bond together in groups, because we act under a compulsion, a biological imperative, to attempt continually to recreate tolerable con-ditions of life, even though this is now technically impossible. The important thing is the sign under which these groups form, the totem which they choose: and here Manson's murderousness is clearly less developmental than, say, Madame Blavatsky's theosophy, or than some kinds of Christianity, or even than a plate of spaghetti. 'Everything is going to become unimaginably worse, and never get better again'[19]; but with a bit of luck, and sufficient benevolence, we may avoid noticing that this is the case. The flippant and the sombre go hand in hand in a structure which is indeed schizophrenic, although aware of its own contradictions: it is as though, when the holocaust comes, we can 'survive' by having trained ourselves to live all the rest of our lives in the split second before incineration. But there is also a faith in the corrosive power of ridicule: that somehow, by means of incantations such as, indeed, the very title of the book, we can set up a force which will rock the institutional foundations and break open the walls of the Pentagon.

The problem of metaphysical solipsism is referred back to the actual conditions of life, and the cry of the hoped-for future becomes 'Lonesome No More!', which then in turn becomes the subtitle of Vonnegut's next fiction, *Slapstick* (1976), which is 'about desolated cities and spiritual cannibalism and incest and loneliness and lovelessness and death'.[20] It is a narrative of the double and of the Frankensteinian monstrous birth; the twin central characters are too Neanderthal, too hideous to survive and are thus immediately entombed. Together they constitute an all-embracing psyche; kept apart by vicious circumstance they are unable to operate in this way and become instead figures for lost hope, a potential which America declines to accept. As in Lessing, the group mind and its possibilities for development and interpretation is the feared object; not only in the shape of the twins but also as the Chinese who, in the wings of the text, are overcoming individualism and, as a result, passing into realms of experience where the West cannot follow. In the process, they are also miniaturising themselves, and there is a complex and doubtful connexion between this and the several evils which descend on the planet; gravity becomes irregular and unpredictable, and diseases appear, diseases which may perhaps be the operations of an exasperated nature or, alternatively, the 'result of inhaling and ingesting invisible Chinese communists'.[21] 'Going to China' becomes an image for suicide, because nobody who goes there to find out what is going on ever returns; but whether this is because of some dreadful fate which awaits or because something is happening in China which makes American individualism forever unpalatable remains open to doubt. Certainly the Chinese eventually withdraw their by now microscopic ambassador from the US because, as he puts it, nothing is going on in America or the West which is any longer of any feasible interest to the more advanced group mind.

Wilbur and Eliza, the twins, incarnate the trace of the self-sufficient relationship, and are thus partially freed from the bonds of mortality. But they find themselves in the paradoxical situation of the traditional monster; feared but tolerated so long as they pretend to be idiots, once they decide it is worth letting the world know the full extent of their mental powers they are forced apart and 'reduced to size'. One consideration which at first keeps them from realising or expressing the extent of their powers is that they do not wish to disrupt the lives and expectations of those who have been appointed to take care of them:

Consider: We were at the center of the lives of those who cared for us. They could be heroically Christian in their own eyes only if Eliza and I remained helpless and vile. If we became openly wise and self-reliant, they would become our drab and inferior assistants. If we became capable of going out into the world, they might lose their apartments, their color televisions, their illusions of being sorts of doctors and nurses, and their high-paying jobs.[22]

This is the circle of dependency, the assumed understanding on the part of the child that his or her weakness is an essential part of a relational system which will fall apart as they step out of their allotted roles. It is, in fact, the twins' millionaire parents who are obsessively described as young; it is as though they have come through the full circle of material acquisition which has now left them re-childed and irresponsible, and the monstrous birth is the mark of the impossibility of proceeding any further with this terminal cycle. With the planet squeezed dry of resources by the Rockefellers and the Fords, the only way forward lies through the emergence of the new rough beast(s).

But Eliza dies, and Wilbur is left bearing the scarred promise; the rest of his life, culminating in his election as President, passes in a kind of dream as his power seeps away. Yet this dream, and the concomitant atrophy of society, has its own compensations: 'I found the hospitality of my mind to fantasy pleasantly increased as machinery died and communications from the outside world became more and more vague'.[23] So the text moves between two richnesses. In the beginning, we have the spreading wealth of the primal scene: not only the twins, but the death-wish the parents visit upon them, the doubt in relation to the doctor who is (re)placed in charge of their upbringing, the ready absorption of the available wisdom of the West, the mansion which not only entombs them but also provides them with an entire apparatus of secret routes through which they can find their way to a kind of maturity without passing through the conventional channels. But because the severance of the (double-)jointed mind makes this scene inaccessible, this initial richness comes to take on another, clouded form, as the dream-knot, the series of cataclysmic events which can be arranged in no causal order and which reaches down into its own unknowable. As knowledge fades, Wilbur becomes increasingly able to take a kind of temporal power; but as he does so, the site of that power is wrecked, and so is his ability to provide himself with a satisfying account of history.

And so the narrative breaks, is fractured at the point at which the questions might begin to be answered, and Wilbur's voice disappears; the final section of the book brings on another voice, but it is unattributed and so we pass through into the void which follows the death of relationship.

For Wilbur, this seems to bring on a delayed attack of childhood ritualism:

> Because everything had dwindled so quickly, and because there was no one to behave sanely for any more, I developed a mania for counting things. I counted slats in venetian blinds. I counted the knives and forks and spoons in the kitchen. I counted the tufts of the coverlet on Abraham Lincoln's bed.[24]

And yet this reduction comes at the same time as the realisation of the group dream: Wilbur's only significant act as President is at last to put into practice one of the schemes which he and Eliza had dreamed up years before at the time when they were wise, and to assign every person in the country to an arbitrarily chosen extended family. Salvation arrives, in the sense that the trace of familial longing is at last accommodated, but in an arena aside from parental conditioning: a massive transition into family shape is made possible without the concomitant Oedipal knotting. But it arrives too late, and the structure which is meant to provide free flow is installed after the breakdown of the material means of communication. The yearning for home thus remains, and the massive structures of dependency remain unbreakable. Towards the end, Wilbur, the ageing and powerless President, is summoned to see one of the warlords who have arisen to fill the vacuum:

> It was such a comically trite historical situation, I thought. Aside from battles, the history of nations seemed to consist of nothing but powerless old poops like myself, heavily medicated and vaguely beloved in the long ago, coming to kiss the boots of young psychopaths.[25]

The model twins are Laurel and Hardy, bound together by nothing more (or less) powerful than obedience to an unchangeable set of behavioural conventions; but the generational knot is not slipped so easily, even though Wilbur thought he had been careful not to reproduce himself. He finds nevertheless that he has a grandchild:

So, when Melody gave him shy but convincing arguments that she was an actual blood relative, he had a feeling that he . . . 'had somehow sprung a huge leak. And out of that sudden, painless opening . . . there crawled a famished child, pregnant and clasping a Dresden candlestick'.[26]

The candlestick is the broken and useless phallus;[27] Wilbur is the 'King of Candlesticks', named for his huge but useless collection, and there are no more candles. Dresden, of course, refers us back to *Slaughter-house-Five* (1969) and the archetypal revelation of the terminal violence of patriarchy: the absent flame and the absenting fire-bomb, self-destruction and the pointless destruction of civilisation again entangled in the inability to form communicating groups.

Jailbird (1979) has no subtitle because it carries no alibi; far from being 'elsewhere', Walter Starbuck was indeed precisely on the scene when it happened, the scene of Watergate, which figures here as the unmasking of childhood lies – although even on that scene, his role has been publicly forgotten, as has his previous part in testifying before the McCarthy tribunals. His crimes are venal: his assistance to Nixon was largely unwitting, or at least passive, while his evidence against his erstwhile comrade Leland Clewes, the Alger Hiss clone and ruined golden boy of WASP America, remains ambiguous. It is one of the several truths we are not vouchsafed, but this matters little to Starbuck or to the structure of the text, because essentially *Jailbird* is the narrative of shame, of unsuppressable embarrassment, and its occasions matter little. In the beginning, he is in jail, and so he is at the end: whether he deserves this fate has long passed his comprehension, because it is all too clearly a likely consequence of an intolerable economic and political order. It is not that Vonnegut is seeking the consciousness of Watergate; rather, that he is painfully probing that self-wounding which has histori-cally meant that no such consciousness exists, that Watergate becomes the throbbing trace of a dream of power, in which nevertheless the figures of actual power continually pass us by while we are prevented from questioning them by their clear possession of credentials – Harvard, wealth, the White House. If Starbuck comes to know that these claims are false, he is nonetheless at a loss when it comes to replacing them. It may indeed transpire that most of the real power in the US has passed into the arbitrary realm of the RAMJAC corporation and its ghostly operatives, but even this paranoiac awareness fails him when he discovers that in fact the corporation owns only 19 per cent of America; even big business cannot constitute a total explanation of the prior betrayal.

The recurrent motif of excessive smoking is also double-edged: it is true that it images shame as cancer, the numbing of responses so that differentiations are obliterated and cells cannot separate themselves but are condemned to a bit part in the carriage of death, but also for Starbuck it signifies merely burns in his best and only suit, and also the unassailable memory that it was only this excessive deference to habit which got him noticed by Nixon, whose adviser on youth affairs he ostensibly was. And thus the chain of generational reversals, with which we are by now becoming familiar, begins again. Vonnegut refers in his prologue to a pretext which enshrined the story of the relations between himself, his father and the category of potential. Everybody, in heaven, has a choice about their (unchangeable) age: the father chooses to be nine, Vonnegut to be forty-four, and the result is the pre-image of embarrassment:

> He was lemurlike as a nine-year-old, all eyes and hands. . . . Bullies liked to torment him, since he was not like other children. He did not enjoy children's talk and children's games. Bullies would chase him and catch him and take off his pants and underpants and throw them down the mouth of hell. . . . Whenever Father had his pants stolen, he would come running to me, purple with rage. As like as not, I had just made some new friends and was impressing them with my urbanity – and there my father would be, bawling bloody murder and with his little pecker waving in the breeze.[28]

Walter himself, trying to bring some order to the Nuremberg trials, is seen by his future wife, an ex-inmate of the camps, as an eight-year-old. The instances could be multiplied; but again, they have their function as themselves pretexts for the formation of an alternative family. Because Walter, in his long-spent youth, knew (largely carnally) the present major stockholder of the RAMJAC corporation (Mrs Jack Graham, signified as hermaphrodite), therefore everybody he meets on his passage from jail and who shows him the least kindness is implicated in his temporary resurgence within that corporation. This body of eventual Vice-Presidents, casually met during a Joycean morning in New York which expands to take in the universe, is not an especially close or trusting one; but at least it does, for a moment, allow Walter to recapitulate and assuage the years of (solitary) confinement.

Or we can put the cyclical narrative another way, as the oscillation between rival models of exploitation and hypocrisy. In the beginning (as one aspect of the myth of origins) we have the Ponzi schemes of Carlo di Sanza, one of Walter's fellow-jailbirds, which are a variant of pyramid selling and thus encapsulate the instability and terminality of capitalism. At the end we have the myth of the heavenly audit: each soul, as it enters heaven, is informed that he or she did, after all, have chances – perhaps they passed every day a collection of gold bullion stored under a man-hole cover, or living in a derelict hut in the Appalachians they in fact spent their time over the largest deposit of nickel in the world – but when the ghost of Einstein, appalled at the impossibility of supposing that we were all, therefore, missed millionaires on a cosmically expanding economic scale, complains to God, all he gets is a furious archangel telling him not to gum up the works. But the twinned myths are identical: we are required to solace ourselves by a fantasy of continuous expansion, which is also the solace offered us as surrogate for the induced paucity of personal relationships. Only invest (in our children) and we will be exempt from the fate of resource starvation. Mrs Graham, manager of empires but living as a paper-bag lady to avoid the operatives of envy, says that she needs 'solid information', that she needs to know 'what was really going on',[29] thus echoing the wish-cry of Vonnegut-texts from beginning to end; but the quest is hopeless.

She actually spends her time circumambulating the height and the depth, attempting to square the circle. The depth, the maze of secret passageways under Grand Central Station, offers her only a miserable death, the height only an equally miserable betrayal. But the height is (as it is societally for Vonnegut) more interesting; it is represented by the interior of the peculiar superstructure on top of the Chrysler skyscraper, a metal pyramid with elongated heart-shaped windows, whose insides Vonnegut fills with the obvious correlate, the sales offices of the American Harp Company. But not only are there harps there, symbols of auto-destruction since, we are informed, the tension in harps prevents them from ever becoming investments, but there are also pro-thonatory warblers, the incarnated 'jail-birds', 'released' into this 'open' (but closed) space because their droppings are uniquely containable. Habituated to shitting in other birds' nests, they therefore become uniquely human.

Over all this hovers another myth of origins, a primal massacre of the

American labour movement, a scene portrayed (in the prologue) in almost total silence, which thus prefigures the further linguistic complications of the text. Alexander Hamilton McCone, the relatively humanistic son of the deathly capitalist, is converted by his participation in this scene from an averagely traumatised stammerer into 'a bubbling booby of totally blocked language'.[30] Naming is to a large extent a matter of anagram, although these anagrams are interminable in that they continually point beyond themselves. Cleveland Lawes, himself a lower-class black anagram, eventually gives vent to his fabled ability to speak Chinese. 'How do we know he wasn't ordering sweet-and-sour pork?',[31] asks Sarah, who incarnates the displacement of sexuality into language. She treats every manifestation of sex as a joke, inverting Freud; and she and Walter, replaying their past love ('I am a recidivist', he finally announces in the nearest the text gets to a staged revelation), converse only in prerun jokes which are reasonably mistaken by her husband as sex-play. The circles are endless: her husband is the man who partnered Walter in the game of bluff and betrayal years earlier from whose effects they are both still suffering.

The series of texts overall thus enacts hope against hope: the sombre assessment locked into the laughing vaulting. The too omnipresent might also be the too ridiculous: all the ramifications of socialist practice might, after all, count for less than the sudden revelation of the intolerable. It is thus that the primary psychic mechanism becomes coincidence, and/or the simultaneity of time: the tying up of all these knots of lives in the shaking hands of international finance must surely (mustn't it?) reveal to us that domination is rooted in our own capitulation in the urge towards logocentrism. But against this centripetality, what can we display but the random? By pushing coincidence to its inmost margin, and by suggesting that all these manifestations are perspectives on a single phantom, we must be able to banish, because when a ghost is approached from all sides what we perceive, through the transparency, is each other. So runs the wish, along with the concomitant hope that this revelation will be enough to reassure us of both our solidity and also, more importantly, our commonality of interest.

What stands in the way is the father, not as authority but as the reverse, as a prior attempt at liberation which failed. The father of these texts (Vonnegut's father, Vonnegut as father) is in retreat: what he has experienced as impregnable does not recommend itself for our attack, and thus the doubleness of movement. Thus the lack is the female: in

Jailbird, we learn (continually) that Walter has loved four women, but what becomes apparent is that he has divided his desire for the passional self and thus weakened it, multiplying his mothers and sisters to the point where they are bloodless, and thereby sealing his own isolation – and thus, textually, ours, as we are confronted with an alienated plural whose voice can never be heard.

Section B:
Practice and theory

6 Fears of surveillance/strategies for the future

> The longer I continue, the more it seems to me that the formation
> of discourses and the genealogy of knowledge need to be analysed,
> not in terms of types of consciousness, modes of perception and
> forms of ideology, but in terms of tactics and strategies of power.
> Tactics and strategies deployed through implantations,
> distributions, demarcations, control of territories and organisations
> of domains which could well make up a sort of geopolitics . . . [1]

One thing which seems valuable in relation to these fragments of the
social text is to develop some of the connexions between the Foucauldian discourse of knowledges and powers and the contemporary
discourse of fictional futures. This is not simply an issue of critical
method: the Foucauldian 'obsession' with translation into geographical
metaphor and the impulse in much of the fiction to use the mechanics of
time to reshape (outer and inner) space to conform to the projections of
desire can also be seen in parallel.[2] According to Foucault, the major
change of modernity has been the replacement of power modelled on
real or hypothetical sovereignty by power through surveillance, the
implantation of devices for recording and monitoring in every local site[3]:
under these circumstances, we can follow the tactics of the 'literary' as it
seeks not to validate but to escape omniscience. The text itself, whether
in the hands of Big Brother or as the Little Red Book, is implicated in
the processes of surveillance, and has to perform increasingly complicated manoeuvres to avoid entanglement in a military/commercial
complex. Foucault's achievement has been to effect a dissociation
between the concepts of power and the category of repression:

> What makes power hold good, what makes it accepted, is simply the
> fact that it doesn't only weigh on us as a force that says no, but that it
> traverses and produces things, it induces pleasure, forms
> knowledge, produces discourse. It needs to be considered as a

97

productive network which runs through the whole social body, much more than as a negative instance whose function is repression.[4]

The fictional future needs to be placed alongside Foucault because there the 'spirals of power and pleasure' are laid bare:[5] to read *Brave New World* merely as an instance of repression is to deny the force of a dialectic, the pleasure of a text which holds us closely and safely in the bosom of Big Brother at the same time as permitting us the indulgence of rebellion.

It is the study of the detailed workings of textual pleasure which has characteristically eluded the critical histories of the future in their assumption of unitary and linear development from an assumed structure of the present:

> . . . the engaging novelties of these brave new worlds tend to mask the primary fact that all didactic stories about the future begin from the possibilities considered to be latent in the contemporary world. The archaeology of the genre reveals that, level by level and period after period, the perennial question about the best arrangement of human society is at the centre of this intensely self-conscious and exceptionally varied form of fiction.[6]

This discourse of 'problems' and 'solutions' rests on a conception of the Real as revealed through the detailed workings of social and especially scientific and industrial history, and thus asserts that the relevant structures of power to which the fiction of the future addresses itself are global. Against this we need to place the Foucauldian vision of a controlling 'panoptism':

> . . . an ensemble of mechanisms brought into play in all the clusters of procedures used by power. Panoptism was a technological invention in the order of power, comparable with the steam engine in the order of production. This invention had the peculiarity of being utilised first of all on a local level, in schools, barracks and hospitals. This was where the experiment of integral surveillance was carried out. People learned how to establish dossiers, systems of marking and classifying, the integrated accountancy of individual records. Certain of the procedures had of course already been utilised in the economy and taxation. But the permanent surveillance of a group of pupils or patients was a different matter.[7]

On this analysis, what has been essential in the progression of fictions of the future from the eighteenth century has had less to do with their insistence on the relations between societal development and specific invented mechanisms – the balloon, the submarine, the computerised file – than with the locations offered within the texts for narrator and subject; the global view of the eighteenth-century political propagandists and, in self-conscious form, of Verne's world-encompassing heroes, encapsulated in Phileas Fogg's covert vindication of the planet as a single system, interlocking as neatly as an ideal train timetable, has been gradually replaced by a view from the ground, from the local site of power. Change in the set of knowledges on offer in the global supermarket/university/operational research establishment is often experienced in the text as it produces instability in the power relations of the local hospital/school/plant research institute.[8] It is from there that the heroic future self sets out to investigate change in the wider network, and often his achievement is partial: forms of power collapse and are replaced without the aid of full comprehension – after all, accessible modes of knowledge are being replaced by 'operational codes, logistic curves, systems analysis, trend extrapolation, morphological research, relevance tree techniques',[9] all the apparatus of new discourse which Pynchon deploys to reveal a new – and to a large extent arbitrary – history of the past: the fictional text itself, bounded by concepts of the literary and by the demands of an audience to whom most of the discourses of power have become foreign, can only reflect this in shadow form, thus also enacting the wish that a feared specialisation will collapse under its own pressure and allow again the emergence of an empty site – the island, the desolated city, the institution reshaped as a play area stripped of adult meanings – against which backdrop the 'free individual' can begin again, secure in a 'knowledge' that the forms of surveillance have broken under their own weight. Thus what appears as a search for prediction, for knowledge *of*, becomes a cover story for a different wish, for the return of a 'cloud of unknowing' such that there is no knowledge *by*: in the wished-for world, we will no longer be subject to credit checks, data accumulation, domestic policing; the discourse we have 'naturally' available to us will again become adequate as a guarantor of individual power. At its simplest, a major governmental imperative of the last three centuries, the imperative of the census, will be negated, and nobody out there will know how many of us there are, or therefore how many different shapes may be assumed by the hitherto confined subject.

Fahrenheit 451

> When I was a boy my grandfather died, and he was a sculptor. He
> was also a very kind man who had a lot of love to give the world, and
> he helped clean up the slum in our town; and he made toys for us
> and he did a million things in his life-time; he was always busy with
> his hands. And when he died, I suddenly realised I wasn't crying for
> him at all, but for all the things he did. . . . He was part of us and
> when he died, all the actions stopped dead and there was no one to
> do them just the way he did. He was an individual. He was an
> important man. I've never gotten over his death.[10]

In Ray Bradbury's text (1954), the association of 'Granger' with the
husbandman of the Lord, the good tenant-farmer who makes the most
of his talents, discloses the affinities between Granger's grandfather and
Montag, 'Saint Monday', holy relic of a world before the enclosure of
space and time. In that world, the skill of shaping could move and
distribute itself freely down the channels of power: sculpting and town
planning were fused in a universal concept of 'good works'. Yet the
books have an uneasy relation to this concept of communicational flow,
and this is the site of irresolution in the text: channel for experience, but
also blocking artefact, the book is not a direct means of transmission but
a double symbol. 'They weren't at all certain that the things they carried
in their heads might make every future dawn glow with a purer light, they
were sure of nothing save that the books were on file behind their quiet
eyes, the books were waiting, with their pages uncut, for the customers
who might come by in later years, some with clean and some with dirty
fingers':[11] transmission into the present is subordinated to the demand
for a channel direct from past to future, and what is encoded is the fear
of a present too tarnished for revelation. The only way to escape
surveillance is through a separation: the conscious contents of the mind
can be allowed to remain trivial – *must* remain trivial if they are not to be
usable by the probes of authority, the deadly scenting of the Mechanical
Hound – provided we can cheer ourselves up with the thought that,
below the surface, the wisdom of ages is stored, un-conscious, providing
the source for an unimaginable future educational practice.

The literary thus hides itself and sulks; but in fact, it has already been
taken over, reduced itself to quantification under the thin guise of
quality control:

Do you know why books such as this are so important? Because they have quality. And what does the word quality mean? To me it means texture. This book has *pores*. It has features. This book can go under the microscope. You'd find life under the glass, streaming past in infinite profusion. The more pores, the more truthfully recorded details of life per square inch you can get on a sheet of paper, the more 'literary' you are.[12]

But this is a capitulation in the discourse of data, and the text knows it: only in the future can the streaks on the tulip be other than numbered, and in the meantime the text must pass the time on the shelf of a human library. Secrecy and the existence of an élite of 'Voluntary Nobility' become the mirroring response to the freemasonry of the firemen:[13] what is enacted is the academy, cheated of access to power, turning into a temporary consumer, absorbing back into itself the sweetness and light which a blackened world rejects. In *Fahrenheit 451*, the controlling wish is for the validation of the unaccompanied word, for the refusal of the hieroglyphs of commercial and political persuasion represented in the televisor and the White Clown; the text realises that what is proposed can therefore be nothing less than a change in the processes of time and space, a switch from the domestic interior and the programme note to the wilderness of unsurveyed leisure.

What Foucault suggests is that this opposition can be seen as a reflection of the ways in which, operating in our minds and bodies on behalf of the sources of power, we exercise surveillance over ourselves, in the name not of repression but of pleasure. The new mechanism of power 'is constantly exercised by means of surveillance rather than in a discontinuous manner by means of a system of levies or obligations distributed over time. It presupposes a tightly knit grid of material coercions rather than the physical existence of a sovereign.'[14] Within this system, it is obvious that the televisor represents the tightly knit grid; what is less obvious – and is, indeed, partly suppressed by the text – is that the charge of pleasure connected to the book derives from the wish for an older system of sovereignty and domination. The book, after all, is apparently free from time: it can be picked up and put down, parts of the memory can be rerun at will. But over this illusory freedom hovers the domination of culture, the internalisation of an allegiance which is feudal in its intensity, no less slavish in its resistance to change.

The pleasure of the unaccompanied text in *Fahrenheit 451* is caught up in an unarticulated set of gender assumptions: what female reliance on the televisor is said to effect is the breakdown of the family, but what lurks behind this is an unacceptable challenge to male authority, and it is this which Montag flees to be with a new Rosicrucian 'brotherhood', leaving the women to an endless round of coffee mornings. It is only the man who can be truly scorched by the flames of experience: their heat is contrasted with the steady white light of the screen, and we are invited to collude in a masculine but sexless resurrection. After the cataclysm,

> The other men lay a while, on the dawn edge of sleep, not yet ready to rise up and begin the day's obligations, its fires and foods, its thousand details of putting foot after foot and hand after hand. They lay blinking their dusty eyelids. You could hear them breathing fast, then slower, then slow . . . [15]

Womb envy is present in the tucking away of the seeds of the future, the return to a modified tribal vision where male obligation is rendered palatable by a clutching of creativity to the masculine self in a Hemingway-esque projection of hunting and poetry: here, all the books are garnered away from the dangerous city, but the passivity of the televisor is in the end replicated by the passivity of continuous and pointless rememoration, an endless wandering in search of the lost secret of reproduction and birth.[16] The text turns in on itself, and the fear of the complexity of knowledges is drowned in a 'child-like' sleep in a space without organisation or direction.

The Sirens of Titan

The conflict of discourses projected in *Fahrenheit 451* is between surveillance and disclosure, in the forms of the multiple implantation of secrecy and the reservation of a powerless power to a bracketed unconscious which will somehow foster the future. In Vonnegut's *Sirens of Titan* (1959), the ramshackle Army of Mars sparks our pleasure in the imminent failure of surveillance techniques, and the tissue of imaginary quotations vindicates a more haphazard historical and biographical discourse at the expense of the forms of organisation. The musical discourse of the inhabitants of the caves of Mercury marks a further step in the nostalgic regress: here is the unitary voice of the single sheet of parchment, incomprehensible to us until we realise that it is the voice which speaks our name, which spells out in visual form our process of self-differentiation. Unk may have lost his 'signature'; but it is in safe keeping in the caves of birth and death, deep below the fires of Mercury, which symbolise the formlessness from which we need to be protected.

The terror of total organisation which is thus displaced appears again in Salo, to whom the planet is a text, and a functional one at that; but even the mighty and impersonal power represented in the machine from the stars is not proof against the discourse of the thoroughly, and traditionally, individuated subject:

> 'The machine is no longer a machine', said Salo. 'The machine's contacts are corroded, his bearings fouled, his circuits shorted, and his gears stripped. His mind buzzes and pops like the mind of an Earthling – fizzes and overheats with thoughts of love, honour, dignity, rights, accomplishment, integrity, independence – .'[17]

Thus both the military and the technical are subjugated to a victory for humanising chaos; the reader is invited to suppose that the discourses of pure instruction, threatening though they might appear, will cease to be effective when confronted with the irreducibly individual, the 'constant' prophet of survival.

The price paid is a heavy one: a spatial removal, from Earth through Mars and Mercury to Titan. The complex power structures of over-population are replaced by the simplest model of all, military obedience; then by a world where both power and knowledge have disappeared and been replaced by the single, self-satisfied hieroglyph; and finally by the family, seen as the site of the suicide of the machine and the resurrection of affect. The next stage on the parabolic loop, of course, is Tral-famadore itself, but not for us; instead, satisfied by the vindication of domesticity and its triumph over design, we are returned to an am-biguous death – ambiguous not principally in terms of the closing dream, but in that Malachi Constant, secure in the return of his name, appears to need no longer to fear reduction to a statistic.

Even the harmoniums of Mercury set Unk an 'intelligence test' and, feeding as they do on the song of their planet, are given as potentially implicated in the gathering of 'intelligence'; but for them power and knowledge are dissociated, for 'the messages were written, of course, by Winston Niles Rumfoord, who materialised briefly on Mercury at fourteen-day intervals. He peeled off harmoniums here, slapped others up there, making the block letters.'[18] This process of artifice is contrasted as ironically benevolent to the epochal discourse of the

Tralfamadoreans, but only because the operation of unchallengeable power is here accompanied by aesthetic pleasure: to the functionalism of Tralfamadore is contrasted the possibility, in Rumfoord, of a poetics of power, versification and rhyme writ large in the recurrent and symmetrical operation of the 'chrono-synclastic infundibulum'. Rumfoord has seen the cycle of predictability, but he cannot use it: as readers, we are safe from surveillance and machination because Rumfoord is as much a victim of the poetic and arbitrary as are we.

There is no global power-source in *Sirens of Titan*, but no validity is granted to local knowledges either: pleasure is invested in the hope that, however perfect the quality and quantity of information may become, it can gain no purchase on the Möbius strip. Thus we are invited to share in a peeling back of layer after layer of apparent control: fallibility is spread equally through the interlocking systems, and the pain of subjection is dissolved, Big Brother reduced comfortingly to a fellow-victim of circumstance. We do not need to escape into the dark of *Fahrenheit 451*, because the future is given as convergent: as the levels of discourse multiply, they undercut each other. This is the illusory perfection of military and diplomatic intelligence which is supposed to render war unnecessary: there is no Mechanical Hound, only Kazak; no production of meaning but only the endless recurring palindrome which in time vanishes in the flare of its own instability.

> We can make the centre of a man's memory virtually as sterile as a scalpel fresh from the autoclave. But grains of new experience begin to accumulate on it at once. These grains in turn form themselves into patterns not necessarily favourable to military thinking. Unfortunately, this problem of recontamination seems insoluble.[19]

Regimentation is destined to fail, the pain from the antenna can always be fought: the thinned discourse of subservience and domination is incapable of reducing the self to commodity. Thus the only valid texts are those with actants, heroes; and narrative, even if the hero loses name and world, is vindicated at the expense of the specious 'authorities' who claim access to the system at the heart of time. Yet what is at stake is only a distribution of powerlessness: Rumfoord has all the time in the world but his spatial manifestations are strictly bounded, Malachi Constant is granted supernatural mobility and spatial exemption, but his time runs out. Twin hopes of transcendence are shown as self-cancelling, and even the sirens of Titan, the Muses, the point of validation for the continuous poeticisation of the universe, end up covered in algae, buried in their pool, again bypassing an unwholesome present in favour of a future awakening.

'Morris in Chains'

Fahrenheit 451 and *Sirens of Titan* present us with a triple discourse: within the narratives are framed condensed representations of the feared discourse of power (the unredeemed automatism of the firemen, the handbook of the Army of Mars) and of the wished-for discourse of the freed subject (recitations from the classics, the quirky histories of the future). Robert Coover's 'Morris in Chains'[20] dissolves the narrative chain back into discursive opposition, presenting us with Morris's first-person singular against the curious first-person plural of the anonymous representative of pursuit. The clarity of this clash is delusive: Morris's discourse is bracketed, not to exclude the reader but to slot him/her into the proper place, as the otherwise non-existent addressee of Morris's musings. Yet, as an audience, we are divided: for while our singular and private subjectivity is being unwittingly addressed by Morris, our public selves, our selves-as-plurality, are the recipients of the broadcast messages of Dr Peloris's team and are thus placed in uncomfortable proximity to the systems of information and power:

> Through the tense days that followed, Dr Peloris and her handpicked staff of highly trained urbanologists, high above the City, pored over the dossiers of previous forays. Polly and the other systems analysts made octal and symbolic corrections to the operational program, broke down old software systems and reassembled the data under new descriptors, and came up with a new standard programming package for the project, now known as Project Sheep Shape.[21]

The female is, as in *Fahrenheit 451*, still embedded in the city but is now mistress of its discourse, the agent of a feared redistribution of power, behind the televisor instead of in front of it: what is *shown* on the screen is the squirmings of Morris, guardian of the last free spaces. The fate of the male is to provide a little spectacle before the inevitable castration, a small drama of pointless singularity before being 'turned over to the urbanologists'.[22]

What Morris threatens, or promises, is again recontamination: 'perhaps due to an underestimation of the adversary's perverse vitality, those early expeditions were all too often subverted by disorder, what we can now see as an undeniable disorder.'[23] Morris is, of course, the goat, the 'stubborn beast flesh' which grows back again even in Doctor Moreau's haphazard laboratories:[24] the apparent freedom granted to the reader in the unattributed clash of discourses is itself a paradoxical illusion of liberty, for here the loading in favour of the singular and resistant subject, the weight of Eros, is immense, the opposition unredeemed even by the ignorance which characterises the firemen and the lesser bosses of the Army of Mars. And here again we can trace the lineaments of the lost sovereign: Morris heads an alternative empire, of sheep – he 'included them, they him, his speed was describable only by theirs'[25] – and in him the untrammelled male ego has a last fling until, inevitably, brought down variously by women, both doctor and witch. His desires are modelled on the ram, his alternate form of plurality a cover story for dreams of unchallengeable polygyny: in this sense, he has created the conditions for his supersession by an organisation of women, although the text does not explicitly offer us so ruthless a view.

The displaced heart of the text is the unnamed representative of scientism, the happy member of Dr Peloris's smooth team, and it is he who is Morris's true successor, the future male acclimatising himself to a subordinate role within which, nonetheless, he controls the Ministry of Information while his female seniors are occupied with controlling the hardware. The wreck of the phallic which apparently occurs on the body of Morris slyly suggests also the ruin of woman: Dr Peloris's headquarters are 'high above the City'[26] where overview fades into remoteness, and we are invited to share with this small, unnamed narrator a series of intimations that the old Eve will recur, that this apparent transfer of power is an interregnum. We may well take pleasure in Morris's run, as we do in those forces who, for Zamiatin, resist the ban of the 'Green Wall', resist the taming of the wild:[27] but we are simultaneously being induced to take pleasure in a joke at the expense of women, in an expression of the conviction that the assimilation of women to power is unstable and doomed: 'though he remains in chains, Morris's story may not be ended'.[28] The suggestion is that these complicated systems of information and operations of power are built on the will of the female, and thus the process of societal change is reversed, and we are left to await the coming of the new masculine millennium.

... evident correspondence between human personality and group behaviour appears ... strikingly on those occasions when some major anxiety erupts into alarming accounts of the cataclysms and disasters that will descend upon the nation or the human race; and then there follows a period of collective neurosis when the future takes on the appearance of the dominant fear.[29]

What this bland account ignores is the extent to which the feared material may be displaced: thus in 'Morris in Chains' a masculine fear of castration associated with unemployment and the rejection of fathering stereotypes is displaced into an ironised fear of women, and the problem of complicity with the machines may be evaded.

Thus Morris becomes the prototype of an instinctual and organic knowledge, as against the computer banks of his enemies; yet it is for Morris himself that hierarchy is unquestioned and unquestionable, while his pursuers represent a more flexible specialisation. Their knowledges make no sense separately, while Morris's makes no sense socially: thus again the irreducible subject is condemned to a temporary impotence, but lodged within a reassuring post-romantic discourse which, we know, can have no real end because it *is* the discourse of the 'literary'. Surveillance can produce Morris as victim and captive, but it cannot produce meaning: Morris has the last word, and it consists in reducing sense to nonsense, substituting a run of alliteration and assonance for the chirpy team-spirit of the alternative narrator. The lines along which the text projects a future are looped back to myth in an assertion that old battles and strategies will never change, that the sovereign ego cannot be socialised; parentally, all that has happened is that Morris has become the hounded and eventually impotent mother, Dr Peloris the stern but successful father, while the plural narrator and his implied siblings settle down again into an essentially unchanged family formation, secure in the understanding that the great events are carried on above their heads and relayed to them only through the public information services.

'The Balloon'

The private character of these wishes, of their origins, deeply buried and unknown, was such that they were not much spoken of; yet there is evidence that they were widespread. It was also argued that what was important was what you felt when you stood under the balloon; some people claimed that they felt sheltered, warmed, as never before, while enemies of the balloon felt, or reported feeling, constrained, a 'heavy' feeling.[30]

In Donald Barthelme's 'The Balloon' (1966), the oldest 'invention' returns, that scientific development which in the West first provoked the extension of a myriad lines into the future. In its original incarnations, the balloon was instant communication, harbinger of a fully global economy, transcender of social division, pathway to the stars: by its form the intricate patterns of controlled space were relativised and negated, from its balcony the track of empires could be followed and knowledge could be totalised and placed in the hands of that cadre who were later to become Wells's beneficent aviators.[31] But here, the transformation of space is itself transformed into a discourse about projection and fantasy: 'the balloon, I said, is a spontaneous autobiographical disclosure, having to do with the unease I felt at your absence, and with sexual deprivation ... '. Yet this attempted closure is not presented as absolute; in the detail of the reactions to the balloon we can again trace the lineaments of a paranoiac subjectivity, and of a form of surveillance so close that its contours follow exactly the geography of the 'lower' world. 'Each intersection was crucial, meeting of balloon and building, meeting of balloon and man, meeting of balloon and balloon', because those numerous meetings reflect the shapes of acceptance and rejection, the contortions to be adopted by the body in response to an overarching knowledge which itself repels investigation: 'it was suggested that what was admired about the balloon was finally this: that it was not limited, or defined.'

The trajectory of the narrative is from agency, through a common subjection, to a fantasised agency offered merely as provisional, a hypothesis about relatedness. Thus the history of the encounter between balloon and city replicates the history of a more massive encounter with power: from the happy consciousness, for which the agencies of the state are securely within human control, through the deflating misery of a seepage of power from individual to apparatus, into that realm where reality-testing is abandoned and we lay ironic claim to a power and knowledge from which, in fact, we are irrevocably alienated.[32] And within this matrix is situated the whole complex of discourses of desire, as the population of the city offers its various attempts at accommodation with an inexplicable dominance: 'one man might consider that the balloon had to do with the notion "sullied", as in the sentence "The big balloon sullied the otherwise clear and radiant Manhatten sky". . . . Another man might say, "Without the example of ——, it is doubtful that —— would exist today in its present form".' What is clear throughout this profusion of 'exempla' is that the genesis of these discourses is bound at root to an accommodation with power: that without the context of a suddenly mirrored world, syntax could not emerge, for syntax is a way of shaping the shapeless, of rendering the indeterminate outline of the balloon in some way conformable with the shapes of the known city beneath.

Thus the desire is not to remove domination but to adjust our perception so that it becomes acceptable, which involves a multiplication of invented functions and uses for the balloon, and simultaneously a multiplication of the points at which the balloon (power) touches the regular shapes of life:

> Once knowledge can be analysed in terms of region, domain, implantation, displacement, transposition, one is able to capture the process by which knowledge functions as a form of power and disseminates the effects of power. There is an administration of knowledge, a politics of knowledge, relations of power which pass via knowledge and which, if one tries to transcribe them, lead one to consider forms of domination designated by such notions as field, region and territory. And the politico-strategic term is an indication of how the military and the administration actually come to inscribe themselves both on a material soil and within forms of discourse.[33]

Just so each of the formations of knowledge deployed by the city's population is bound up with a deepening capitulation in the balloon's unjustifiable and ineffable power: the very shapes of knowledge conform to the interpretations which the properties of the balloon allow. And even the form of Foucault's prose is mirrored in the discourse of the story:

> The upper surface was so structured that a 'landscape' was presented, small valleys as well as slight knolls, or mounds . . . Sometimes a bulge, blister, or sub-section would carry all the way east to the river on its own initiative, in the manner of an army's movements on a map, as seen in a headquarters remote from the fighting.

What is proffered is a doubling back of the techniques of surveillance: as the balloon shapes itself to the terrain, so we assume for ourselves the function of producing meaning from its random movements; we come to know it under the impulse of the fear that it might be getting to know *us*, and accommodate our lives to the tightening interface between the material of the city and the group fantasies and myths which are shown performing ideological operations on the balloon's surface.

As often with Barthelme it is barely the case, of course, that in 'The Balloon' we are confronted with a discourse of the future; or rather, here the invention of the future is telescoped into the single arbitrary event which tests out as in a laboratory the tracks of knowledge along which we shall seek to understand the new world, and thus the processes by which, as with all modes of knowledge, we shall seek to suck the balloon back into ourselves, to reabsorb the threatening presence and to succumb to the illusion that the threat of superior power is merely the materialisation of an intelligible desire. On this surface, marked by a 'deliberate lack of finish', our strategies for coping with the unexpected can be mapped with the precision of a diorama: the power of the balloon can be illusorily dissipated by the apparent allowing of a plurality of interpretations which ends by asserting that none of these accounts has any *specific* validity; that all our imaginings and plans are only a sequence of attempts to give shape to a power which is, in any case, irreducibly *there*.

Sovereignty and surveillance

These four instances offer us some hypotheses about surveillance and spatial arrangement, and thus give a rudimentary map of the strategies available for the subject and of the unconscious desires which control and determine these strategies. What is significantly lacking is what Foucault calls the 'insurrection of subjugated knowledges'.[34] In *Fahrenheit 451*, Montag is satisfied with the trappings of a justifiable barbarism (how to light a fire, how to exist in a group) but the knowledge sewn up in books and memories is not for him, but for the benefit of an unimagined future state. In *The Sirens of Titan*, the shreds of understanding picked up on Malachi Constant's loop through the universe are received only by a shattered and divided brain, and evaporate when he is sited again on Earth. Morris's knowledge is largely irrelevant to his conditions: he does not herd sheep because that way lies an escape, but because he has always herded sheep; he stands not for the unpredictable but for an easily reducible subjection. Under the balloon, the narrator settles for an unvalidable impulse to dominance: no system or theory can 'take' or impress its shape on the gasbag of power. And indeed, as we have already seen, on the concrete island Maitland accepts that there is not even the alternative romantic knowledge to be gained through difficulty and pain; although his circumstances are hard, he and we know that what he confronts is not death, that the surrounding triangle is protecting him as well as hemming him in.

The pleasure of these texts of the future thus comes to reside in a kind of trickery, in detailed observation of the fictions the psyche will conjure up under the pressure of powers and knowledges which cannot be fought, and we are encouraged to share ironically in a series of self-deceptions.

> And they will have no secrets from us. We shall allow or forbid them
> to live with their wives or mistresses, to have or have not children –
> according to whether they have been obedient or disobedient – and
> they will submit to us gladly and cheerfully. The most painful
> secrets of their conscience, all, all they will bring to us, and we shall
> have an answer for all.[35]

The Grand Inquisitor reminds us of the birth of fictions of the future coincided precisely with the emergence of the Gothic, and suggests that, although we might be drawn into identification with Winston and his many avatars, this is only part of the story: while the subject as individualised hero is experiencing reverses and successes, the subject as superman is also deriving pleasure from the act of surveillance, from having this other, puny self at its mercy. And this suggests a root for our capitulation in surveillance: that through it we are given another whole nexus of imaginings, in which we are ourselves at the controls of the computer, and can make whole lives flash before us in coded form, can drown the awkward Others in a flood of information. There is no room, even in fantasy, for two thousand million sovereigns, but two thousand million computer operatives can coexist more happily: the power emulated is no longer that of the supreme individual, but that of the skilled technician, happily located at one of the myriad apparently power-laden intersections of panoptism. As Foucault says, the time of the 'universal intellectual' is over, replaced by the kinds of knowledge produced by and for the 'specific intellectual':[36] what remains to be seen, and what so many of these texts play with, is whether this change is in fact a further device of the state, whether, under the guise of specific effectiveness, the internal agencies of power are in fact acting to reduce options by a further mystification of the discourse of power, such that control is removed from human hands altogether and offered instead in the forms of necessary fire surveillance; imponderable manipulations of time; that which is essential for the health and salvation of the city; the multi-dimensional balloon. Clearly, for these devices to work, they must operate not only through repression but also through the provision of viable alternative pleasures; in the fiction, we can sample these pleasures, casting ourselves both as subjects and as operators of the future state, and still observe that which will be unobservable in the presumed coming realm of total organisation, the shapes into which we must be bent for convenient commodification and for painless insertion into the intersections of power and knowledge.

7 The politics of fear

When dealing with texts of this type, it has to be borne in mind that in British culture at the present time the force of a certain kind of urgent politicality has largely drained away from the literary text, and from film, although it survives still in theatre and in the related mode of television drama. This is partly the latest manifestation of longstanding Americanisation: US domination of film is obvious, but it exists also in the 'literary' market, in only slightly subtler forms – the modelling of the bestseller, the increasing assimilation of authorial publicity to US modes, the wholesale adoption of 'genre' sales definitions, the hegemony of a metropolitan critical apparatus. In terms of cultural production, Alan Bleasdale's *Boys from the Blackstuff*, the outstanding political representation to date of the 1980s, holds on to the remains of an alternative tradition: the force of the regional disaffections of Liverpool and Birmingham, an insistence on limiting the conventions of articulacy, a more flexible dealing in the interface of comedy and tragedy, a spreading of heroisation which resists fantasies of the all-powerful ego. The 'blackstuff' itself condenses these elements: tarmac, of course, and thus the supersession of the expansionist planning of the 1960s and early 1970s, but also the 'Black Country' where grime obscures technology, and 'black' as 'blank', non-reflective, bland as Yosser Hughes's face as he reflects in incomprehension the bitter contradictions of monetarist dehumanisation.

But what is left on the big screen and on the printed page is not, of course, content-less: instead, we find there a terrain of melodramatic symbolisation rather than of political realism, within which occurs a continuous spinning-out and modulation of images of fear. The earlier attempts to capture Western fears in a handful of dust – late eighteenth-century German fiction, the English Gothic, Eugène Sue's urban mysteries, the early German silent movies, Universal Studios, Hammer – seem mere aberrations set alongside the dominance of 'horror' in the

113

1970s and early 1980s, the intensive packaging, between lurid green and red covers, of the displaced forms in which we revisit individual and societal trauma. *Frankenstein* and *Dracula* are still granted fresh embodiments, demonstrating both their own imagistic flexibility and at the same time the essential continuity, under capitalism, of the anxieties about class and gender warfare from which they sprang;[1] but alongside them we have a new range of fantasies, for which we need to account, not in the floating terms of a literary discussion of symbolism but in terms of power and the material base.

There is a key to be found in that most cheering of invasion films, Steven Spielberg's *Close Encounters of the Third Kind* (1977), and its dealings with panic and psychic accommodation. The shape of the film is a trajectory from technological overload, through an attempt to find salvation through the primitive and the excremental, to a ritual purification. Visually: from the jagged and diagonal images of air traffic control, through the dirt and rough edges of mountain-building, to the order and symmetry of the final controlled and built encounter. Acoustically: from the interplay of jerry-built jargon, through obsessional monologue, to the simplicity of melody. Thus what is apparently demonstrated is a putting away of the things of childhood and an achievement of maturity and harmony for the species.

But something darker is nonetheless present in silhouette against this clearing sky. The fantasised future species, for instance, is one from which reproduction appears to be exiled, the home of a kind of gender apartheid. The masculine 'spirit of adventure' is validated and trans-formed into a wished-for experience of new worlds, while the feminine condemns itself to mundanity several times over: the wife is left behind in the male race for approval from 'parental' aliens, and the female fellow-initiate who replaces her willingly resigns her place in the here-after. In fact, adjuvants in general have a hard time in this fantasy of technological success;[2] the hero progressively strips himself of contact, to the point where he and he only, the pure and isolated ego, is capable of travel. Otherwise, only the magus is saved from plotted oblivion; but, played by a real film director, he is one step removed from the action, a benign creator whose role is to admire the indomitable competitivity of his chosen son, and to construct the backdrop of design against which the hero's fate may be most aesthetically played out.

It is, in one sense, the film of the eternal golden braid:[3] Gödel, Escher, Bach, mathematics, visual illusion and music are offered as the guarantee of permanence, a permanence which seems to imply the absolute disappearance of the body and consequently of material demands, and a traditionally Pauline form of resurrection, Pauline also in its suppression of the possibility of women with vision. Where our hero sees the contours of the sun, his female companion is merely blinded; where he is offered life eternal as a reward for his anal persistence, she is rewarded only with the return of what is already hers, her child, and must be grateful.

And according to the film, this traditional displacement of materiality into spirituality is not incompatible with the military. Soldiers may huff and puff, even be a little rough in their manners, but in the end they are not only benign but, incredibly, fully adequate to the task in hand: to the shape brought from the stars, they can bring an answering shape in a beautified dialogue of invaders, a ritual dance from which the female is excluded. Flowers, as we know, offer their rich visual patterning as guidance for fertilisation, and in this sense the brilliantly lit runway offers itself up to the landing of the strange craft. But the runway is not public, it is hidden, and it is on the far side of the mountain, the mountain which we have been continually shown as a model in excrement. The sexual act thus described is not genital but anal, and at that not fully achieved, a fluttering contact undertaken in secrecy. Domesticity and marriage are semiotically opposed to this meeting of males in the scene where the hero throws refuse through his kitchen window, to the accompaniment of traumatised silence on the part of mortal neighbours: clearly, that which holds us back from contributing to military development must be discarded, because in the end Western defence policy is benevolent and will assure us of our rightful place in the interplanetary hierarchy.

The aliens arrive, not with a message of change, but with confirmation, in the shape of the returning lost, most of whom are military heroes, that the aspirations of the West are in tune with cosmic design. It is through war and speed that these have found their vision; small wonder that their return is into a sticky pool of sentiment, for what we are being shown is the American ideal, having been sent for hallmarking by a higher power, coming back having passed its test. Out there, the purity of metal and electronics has found a like national mind. More than this: the theory of capitalist cycles (Britain/nineteenth century/engineering, U.S./early twentieth century/cars and aircraft, Japan/late twentieth century/electronics) is thus adjusted neatly to counteract the supersession of the American dream; for these 'aliens' are unmistakably orientals. The brief episode of the black guard demonstrates the convenient exclusion of 'inferior' races from this Nirvana; in this peaceful rerun of Pearl Harbour, only master-races need speak. For, at one level, what we are being told, silently, is that only they are capable of the full intercourse symbolised as the 'third' kind, however mechanically aided that intercourse may turn out to be.

The 'hands across the Pacific' scenario is accompanied, again through the presence of Truffaut, by a gesture of allegiance to the 'old West' of Europe. Prohibited, through economic stringency, from full participation in this ideal union of power, we are nonetheless allowed to put our ancient wisdom to use, teaching, as it were, the glass bead game to those with enough money to buy the necessary equipment. In this fantasy of American stability and maturity, there is another essential element in the repertoire, which is the overcoming, so necessary in the decade after Vietnam, of the threat from disaffected youth. The key representation here is the ageing hippie and 'veteran' who makes a fool of himself and his cause in the presence of a galaxy of Air Marshals; the culture of dream is thus revealed as insufficiently disciplined to qualify for the obsessiveness necessary for survival. True, the police too are portrayed as stupid enough to drive off the end of the road in their hunt to pin down the intruding object; but their plight is also represented as tragic, for they too participate in the drama of uniformed authority which the film ideologically sanctifies.

It is perhaps not surprising, in view of science's failure of image, that such fables should be produced to lure the young into technological jobs, or that multilingual translation should be included prominently among them. After all, so the film says, an old cottage is an unsafe place to be these days, where ventilators rise unbidden out of the ground and a cat-door is large enough to permit the Alice-like escape of a child. It is part of the same ideological argument that our hero's artistry and sculpture are useless as sources of revelation until validated by television; just as good intentions cannot achieve penetration without the assistance of the technically skilled. As audience, we are thus placed in a paradox; for we are encouraged to take, in our sympathies, the path of service and to see ourselves, not as ego, but as part of the fuel which will propel that ego to the stars and confirm American hegemony. How, in a class-divided society, could it be otherwise? Equality of opportunity has no place in this refined world, although our masters will see to it that nobody has the temerity to intrude between the participants in the final council; men in white coats, representatives of what is left of an intelligentsia, are shown as accustomed to scuttling for shelter, lest what they see inappropriately drives them to terror.

One of the political wishes thus enshrined in our hero's long narrative is to maintain divisions unquestioned; to connive at the preservation of WASP superiority. Another is to avoid questioning the wisdom of the 'adult', and this is parodically reinforced in the nonsensical precision of the closing 'son et lumière', even if that wisdom appears to include a taboo on sexual activity, on Eros in any of its destabilising manifestations.[4] After all, such activity would be unnecessary in the state of grace towards which our political masters are gently leading us, a state of grace which the aliens effortlessly figure for us by cloning the absent boy and announcing this immaculate conception, or series of conceptions, with the trumpets of Revelation.

I take Close Encounters of the Third Kind, then, to be an act of political advocacy which works by conjuring up unconscious fears of the future and of invasion and transforming them into the grounds for trust in the political establishment of the West. In its offering of a space for fantasised public success, it seeks to harness drives and energies to the forwarding of the state machine and the validation of state priorities. The ideological operations of Stephen King and Stanley Kubrick's The Shining (1980), while cruder, are equally revealing, touching as they do on cardinal problems of surveillance and privacy. We need to assume again, with Foucault, that the massive, and massively complex, surveillance of everyday life, the formation of which has been a large part of the history of the last three centuries, has been possible only through the provision of concomitant pleasures; and thus through the manipulation and alteration of desire.[5] It is thus necessary that privacy be presented as claustrophobia, so that surveillance can figure as a kind of relief; and this is The Shining's ideological terrain, within which marriage becomes the site for an implicit advocacy of guidance by higher authority.

The focal couple is removed from communal life and provided with an optimal set of conditions. They have complete material security and a simple time-bounded task, a will to refresh and to create a newness. The hotel which is the site for this new beginning, of course, also imagistically sets off warning signals: this is the Hotel de Dream, Hotel California, the Chelsea, Heartbreak Hotel, the place where fantasies can emerge which will not stand external testing. What happens really bears only the flimsiest of relations to the supernatural, a covering which is characteristic of the horror genre: more centrally, the film offers us a series of escalating images of marital violence, the head thrown back in a rictus of fury, the long fall down the magnificent stairs, the evolving tissue of misunderstandings, the undermining lies given to us in the writer/husband's meaningless manuscript, the steady accretion of ritualised phrases which reveal the collapse of discourse, the failure to produce meanings. All this time, rescue is arriving, the black man with insight into what may be happening in the mountain fastness (the representative of 'domestic' wisdom – he is a cook – who will bring enlightenment); but then this enlightenment is shown to be savagely unavailable – a single blow from an axe disposes of hope, and the long journey is bent back into the service of unapproachability.

The suggestion is that the root instability is due to the images of an older sexuality, presented in the 'ghosts' who haunt the hotel: as though the superficial coupling of the marriage is a thin cover over an older struggle, which bursts through the net of civilised discourse, language itself defeated by a hideous rememoration which cannot be accommodated.[6] Thus marriage fails in its attempt to encode the instincts, but takes a brutal revenge on those instincts (the rescuer, in the other connotations of his blackness), only to find that this revenge makes the code itself meaningless (the husband becomes unable to follow tracks in the snow, and dies lost in the maze). The problem is presented as partly about transference: in the absence of an arbitrating third party, the wish for a higher knowledge which will relativise the awful secrets of privacy becomes transferred instead to the child. But here we also catch glimpses of a long cultural narrative, with its origins in the child-worship of the anti-industrial romantics: the powerlessness of the present, the loss of comprehension in the mazes of divided labour, as Hegel and Blake both put it, is given an artificial compensation by reconjuring a lost power in the personal past, a set of intimations of immortality which move us, not towards anger at the economic machine which has corrupted that power, but towards acquiescence as we wait for the next generation to embody the totalising insight which we feel ourselves to be denied.[7]

The evasiveness of this ideological displacement is represented in the contradiction of the child's situation in *The Shining*: the visions of terror which he sees are in fact the displaced images of his parents' lives, and he thus holds the vital evidence which could be used for disentangling, but he is powerless to express it with credibility. The family is the site of a circular repression; the faces of whoredom and rape which the child encounters in the hotel room are figurations of marital sexual life in a specific historical conjuncture – they are his own expression of his father's madness – but he is powerless to feed this vision back into the locked system. Although he provides surveillance, he simultaneously receives the full force of the rejection of that surveillance, and can survive only by turning the gaze of his truth (the 'shining') back on to his father, and thus killing him.

The reason why any of this should be of political significance is that it is becoming increasingly clear that the new conservatism, on both sides of the Atlantic, is operating through a totemic redefinition of the family. The illusory pleasure proffered in this redefinition has to do with power: a party political broadcast on behalf of the Conservative Party demonstrates its statistics on home ownership with a small cartoon in which stereotypical houses, the kind a child might draw, are transformed into equally stereotypical castles. But below that, of course, the intention is to valorise the family only insofar as it can be taken as the site of a resistance to change; and *The Shining* powerfully images for us what the shape of that micro-conservatism is to be, the father substantially unemployed, the mother moving from one condition of terror to another, the child losing his/her way in the mazes of maturation and settling for a simple act of murderous replacement of the adult.

This is not, of course, to grant power to the young, but to lock them into a sterile circularity so that the prospect of change itself becomes the feared object and we retreat into the fascinations of adultery, as the ice begins to set around us and the possibility of the long trek towards co-operative organisation becomes unthinkable. We are invited to settle in for the long, hard winter, and to recognise that Ananke is now in charge, that the scarcities which we might otherwise suspect to be linked to the real questions of economic organisation are as natural as the seasons. The mirror-image of the withering away of the state which the new conservatives offer is predicated on impotence and on acquiescence in that impotence; the fact that there is not room enough for three in the Grand Hotel clearly enough incarnates a Freudian myth, and one of substance, but here it is bent to the service of stasis and death.

Yet despite this, *The Shining* is clearly designed to make us yearn for intrusion, for the arrival of the forces of law and order which can regulate this unacceptable primal scene, and this ambivalence is part of the film's psychological strength. The case of Ridley Scott's *Alien* (1979) is different, largely because *Alien* draws upon and effects modulations within an already well-established genre, the disaster movie, which clearly has its own political purposes and symbolic codes.[8] I take it that the disaster movie is focused on problems of societal leadership, and on the validation of a certain kind of force as the guarantor of survival in a world of shrinking resources. In the typical disaster plot, the questions broached have to do with exchange value in an era in which technological development may be becoming unsustainable: what gifts or skills may continue to be negotiable as the economy winds down? In a film like Ronald Neame's *The Poseidon Adventure* (1972), the answers are clear: representatives of non-dominant groups are discarded one by one to make way for the emergence of a new leader, who has perfectly internal-ised the ideology of monetarism and is consequently unhampered by the weaker considerations which consign women and those with more subtle purposes and apprehensions to oblivion. We are invited to view a predetermined exercise in group dynamics, and to sort out stances according to a script which valorises singleness of purpose and brute determination.

Alien works within this code, but skilfully modifies it in such a way as to provide a more apparently palatable outcome. The group we are shown is a minor development from the tokenism of earlier disaster movies: here we have two women, two members of the working class (the engineers), even ethnic issues comparatively foregrounded. And it is not the strongest male who survives: instead, it is a woman, but this outcome is closely bracketed. She does, indeed, eventually despatch the monster, although the film is visually very unclear about the means, as though it cannot really image this new structure; but since, according to earlier elements in the plot, the higher plan of the encircling military authorities depended on the alien arriving safely on earth, we are left to imagine, rather later, the kind of reception she will receive when she achieves landfall – if she ever does.

To that extent, the ending is a clever trick on women; and this underlines the major obsession of the film, which is incarnated in the emergence of the alien from John Hurt's body in a parody of birth pangs. It is, surely, this scene which is the heart of the film, and nothing which succeeds it replicates this moment of terror. As the monster grows larger, it also grows more familiar, and our sympathy for the characters ebbs away: it is one thing not to be able to trace the whereabouts of a being which moves at prodigious speed and is small enough to evade detection, another to be so incompetent as to fail to observe an alien now fully-grown and highly reminiscent of a medieval devil. It is in its dramatisation of incompetence, indeed, that *Alien* most obviously performs a useful act of ideological incorporation. Kubrick's *2001* (1968) rapidly became an outworn and overgrown myth, as the perfection of technology on which it depended became inconsistent with material developments, and it was this actual defeat of the technological which John Carpenter brilliantly encapsulated in *Dark Star* (1974), with its latter-day hippie crew and pointless control systems. But *Dark Star* was a real threat: produced on a low budget and outside the control of the major studios, it presented us with a deflation of Western pretensions of a kind which, followed to its logical conclusion, might threaten our capitulation in the accretion of defence and technology budgets. The message of *Alien* is the opposite: that if this ill-trained crew is not capable of neutralising the intruder and at the same time performing its mission, then the answer must be better training, so that that mission is not left in the hands of a woman who, although she succeeds on the primitive level of survival, nonetheless fails in that she does not keep up the balance which would enable her to bring the alien safely home, so that he can be used in turn as a weapon in the all-important wars down below on earth.

The debates acted out in films such as these are important because they demonstrate for us possible futures, and they thus illustrate scenarios for which we, as taxpayers and as voters, need to be prepared. What we are given time after time (although *Close Encounters* is a major exception) are emblems of the 'worst case', the situation which must be prevented, even if preventing it leaves us only with a balance of deterrence before which we would normally recoil in horror. When that deterrence is fundamentally nuclear, and proposes catastrophe as its everyday terrain, it is not surprising that the fears which we have to be shown to persuade us into acquiescence become ostentatiously the stuff of nightmare and fantasy;[9] just as, for an earlier generation, Don Siegel's *Invasion of the Body Snatchers* (1956) (now, of course, re-offered in a modernised version) provided the image of indoctrination and societal conformism which made the Cold War seem comparatively justifiable.[10]

The significant change has been in the imagining of the enemy. In the 1950s, it was ideologically possible to slot the Russians into the space which the Germans had just conveniently vacated. As the immediacy of war recedes – for Europe – over the horizon, so new mechanisms have to be found to remind us of the ideological nonsense that nuclear weapons do not 'merely' threaten destruction on a global scale, but can be directed at specific targets; and here, of course, we are in the territory of 'limited nuclear warfare', and of the lies and vacillations encoded in that phrase. Often in those earlier films and texts, the enemy possessed a single and specific strength, and the task of the good and the great was to find the means to oppose it – usually, as in *Body Snatchers* and in Steven Sekely's *Day of the Triffids* (1963), to find a way of stopping a cancerous spread, which was a thinly disguised version of insidious communism. In *Alien*, the being has powers which are unspecific; his threat is predicated on pure malevolence – as it has to be, since no more explicable argument could possibly image for us the unthinkable possibility of a first nuclear strike.

The literary text, of course, gives us as readers a longer time in which to ponder, and therefore conventionally offers more sophisticated arguments about fear, arguments which few film directors – except, perhaps, Michael Powell in *Peeping Tom* (1960) – have risked. The ideological space opened up is thus more potentially malleable, and the transmission between state power and the power of the text more complex. The crucial myth here, I suggest, has already become D. M. Thomas's *The White Hotel* (1981): crucial in that it has engaged with and sparked off debates in the most central areas of literary representation – the intermingling of fact and fantasy, and consequently the relation of the author to historical experience; the question of gender representation; and above all, the relation of psychopathology to narrative.

There are many terrifying moments in the book, from the vertigo and sexual nausea of the opening sections through to the account of Babi Yar. But it is not these which provide the central dynamic of the text, or which explain the critical explosion which followed its publication, and its valorisation by the prize-givers. The root fear of *The White Hotel* is genuinely novel insofar as it has to do with prefiguration, with the possibility that our present fantasies of destruction might actually bring about the holocaust. Within the text, it could be said that Freud receives the blame for this; and it is that sense which is echoed before the fact in the epigram from Yeats,

> We had fed the heart on fantasies,
> The heart's grown brutal from the fare;
> More substance in our enmities
> Than in our love . . . [11]

But again, this appears to be a displacement of the real source of fear, which is about our own connivance: that by adopting a version of determinism which produces the self as victim, we thereby bring about the apparatus of victimisation from which, some time in the future, we will suffer. The hotel of *The Shining*, the house of many windows and many mansions, is here again; the fear is that when we arrive there, in search of purification and of a sexual activity which will be purged of guilt and free from social connotations, we will find that we have indeed brought all our luggage with us, all the terrors and blackness which we had thought to leave behind on the mountain slopes.

The Freud-figure who writes the long central section of the text makes plain this interpretation of the duplicity of destiny:

> . . . I pondered the tragic paradox controlling Frau Anna's destiny. She possessed a craving to satisfy the demand of her libido; yet at the same time an imperious demand, on the part of some force I did not comprehend, to poison the well of her pleasure at its source. She had, by her own admission, an unusually strong maternal instinct; yet an absolute edict, imposed by some autocrat whom I could not name, against having children. She loved food; yet she would not eat.[12]

There is no way of escape from the text. The death instinct, so Thomas claims, is deep within us all – and this has become also a common assumption of less sophisticated horror texts, filmic and literary. Thus a smoothing-out is effected: although on the surface the central figure, by whatever of her various names we choose to address her, is presented as the subject-formation of a specific set of historical and societal conditions, the text in fact generalises out from this, through its mock-theorisations, to impart to us an image of 'the individual' locked within an inexplicable system. And this is simultaneously the meaning carried by the textual form: this history is presented through a series of fragments of discourse, between which there can be little adjudication, and the individual is constituted as a subject by the interplay of those discourses, which grind together to produce their inevitably destructive outcome.

It is evident, then, that *The White Hotel* stands in a direct relation to the theoretical convergence suggested by explorations as apparently divergent as those of Foucault and Lacan; that the text is a dramatisation of the supersession of a credible theory of the freedom of the individual.[13]

But at that point in thinking about the present cultural co-ordinates, a certain vertigo sets in, and one which is familiar to those trying to cling to a meaningful concept of praxis against an increasing emphasis on the constitutive power of discourse.[14] It would not be to the point to enter into that theoretical debate here; but it is very much to the point to bear in mind that the images of terror presented to us by the texts of the contemporary culture are not leftovers from a previous, more melo-dramatic era, but very deeply embedded in those theories of power and knowledge which may, seen from a different perspective, appear to offer us the most incisive possibilities for interpretation of the social forma-tion. *The White Hotel* comes at us directly on the site of intellectual struggle; it would not be an exaggeration to say that the casting of Freud himself as an old-fashioned and blinkered paternalist is an ideological device to divert us from the fact that the fear of determinist prefiguration is precisely the inseparable underside of Lacanian and Foucauldian assertions about the construction of the subject.

But the major argument which *The White Hotel* sparked off was, of course, to do with gender; and the central charge which has been laid against the book is that it is pornographic, in the immediate sense that it deals in the 'graphic depiction of whores',[15] and in the more complex sense that it highlights necessary questions about the purposes of a male narrator who portrays the fantasies, rape and death of an emblematic woman. And it is at this point that we may begin to make significant distinctions between the levels of fear which have condensed around *The White Hotel*, distinctions which may be generalised outwards. First, of course, we may talk about the fear *in* the text, as we have tried to do by naming determinism and prefiguration. But we may also talk about the fear *of* the text, what it is that the text is designed to evade or suppress; and this is extremely difficult, precisely because the very substance of *The White Hotel* is psychoanalysis of a non-political kind, which makes the *political* psychoanalysis *of* the text seem a superfluous activity. The problem is how to bring to bear on this fusion of narrative and analysis the kind of interpretation which we may easily deploy in relation to the obvious 'hidden' of, say, *Dr Jekyll and Mr Hyde* (1886) or *The Island of Doctor Moreau*, with their apparently naive incarnations of imperialism and evolutionary theory.[16] But yet, of course, if we leave the argument there, we are capitulating in powerlessness: symbolically, we are saying that fiction and analysis form a seamless circle and therefore that there is no distinction to be made between truth and lies.

It is this, I suspect, which has enraged the critics: the possibility that a narcissistic text like *The White Hotel*, dense with interpretation of its own meanings, offers them only unemployment. And here, perhaps, if we can begin to close the gap between the gender question and the question of readerly and critical reception, we may glimpse what underlies *The White Hotel*, which is an ambivalence about impotence (and any such ambivalence must of necessity carry a political implication). We are impotent, as readers, in the face of the book: we cannot change fiction, but here also we are reminded that we cannot change history. But we are also confronted within the book by the possibility that impotence may be our only hope (and I am conscious that the floating 'we' has become, of necessity, a male 'we') because the images of power on display are mere cover-stories for the death instinct, for the self and for others. The most benign and the most malevolent of masculine interventions converge: the act of penetration becomes itself the poisoning of the well. And thus, surely, we are back immediately to Greenham Common and to the possibilities of a form of power which will not depend on phallic imagery; but what, and here the fear strikes deep, will the role of the male be in this future scenario? It is as though what is encoded in the text, the wish from which, as Freud assures us in relation to dreams, all the fears derive,[17] is for history to stop, if only for a while: for the five thousand years of patriarchy look interminably long, far too long to be atoned for without suffering, and it may be time for the male to sleep like Rip Van Winkle while history readjusts itself, so that we do not have to go through the torment and – although it is difficult to whisper its name – the revenge.

It could be seen as possible on the basis of these few texts to draw up a brief list of two kinds of fear which lie within contemporary cultural representation. On the one hand would lie those fears which it is in the interests of the state to maximise: the fear of change, the fear of invasion, the fear of the displacement of male hegemony. But if interpretation is to be of any value, it should then be possible to discern below these ideological impositions a further level, the level at which the energy is generated which is then bent into ideological service, however hypothetical our assertions in this area might be. But the problem, of course, is that this model of ideology does not work: as Gramsci and Foucault have ceaselessly pointed out, the dominant class has long since given up working through the operation of unquestioned power, and now rests its case instead on acquiescence;[18] and both the explosive force of *The*

White Hotel and the curiously reassuring impact of horror films derive not from direct repression but from the ways in which we as audience are brought to a sense of how we share in those fears, and thus brought to welcome a version of conservatism as a way of avoiding the confrontation which would occur if those fears were to be tested out in the real world.

If we are to move beyond this inadequate theory of ideology, we need to identify above all the motor principles of this acquiescence, the proffered pleasure in the name of which we appear to be willing, year after year, to grant continuity to a state system which no longer makes any secret of its repressive basis; and the name of this pleasure is survival. The hovering question which endures through these texts – and it is not the question which we experience in, say, nineteenth-century Gothic texts – is about, first, who or what will survive, and second, at what cost. We may run through them again. In *Close Encounters*, it is the trusting male, who has validated his precarious vision by seeing the powerful operations of the state (in the fastness on the other side of the mountain) and has acquiesced in its procedures. In *The Shining*, it is the child, but the child as already traumatised into complicity with the forces of law and order. In *Alien*, we are given the necessary negative confirmation of the image: it appears to be the woman who survives, but we male political sophisticates know that this is not the right answer. In *The White Hotel*, it is again perhaps a woman, but only as irreparably scarred by the operations of patriarchal state power. The answers are really the same; but even if they were genuinely different, it would not affect the structure, which moves us back beyond nineteenth-century fiction, where survival was rarely at stake, to the fact/fictions of Defoe, to the narratives of extreme loss and strength. But even there, the terrain is not the same, and neither is the naming: none of the texts we are considering, nor any like them, could be named for an individual as *Robinson Crusoe* is, for to do so would be to limit their emblematic power. The backdrop of these contemporary texts is not exploration but holocaust, not the difficult possibility of an expanded life but the all too easy possibility of the expansion of death; and this gives us a key also to the current hierarchy of theory.

For those theories which have based themselves, like Barthes' and Foucault's, on the increasing sophistication of power and control are, of course, in one sense already out of date; and they were so before the fact. For it is not only true that the states of the West are accustoming themselves to the exercise of power within straitened circumstances; it is also the case that they foresaw this, they foresaw it all; and to understand the way in which ideology has been reproduced by cultural representations over the last decade we need to assume, not, with the hubris of intellectuals, that we were one step ahead of them, but that they were one step ahead of us, and were already shaping myths which would accustom us to the rule of scarcity. To take an example: the spinning-out of discursive formations which we find in Foucault has as its assumed backdrop an expanding universe; like Giordano Bruno, Foucault speaks of the 'infinite universe and worlds', he works within a set of assumptions about expansion and exploration, and to that extent he concerns himself with a style of state conservatism which was already outmoded in the days of *Discipline and Punish* (1975).[19] The contraction we are painfully experiencing was implicit from the earliest days of the oil crisis; and was there, powerfully imaged, in, for instance, the new skills we demanded of the oil drillers, and economically in the differentials we offered them in relation to their old-fashioned brethren in the other energy industries. For the theorisation of this new universe, predicated on contraction and holocaust, where the heroic premium has already been paid to the survivor, we may do better to take the path Thomas has taken in *The White Hotel*; to return to Freud, in the first instance, but more importantly to return to those theorists of fear and holocaust who had seen Freud already against the background of the old concentration camps, and who saw the plight of the intellectual, the critic, as the fending off of concentration camps of the mind: the Frankfurt School, and particularly Adorno, who has already identified the problem of how to escape from the 'open-air prison'. It is, of course, highly significant that Adorno's real prisons have become transmuted, in the culture of theory, into Jameson's 'prison-house of language';[20] but what the images of fear reveal is that it is not actually possible conveniently to reduce real imprisonment, real victimisation, real destruction to a matter of 'mind-forg'd manacles'.[21]

Goldmann wrote of the necessity of identifying the differentials in cultural attitudes to death, although – since his death – no significant work has been done in that area;[22] but it is precisely these films, these books, which provide us with the materials, because the *substance* of death is fear. We may deplore, in Goldmann and in Adorno, an insufficient attention to the fundamental issue of class, but we do so at our peril, because it is clear that, whatever the reality of class and of the control of labour, the welfare states of the West have spawned precisely an analogous repression, and it is now possible for cultural producers to bypass class altogether. As critics, we may choose to return to it, and we could, indeed, identify class as a crucial absence in the field of representations of fear – although the Western governments have *already*, before the fact, moved a long way towards destroying – as Adorno was saying many years ago – the *awareness* of class.[23]

But if a principal point about these representations is that nowhere do they touch on the questions of class and control, then in their assumption that the terms of a class analysis have been superseded they clearly find a resonance in popular consciousness. The question they continually posit is instead about survival, and the fact is that survival has become the principal term in which the dominant ideology seeks to substitute for an awareness of class. To the extent that we are brought – deliberately – to consider ourselves as equal victims of an arbitrary potential holocaust, we must also circumvent the important questions of access to present power. And what this reveals is what Adorno suspected all along: that the Third Reich prefigured an all-encompassing revision of class relations, whereby our mundane fears of exploitation can be made to appear trivial alongside the fears of the millennium – and it is into the service of this argument that Thomas brings Freud.[24] And this collusion between the imaginary and a certain version of psychoanalysis is prevalent elsewhere, across the cultural strata, from the pop psychology of the 'video nasties' to the painstakingly traced psychopathologies of writers like Ian McEwan and Adam Mars-Jones.[25] But what this collusion suggests is that it is all too easy, in an era when the major state effort is to persuade us of the invalidity of class analysis, to substitute for this an emphasis on an unchangeable thanatic impulse; and also that, on the other hand, the analysis of fear is far too significant a matter to be left to the psychologists. As we are brought to consider ourselves merely as candidates for survival, so our engagement with the political complexities of the present are worn away, and we are prepared for the terminal return of a brutish individualism.

Section C:
Trajectories through language
and culture

8 *W. S. Graham:*
Constructing a white space

In trying to follow some of the windings of the unconscious in contemporary texts, I have been mainly following two major clues: the modes in
which desire is accommodated in the forms of the projected future, and
the occasional but revealing collusions of textual practice and theory of
discourse and power. But where these forms move together, of course, is
in the trajectory of language itself, and symptomatically in the condensa-
tions of poetry. To try to look at this trajectory more closely, I have
chosen to look in detail at the work, over three decades, of one poet,
W.S. Graham, whose work, it appears to me, traces the encounter of the
troubled consciousness precisely with the new forms of control which
are represented, on one side, by the machinations of state power and, on
the other, by the emergence of a theoretical conventionalism which
resists materiality.

In critical discussion of Graham, a tradition is already emerging: he is
seen as a poet dogged by bad luck. It was bad luck that his early work fell
so heavily under the influence of Dylan Thomas; bad luck that his most
considerable volume of poems was overshadowed in its year of publication by Larkin; altogether bad luck that he should choose to write in a
vein deeply counter to Movement norms. But there is – and here we
already touch on Graham's own themes – a limit to the accidental; we
cannot best get at the importance of this highly individual body of poetry
by claiming to pare off its excesses, by treating the early volumes as mere
training, or by – and this is where the conventional approach appears to
have ended up – simply regarding Graham as better the less he writes.[1]
Critically, he has been turned into a monument to linguistic suffering
who, by his silent contortions, provides us with a signal reminder of the
fate of the unattached consciousness. I want to suggest instead the
specific trajectory which Graham's poetry describes. Over the course of
seven slim volumes, we can see his writing moving, sometimes hesitantly
and sometimes with exultation, from the full to the empty sign; from the

plenitude of connotation to the bounded spaces of denotation; from white heat over the 'white threshold' to the white degree zero.[2] From an inclusive consciousness which 'seems to have no circumference, and to merge with whatever he writes about',[3] Graham moves, and in moving moves *us*, towards the deconstruction of the subject, a measured and ironic dissection of himself and his reader; like the magician in Coover's 'The Hat Act',[4] he enrols his reader as his professional assistant and then proceeds to dismember him, although unlike the magician he does so not in front of a large paying audience but in the pursuit of apparently more private and, perhaps, vengeful satisfactions. For Graham is not a comforting poet: over the years he has demonstrated in his poetry an increasingly anxious pallor before the unlocked might of language, and there can be little doubt that he means to allay some of this unease by passing it on.

With hindsight, then, we can see the first four volumes – *Cage Without Grievance* (1942), *The Seven Journeys* (1944), *2nd Poems* (1945) and *The White Threshold* (1949) – as an initially rather cheerful encounter with the contents of Pandora's box. Graham here revels in poetry as if in a child's playroom: adjectives and prepositions are profuse, words change their syntactic function with deliberate sleight of hand, complex and repetitive forms are whirled before our eyes.

> I worship a skylift of Narnain blaeberry globed
> Priestlike sealed in a tensile sac in a nerve
> In the vein-geared bubble of vision.[5]

Meaning, for the early Graham, is liquid: sweet and dangerous, it is to be contained in poems as in a grapeskin, available to the 'tongue like a stamen'[6] which can blindly share the verbal euphoria. Thus although many of the poems in *Cage Without Grievance* are syntactically strange, they are not loose but taut, crammed with too many connexions, too many separate relations between words, complex, showy and pointless like the Brussels Atomium. And, clearly, Graham is aware of this: the imagery of poems like 'Over the Apparatus of the Spring is Drawn', 'As If in an Instant Parapets of Plants', 'There was when Morning Fell' is unified round a single concern, the relation between 'natural' exuberance and architectonic structure. 'Over the apparatus of the Spring is drawn/A constructed festival of pulleys from sky':[7] the world of these poems is riotous with foliage, but it is curiously stagey, full of arbours from *Midsummer Night's Dream* in which at any moment part of the scenery might fall away to reveal, as in Ballard and Vonnegut, a world of rather primitive machines. And this sense of the interpenetration of the free-flowing and the prearranged or determined is, in a shadowy way, related also to the poet's own identity, even at this early stage:

> After, when who I was
> Stands rarer and as fair as natural hawk
> My death will need no roof
> To trellis Spring's horizon from my head.
> Laid out with bloodshot pennies on my mind
> My dead discovery in evening corridors
> Shall bring this crossbeamed sycamore of steel
> To brace my crowded heart.[8]

Almost hidden within the contorted syntax, as within an over-lush forest, there lurks a fragile ego, incapable on its own of withstanding the sheer press of the outside, looking toward death, or at least the certainty sanctioned by the approach of death, as a crunch or breakwater. There is irony in the insertion of the word 'natural': where for Ted Hughes the associations of the hawk with freedom, blood and cycle might be assumed, for Graham the very category of the natural is dubious:

> I, no more real than evil in my roof
> Speak at the bliss I pass I can endure
> Crowding the glen my lintel marks
> Speak in this room this traffic builds
> About my chair and table for my nature.
> I feel the glass collide with light and day.[9]

Again, some of the difficulty is wilful, and the insistence on subjective relativism callow; what is interesting, however, and again it is a keynote of many of the early poems, is the 'collision'. For the world of these poems is not static and unified; it is one in which the ego has to try to shoulder itself a space, try to find standing-room in a world already crowded; but to 'build', to try to establish coherent identity and personal location, is simultaneously to enter into conflict of kinds that one could not foretell in advance. The poetic implications are obvious: Graham is not a believer in the pure word, language is already unspeakably profuse, the stage is already set for an as yet undreamed-of play. The poet can only try to move the scenery about, as 'through all the suburbs children trundle cries'; neither the woods of Arden nor the cries of poverty or boredom reveal anything of the underlying reality of the world.

This set of half-completed metaphors about the secret springs of action and control is strongly present in *2nd Poems*: 'Explanation of a Map' deals in the contrast between surface and deep structure, and 'His Companions Buried Him' offers us two neatly encapsulated images:

> Always by beams of stars (and they disclose
> India Africa China Asia then that furry queen)
> I see Earth's operator within his glade
> Gloved in the fox of his gigantic hour.
>
> . .
>
> Always by beams of stars (and they disclose
> That furry queen who saunters on night's boards)
> I see Earth swing within its own explorer
> Who dangles each star lighting up his map.[10]

In the first stanza, the secret knowledge is of the illusory quality of freedom: the dramas of history are staged for us by technicians, pilots, telephone operators, intelligence men crouched in the thickets. It is they who can fairly claim 'gigantic' purposes, destinies, not the rest of us for whom the 'furry queen' is all we need to know. The last stanza narrows the focus still further: the planet itself is reduced, as in Lessing, to a plaything, the stars to coloured lights, and we, presumably, to the unnamed dying alluded to in the poem's title.

The lushness offered by the visible world and by language is thus illusory: and in this context it is hardly surprising that Graham should next choose, in *The White Threshold*, to renounce these overpowering illusions in favour of a grittier, harsher attempt to break through to bedrock. Calvin Bedient says of the early volumes that the poet 'has backed so far from common discourse that he makes us conscious less of what he sees than of his effort to escape convention',[11] but the poems *feel* more the products of a writer in a cave; in *The White Threshold*, Graham turns his back determinedly on his absorbing but cloudy trophies from the underworld, and moves out to the mountains and the sea. And this is accompanied by another change: for the explosive fullness of massive instantaneous signification he substitutes the more continuous pressure of time: short, effusive lyrics are replaced by lengthy, slender ballads and the terrifying choric structure exemplified in 'The White Threshold' itself:

Let me all ways from the deep heart
Drowned under behind my brow so ever
Stormed with other wandering, speak
Up famous fathoms well over strongly
The pacing whitehaired kingdoms of the sea.

I walk towards you and you may not walk away.

Always the welcome-roaring threshold
So ever bell worth my exile to
Speaks up to greet me into the hailing
Seabraes seabent with swimming crowds
All cast all mighty water dead away.

I rise up loving and you may not move away.[12]

The ballads, 'The Children of Greenock', 'The Children of Lanarkshire', 'The Lost Other' spin out like fishing-lines: in 'The Children of
Lanarkshire' in particular it looks at times as though Graham is deliberately replacing imagistic density with an absent-minded casualness, as
though he wishes to postpone climax as a way of avoiding the overriding
problem of bringing together the scattered and dislocated ego:

And under waters of a monstrous language
Its glow and game writes on the age
Here loud with beast and flying offices.
And April rising from the laws

Finds in my nosed and fostering pocket
Kingcup myrtle lintroot for my foot.
And a good black thorn for my head.
And a linty to sing at my deathbed.[13]

The last two lines are fragments of the past, not writable by the
individual poet, and this is surely the point: Graham has now identified
that hidden force which surreptitiously makes and remakes the world
behind our backs (or when we leave the theatre each night) as language;
he has realised that the discourse in terms of which he is trying to write
has itself a 'monstrous' and material presence which presses heavily
upon the poet.

The movement into the open air is not altogether successful: his
rhythms, certainly, are liberated by this unclogging of the arteries, but a

poem like 'The Search by a Town', which promisingly begins 'This step sails who an ocean crossed/And mountain climbed', nonetheless becomes redolent of Blake's doomed and circular 'Mental Traveller':

> For ever as the seeker turns
> His worshipping eyes on prophetic patterns
> Of shape arising from all men
> He changes through, he shall remain
>
> Continually stripped and clothed again.
> The morning loses sound and man.
> The glow invents the worm. His saint
> Invents his food and feeds his want.[14]

The self here moves together and apart in purposeless gyration, solving problems in the external world which have in fact arisen purely through its own structure. The sea proves even more problematic: it allows Graham the minor triumphs of 'Shian Bay' and 'Gigha', but it also prompts the reflections at the end of the third of the 'Three Poems of Drowning':

> Now in these seas, my task of the foam-holy voyages
> Charted in a bead of blood, I work. I answer
> Across the dark sea's raging bridges of exchange
> Proclaiming my own fought drowning, as loud laid under
> All arriving seas drift me, at each heartbreak, home.[15]

From Pandora's box to Chinese boxes: the complex poise of the ending, whereby we are not certain whether the homeward drift connotes safety or failure of communication, or whether we are intended to see the two as necessarily interwoven, is precisely the poem's problem: whether the very *achievement* of that 'complex poise' is not itself a betrayal, a refusal of communicative direction and a consequent submergence in the endless and pointless flow of the sea. Might it be the case, Graham is asking, that the density of language ends by stripping *us*, as subjects, of meaning?

Because *The White Threshold* marks out the beginnings of new formal directions for Graham, what tends to have been underestimated in it is its often successful deployment of the older mode of plenitude, notably in the 'Two Love Poems' and 'The Bright Midnight', in which the resonances from Dylan Thomas remain but are set against a different kind of voice, derived from Hopkins and from the seventeenth century, almost as though, despairing at this time of finding his own voice amid the newly revealed labyrinths of language, Graham at least determined that he would test the Thomas fluidity against a poetry of sinew:

> Since there (spun into a sudden place to discover)
> We first lay down in the nightly body of the year,
> Fast wakened up new midnights from our bed,
> Moved off to other sweet opposites, I've bled
> My look along your heart, my thorns about your head.[16]

The voice is not in itself original, but hearing a dialogue between Donne and Thomas is nonetheless an adventure of language, another step out of the forest; but it is also, of course, a revelation of further depth within the sign, depth which can be interpreted as unconscious resonance or duplicity.

We may thus take Graham's early works less as variously successful or unsuccessful isolated attempts than as the complicated and hesitant beginnings of a narrative which can be seen running through his texts. I am therefore less concerned with the quality of individual poems than with the directions of a large poetic enterprise, and with getting our bearings in Graham's world before coming to firm decisions on the identity of the objects within it. It is in this sense that we need to follow this hazy and winding narrative through his three more recent books, *The Nightfishing* (1955), *Malcolm Mooney's Land* (1970) and *Implements in Their Places* (1977).

The structure of *The Nightfishing* is complex, and important because the volume as a whole represents an attempt to bring the overflowing world of experience into relation with meditation on the draining away of the ego:[17] the sea gives, but the sea takes away. The central long poem, 'The Nightfishing' itself, contains a central section in which we are immersed in immediate experience, but this is framed between sections designed to cast doubt on the sufficiency of the unreflective empiricism which such description entails:

> The rigged ship in its walls of glass
> Still further forms its perfect seas
> Locked in its past transparences.[18]

When Bedient says that 'few poems in the language resonate with so full and immediate a response to life',[19] this is certainly true of the central section: but that section is presented less for absorption than for criticism. Graham seems to see it as representing one, wished-for, way of achieving wholeness; yet also as a way impossible or illicit in the real world, achievable only within the framing confines of poetry. Thus the relation between the fully described experience and the half-hearted and half-glimpsed relations to nature which are permitted us in everyday life remains an ironised one, and this is pointed up by the other poems in the volume, which by no means share the easy, complicit tone of the fishing description.

In the first section of 'The Nightfishing', the poet is 'called' by 'the quay night bell', but his response is ambiguous:

> I bent to the lamp. I cupped
> My hand to the glass chimney.
> Yet it was a stranger's breath
> From out of my mouth that
> Shed the light. I turned out
> Into the salt dark
> And turned my collar up.

Ostensibly the narrator makes his way down to the herring-boat; but at the same time the poet embarks on his own descriptive voyage, thus assuring us that the poetic mode he is about to use is in no way to be seen as 'natural', but instead as an artificially constructed work which may gain the weight to stand firm against the erosions of memory and the intrinsically fragmentary nature of perception and reflection. And indeed there is a further more troubling level at which we are brought to doubt whether either of these journeys are happening in any realm other than that of dream:

> Far out faintly calls
> The continual sea.
>
> Now within the dead
> Of night and the dead
> Of all my life I go.
> I'm one ahead of them
> Turned in below.
> I'm borne, in their eyes,
> Through the staring world.
>
> The present opens its arms.

Graham manages to find new uses for ancient imagery: if the sea is dream, how can we find in it any source of purchase? Yet this is the point: for only at sea are we freed from the 'arrangements' that take place in unseen glades, only by plunging into flux can we escape the crushing massiveness of linguistic preformation. And so, says Graham, 'we'll move off in this changing grace. /The moon keels and the harbour oil/Looks at the sky through seven colours'. What the last phrase establishes is that the escape which the sea represents is an escape from a particular kind of perceptual separateness: the central description is based, not on the poet looking at the sea, but on a dialectical relationship including an attempt, reminiscent of Hopkins or of Keats's 'in-feel',[20] to see and feel through the sea's blue senses: 'Our bow heads home',

> Into the running blackbacks soaring us loud
> High up in open arms of the towering sea.
> The steep bow heaves, hung on these words, towards
> What words your lonely breath blows out to meet it.
>
> It is the skilled keel itself knowing its own
> Fathoms it further moves through, with us there
> Kept in its common timbers, yet each of us
> Unwound upon
>
> By a lonely behaviour of the all common ocean.
> I cried headlong from my dead.

In *The White Threshold*, Graham had approached an impasse: on the one hand he sensed the power of language to resist purposive shaping, while on the other he took on the responsibility for agency which writing entails, thus sharing language's historical guilt. Here we see him trying to shed that guilt, trying to enable the sea to write itself, humbling himself before the power of the word and allowing the waves of description to roll over him, as if hoping that he could by those means exhaust the enemy.

What is produced is change in the poet, and particularly in his sense of place:

> So this is the place. This
> Is the place fastened still with movement,
> Movement as calligraphic and formal as
> A music burned on copper.

> At this place
> The eye reads forward as the memory reads back.
> At this last word all words change.
> All words change in acknowledgement of the last.
>
>   . .
>
> Here is this place no more
> Certain though the steep streets
> And High Street form again and the sea
> Swing shut on hinges and the doors all open wide.

But whether this change solves any problems remains ambiguous: in one way the poet's immersion has devalued other experience, enabled a metalanguage but at the expense of the sense of home. Immersion in the Other has produced not reconciliation but exile; the haunted stillness of the port enshrines traces of the poet as he was before, progress is subverted into a doomed attempt at recapture.

> Home becomes this place,
> A bitter night, ill
> To labour at dead of.
> Within all the dead of
> All my life I hear
> My name spoken out
> On the break of the surf.
> I, in Time's grace,
> The grace of change, am
> Cast into memory.
> What a restless grace
> To trace stillness on.

The attempt to use the sea as image and touchstone, to generate energy from its stored metaphoric power, has partly backfired: the sea now has added to its blind power a voice, whereas the fecundity suggested during the actual voyage dries up on the poet's tongue when he returns to land. The sea has caught the poet as the poet has caught herring: as he hauled them up to the surface in nets of words, attempted to impose precision and order, the sea fought back. 'Far out faintly calls/The mingling sea', mingling in defiance of order and integration, calling out with the voice of language itself, imprinted with the thousand other voices which impede our direct vision of the word. Under these circumstances, the poet's fragile ego cannot survive: change, after all, is the sea's realm, and the human being cannot bear this much of it:

> So I spoke and died.
> So within the dead
> Of night and the dead
> Of all my life those
> Words died and awoke.

But the death of the ego is simultaneously a kind of non-human liberation, for the poet dies so that the word may have its own life. The thought is an alarming one: Graham implies that language feeds, vampire-like, on death, on what is irrevocably past.[21] Catching the herring was a present act: but no matter how immediate, to write experience remains a distortion, a savagery, and one within which the poet finally consumes his own substance, leaving phantom words hovering over the resultant double absence.

The 'Letters' and 'Ballads' meditate variously on this collection of themes, some less pessimistically than others. 'I am/Trusted on the language', begins 'Letter II', but this hope turns into an agonised pleading with the bonds of the past:

> Take heed. Reply. Here
> I am driven burning on
> This loneliest element. Break
> Break me out of this night,
> This silence where you are not,
> Nor any within earshot.
> Break break me from this high
> Helmet of idiocy.[22]

Implicit in many of the poems is an inverted model of communication: when Graham utters words, he loses them, and utterance thus demonstrates not communication but isolation. It is language itself which has power, mostly for destruction, always for obfuscation; far from freeing us to make contact with others, it effectively bounds us, reminding us whenever we choose to collaborate with it that only by its permission can we prepare a meaning.

Cast in this gold
Wicklight this night within
This poem, we two go down
Roaring between the lines
To drown. Who hears? Who listens?[23]

The obverse side of the close involvement of the herring fishing scene is withdrawal and violence, reflected in the crudity of 'Baldy Bane':

Through the word and through the word,
    And all is sad and done,
Who are you that these words
    Make this fall upon?
Fair's fair, upon my word,
    And that you shall admit,
Or I will blow your face in glass
    And then I'll shatter it.
Lie over to me from the wall or else
    Get up and clean the grate.[24]

If words cannot be used for communication, perhaps they can at least be effective weapons; but the impotently threatening figure of Baldy Bane, drunk and powerless, undercuts even this possibility and gestures towards the frozen wastes of *Malcolm Mooney's Land*.

Malcolm Mooney's Land contains several significant genre successes: the elegy for Peter Lanyon, 'The Thermal Stair'; the love poem, 'I Leave This at Your Ear'; even the splendidly kinetic and colourful portrayal of a fruit machine in 'Press Button to Hold Desired Symbol', despite the dubious nature of the underlying set of puns. But these are suspended, as in aspic, in a world largely without outward-going vitality, a world which recognises only immobility as a possible posture of defiance. The co-ordinates for Graham's vision here are, on the one hand, the Antarctic scenery of the title poem and, on the other, the long series of circular or regressive linguistic meditations which run from 'The Beast in the Space', through 'The Dark Dialogues', to 'Approaches to How They Behave' and 'Clusters Travelling Out'. Those poems which escape debilitating introspection are the rareties, sparks cast off by the hammer with which Graham seeks to pound a glimmer of truth out of the distortions of the word; yet the paradoxical strength of the introspective poems is that the poet is fully aware of the debility, is able to take the tonal thinness and, largely by use of his twisting, squirming short lines, stretch it beyond expectation. The effect is of a discourse virtually shorn of predictable sources of interest – compelling imagery, character formation, narrative – which nonetheless succeeds in exciting us by its absolute determination to attend to words in a self-reflexive way, no matter what the danger.

And there is danger in 'Malcolm Mooney's Land'; the landscape reminds us of those frozen wastes through which Frankenstein and his monster presumably still endlessly pursue each other, hoping against hope for an answer to Oedipus' little difficulty. The explorer who is the supposed author of the poem seems deeply uncertain of the line between the human and the monstrous: 'Elizabeth/Was in my thoughts all morning and the boy',[25] but later Elizabeth becomes the 'furry/Pelted queen' whom we have met before in the glades of illusion. Out here in this uncertain land she is joined by a cast of other familiars, the invisible fox who leaves 'prints/All round the tent and not a sound', the landlice, 'always my good bedfellows', the 'old sulphur bear/Sawing his log of sleep/Loud beneath the snow', the 'benign creature with the small ear-hole,/Submerger under silence'. They and the explorer share a world of minimal sound: the purpose of the journey may be to isolate the smallest of all possible sonic units, freeze them, and see whether by these means some sense may be distilled.

> Enough
> Voices are with me here and more
> The further I go. Yesterday
> I heard the telephone ringing deep
> Down in a blue crevasse.
> I did not answer it and could
> Hardly bear to pass.

Or could it be that sound and the illusion of meaning simply expand to fill up available space, that to cheat ourselves of normal human converse, however inadequate, is simply to allow the sounds of night and ice to take over?

> Out at the far-off edge I hear
> Colliding voices, drifted, yes
> To find me through the slowly opening leads.
> Tomorrow I'll try the rafted ice.
> Have I not been trying to use the obstacle
> Of language well? It freezes round us all.

At this point, language itself has become the tenor for a complex set of interlocked metaphors: language is the great obstacle to knowledge of reality, whether of the world or of others, yet it is also the only available site for activity, and as such it turns into a deadly trap, or rather, perhaps, it harbours within its own striations and folds a host of partially seen dangers. These dangers become brutally realised in 'The Beast in the Space', which is in some ways a more important key to the volume than 'Malcolm Mooney's Land' itself, in that it pares down the poem to an attempted description of its own creative process:

> Shut up. Shut up. There's nobody here.
> If you think you here somebody knocking
> On the other side of the words, pay
> No attention. It will be only
> The great creature that thumps its tail
> On silence on the other side.[26]

The technical manipulators and string-pullers of *2nd Poems* represented an image of language as determined by rigid, para-human rules; the 'Great Beast' of *Malcolm Mooney's Land* shows us instead language at the service of the maliciously inarticulate and inexplicable.[27] The 'sulphur bear' and the 'beast in the space' are reminiscent of the ancient cave-bear in Conan Doyle's story about the Blue John mine, which is a story not about fear but about the absolute frustration its hero feels at being unable to produce any verification for his awful adventure.[28]

> The beast that lives on silence takes
> Its bite out of either side.
> It pads and sniffs between us. Now
> It comes and laps my meaning up.
> Call it over. Call it across
> This curious necessary space.
> Get off, you terrible inhabiter
> Of silence. I'll not have it. Get
> Away to whoever it is will have you.[29]

That which lies between the writer and his implicit audience has come alive: stirred up finally by continual prodding, it has woken to guard that mysterious boundary area through which communication has to flow. It can be, temporarily, tamed, but remains unreliable, random; because it is the spirit of language, it is a human creation, but because we have lost our grip on our own construction it is out of our control. Our alienation, not only from words but from most aspects of our lives, emerges symbolically in 'The Lying Dear', where a poem which starts off by being about sex falls foul of the beast, and ends up catapulted back into no-man's-land:

> Her breath
> Flew out like smoke. Her beauty
> Twisted into another
> Beauty and we went down
> Into the little village
> Of a new language.[30]

Words act as an inverted Aladdin's Lamp, sucking in energy and meaning.

In 'Dear Who I Mean', the only solution offered is silence:

> When the word or the word's name
> Flies out before us in winter
> Beware of the cunning god
> Slinking across the tense
> Fields ready to pretend
> To carry in spittled jaws
> The crashed message, this letter
> Between us. With two fingers
> I give one whistle along
> The frozen black sticks
> To bring him to heel.[31]

The most primeval power of the gods is to name, and to confer life by naming; in Malcolm Mooney's land, symbolised by telegraph poles isolated in the waste, the gods are always ready to take our names away.

> The quick brown pouncing god
> Magnifies towards us.
> He crunches it up like a bird
> And does not leave one word.

If in the early poems Graham practised an excessive expansion of consciousness, dispersed his location and perspective, here he has come full circle: he is a tiny black dot in a white landscape, unable to move and all but robbed of speech. The sparse words come through gritted teeth;

far from being 'trusted on the language', he appears to have scant hope that any of his words will still mean by the end of their impossibly difficult journey through the space occupied by the beast.

In 'The Constructed Space', there is a certain amount of fighting back. If the boundary between sender and receiver is not rigid and immutable, if it contains pockets wherein words can be swallowed, might it not be possible to find our own space somewhere within that masterless realm? Such a space is suggested, not very hopefully, 'a public place/Achieved against subjective odds and then/Mainly an obstacle to what I mean',[32] yet the brilliantly and intricately worked final stanza does after all allow some possibility, sanctioned perhaps by love, or perhaps by sheer shared effort:

> I say this silence or, better, construct this space
> So that somehow something may move across
> The caught habits of language to you and me.
> From where we are it is not us we see
> And times are hastening yet, disguise is mortal.
> The times continually disclose our home.
> Here in the present tense disguise is mortal.
> The trying times are hastening. Yet here I am
> More truly now this abstract act become.

The 'caught' habits of language are finely ambiguous: infected, but also trapped, language itself trapped by the beast but we as speakers trapped within it. Thus a complicated paradox: as in earlier poems, the ego needs first to shape a space for itself, in which something can be abstracted from the literal meaninglessness of the continuous present – a task which art has habitually set itself – yet this very space can become an inescapable enclosure. The phrase 'disguise is mortal' signifies the problem: it is a mysterious shape emerging from the snowy mist, both ends lost in ambiguity, simultaneously affirming hope for demystification and the endlessness of illusion.

'The Constructed Space' remains the highpoint of hope in *Malcolm Mooney's Land*, the point at which Graham comes closest to emerging from 'white-out in this tent of a place'[33] and building some kind of more stable shelter against the cold winds. 'The Dark Dialogues', 'Approaches to How They Behave', 'Clusters Travelling Out' represent a series of attempts to reach out and touch words, but they become increasingly tentative: the clusters end up travelling beyond reach, the attempt to give an account of how words behave remains an anthropological ruin. 'I always meant to only/Language swings away/Further before me'.[34] What is most painful in these meditations is the increasing weight of guilt; Graham becomes almost chilidishly tearful before the accumulating evidence of his inadequacy, and that guilt which he has previously tried to account for in terms of the pre-empting of language by history now starts to fall back onto his own shoulders.

> Before I know it they are out
> Afloat in the head which freezes them.
> Then I suppose I take the best
> Away and leave the others arranged
> Like floating bergs to sink a convoy.[35]

There are other brief moments of strenuous hope, and more of wry humour, especially in epigrammatic form, presumably because a brief sally into monster country scars less badly than a lengthier engagement; but perhaps the overall tone is best summarised in an extract from 'Clusters Travelling Out':

> I am learning to speak here in a way
> Which may be useful afterwards.
> Slops in hand we shuffle together,
> Something to look forward to
> Behind the spyhole. Here in our concrete
> Soundbox we slide the jargon across
> The watching air, a lipless language
> Necessarily squashed from the side
> To make its point against the rules.
> It is our poetry such as it is.
> Are you receiving those clusters
> I send out travelling? Alas
> I have no way of knowing or
> If I am overheard here.
> Is that (It is.) not what I want?
>
> The slaughterhouse is next door.
> Destroy this. They are very strict.[36]

Graham has indeed arrived in the prison-house of language, poetry is reduced to ephemeral communication in a concrete environment; as the slops are emptied, so is language, in the service of Graham's still continuing and appallingly thorough attempt to find the one true, unpolluted, self-referential word which will destroy the beast and magically open the door it guards.[37]

It seems doubtful whether Graham would attribute the difficulty of communication to a historically specific cultural condition, the sparseness of his own words to the draining of meaning effected by, for instance, commercial debasements of language, but of course we remain permitted to investigate such attributions. On the whole, rather surprisingly, critics have not done so; they have preferred to see the changes in Graham's work as indications of a purely private syndrome, and the reviews which greeted *Implements in Their Places* when it appeared suggest a kind of almost morally blameworthy atrophy. 'In what . . . looks like a carefully anxious career, Mr Graham has slowly ground down his work until it is by now concentrated on a small handful of subjects essential to himself', wrote Douglas Dunn, and '*Implements in Their Places* is very much a book for private meditation, no matter how public the theme of communication might seem to be';[38] but both claims undermine the 'careful' dialectic which Graham has built up. The grinding down is performed, not purely by the poet, but in the course of the continuous confrontation between the force of subjectivity and the weight of language; the 'private meditation' may itself be a forced mode, may be the only pocket of resistance left for the poet in a time when the telephone lines are down. The very first poem in the collection is called 'What is the Language Using Us for?', and is a defiant restatement of the earlier pressing themes, an indication that this volume is going to provide no easy escape from an encounter which is now taking on the dimensions of an epic wrestling match:

> What is the language using us for?
> I don't know. Have the words ever
> Made anything of you, near a kind
> Of truth you thought you were? Me
> Neither. The words like albatrosses
> Are only a doubtful touch towards
> My going and you lifting your hand
> To speak to illustrate an observed

Catastrophe. What is the weather
Using us for where we are ready
With all our language lines aboard?
The beginning wind slaps the canvas.
Are you ready? Are you ready?[39]

The resources of Graham's imagery – the sea, the wind, the wastes – are reinvoked in the service of an introductory poem which introduces only its eventually non-existent self; even beginning is replaced by reflexion on the possibility of beginning, bracketed and abstracted in an extreme phenomenological parenthesis according to which the 'thing-in-itself' left for pure apprehension is the pattering of life in language's wainscot, *before* the writer or user himself starts to interfere.

Implements in Their Places is a volume which broadens the site of poetry. Graham's perception of the materiality of language forces him to bring the whole question of the social relation between poet and reader into the arena, and in many of the poems this actually becomes the content. The subject matter of 'Untidy Dreadful Table' is the poet himself in the act of writing; the subject matter of 'Imagine a Forest', a poem written in the second person – singular – is the reader entrapped by the poem's co-ordinates and by his own prior experience of poetry – 'you go in a deep/Ballad on the border of a time/You have seemed to walk in before'.[40] It is not at all that Graham has found a way through the obstacles; it is more that, having observed the monsters which impede communication, he is now concerned to bring up more lights on the stage, to bring us and himself into greater proximity with the beast. But what happens is therefore a set of preparations: the meanings of the title of the volume are multiple, but one important one shows Graham arranging his tools for a further round in the struggle – whether or not that round will come.

This morning I am ready if you are
To speak. The early quick rains
Of Spring are drenching the window-glass.
Here in my words looking out
I see your face speaking flying
In a cloud wanting to say something.[41]

This is the dominant discourse of the volume, and it is in many ways a unique one. What Graham seems to have done is press through an almost adolescent subjectivism and come out on the other side; in order to squeeze through, he has had to – or perhaps more to the point, has determined to – jettison most of the paradigmatic resonance which poetry enables to flourish, as if that were baggage too heavy for the journey (through the Antarctic) and is left with the thinnest and most sinewy of syntagmatic chains, pared to the bone but as powerfully linked as steel hawser.

On the whole, the concentration on the poet's activity is less satisfying, perhaps because Graham has already tapped the vein, than the new attention to the implied reader. 'Language Ah Now You Have Me' makes us begin all over again when we no longer feel we need to:

> Language ah now you have me. Night-time tongue,
> Please speak for me between the social beasts
> Which quick assail me. Here I am hiding in
> The jungle of mistakes of communication.[42]

But 'Ten Shots of Mister Simpson', one of the most important poems in the volume, has power and grace in sinister combination. It seems initially a direct address to the reader:

> Ah Mister Simpson shy spectator
> This morning in our November,
> Don't run away with the idea
> You are you spectating me.
>
> On the contrary from this hide
> Under my black cloth I see
> You through the lens close enough
> For comfort.[43]

Graham's attitude has changed: from a worthy, but increasingly self-pitying, fear and guilt before language, he has moved into a posture of greater aggression: here we are directly threatened by the awful complicity of 'our' November, 'close enough/For comfort'. Why, the poem appears to ask, should the poet be the only one terrorised by the beast? Or, to put it another way, why should we as readers not also be made to feel the threat of unnaming and the meaningless? Graham then swings between Mister Simpson and a further reader:

Look at him standing sillily
For our sake and for the sake
Of preservation.

'Preservation' sounds very like a jibe at Larkin's insistence on the possibility of a poetic conservation of real experience:[44] the alternation between Simpson and a further Other ensures our discomfort, demonstrates that even the élitist complicity offered is itself fake, that language's duplicity does not always merely confound the poet, it can also provide the poet with the means to confound us.

The growing irony in the poet's stance moves at times over the boundaries of literary gentility into sarcasm: at the end of 'Enter a Cloud' Graham, still the stage magician, emerges from behind the curtain to provide a fitting conclusion to his act:

Thank you. And for your applause,
It has been a pleasure. I
Have never enjoyed speaking more.
May I also thank the real ones
Who have made this possible.
First, the cloud itself. And now
Gurnard's Head and Zennor
Head. Also recognise
How I have been helped
By Jean and Madron's Albert
Strick (He is a real man.)
And good words like brambles,
Bower, spiked, fox, anvil, teeling.[45]

At a stroke Graham's abrasive wit scythes through the sterile problems of metaphysics and defines the poem as fiction within self-conscious fiction. Earlier in his career, when asked about his influences, he mentioned only modernist writers, leaving out, to the consternation of some critics, more overt influences like Thomas and Hopkins;[46] whether or not that was a fair account of the poems to that date, his later work has certainly vindicated a similarity of attention to, say, Beckett, and *Implements in Their Places* demonstrates a constant dislocation of form and role which reminds us at several points of Beckett's 'prose'. In 'Johann Joachim Quantz's Five Lessons', a different but related comparison springs to mind: the frozen postures, the stylised speech, the

chill intensity of estrangement are the devices of the new German
cinema of Fassbinder and Herzog:[47]

> Karl, you are late. The traverse flute is not
> A study to take lightly. I am cold waiting.
> Put one piece of coal in the stove. This lesson
> Shall not be prolonged. Right. Stand in your place.
>
> Ready? Blow me a little ladder of sound
> From a good stance so that you feel the heavy
> Press of the floor coming up through you and
> Keeping your pitch and tone in character.[48]

Beckettian fragmentation and neo-Brechtian stylisation are not improbable refuges for the harried consciousness.

Strangest among the poems are the three little horror stories, 'The Gobbled Child', 'The Lost Miss Conn', 'The Murdered Drinker', in which minor newspaper pieces are turned into Graham's distinctive five-lined, non-rhyming ballad stanzas; but more significant is the long title sequence of seventy-four pieces, fragments or epigrams, beginning 'somewhere our belonging particles/Believe in us. If we could only find them'.[49] Rather than attempt the naturalisation which would be involved in marshalling these pieces, Graham has preferred to leave them to stand on their shelves, racked like tools or implements, available for use but not foregrounding their participation in the act of poetry. It is as though we have come to a place where movement has ceased: since such movement might disturb the sulphur bear, release danger and destruction, Graham has become, temporarily, an armourer rather than a fighter: here, he says, are some weapons, but I am not about to dictate their use. And this, of course, confronts us with a choice: whether to believe, with Mister Simpson, that we can take up a passive stance to the problems Graham has outlined, or whether we are fatally embroiled in an active situation. Graham is ironic about our options, and also about our potential: in one poem he leaves us space to write in our own implement, adding after the empty lines:

> Do it with your pen.
> I will return in a moment
> To see what you have done.
> Try. Try. No offence meant.[50]

It is as though, having tried in poems like 'The Constructed Space' to persuade us of the possibility of activity by relatively non-directive means, he is now reverting to more old-fashioned pedagogy. His patience with his audience is fast running out, and we feel increasingly doubtful about the intention of his embraces:

> You will observe that not one
> Of those tree-trunks has our initials
> Carved on it or heart or arrow
> We could call ours. My dear, I think
> We have come in to the wrong wood.[51]

Further reflections are prompted: whose fault, for instance, is the mistake? And what might proceed to happen if this wood is, after all, not the nice safe one which we habitually think of as poetry, but a wood altogether more wild and deep?

In *Malcolm Mooney's Land*, Graham's emptying of the overdetermined and overladen sign was almost completed; greater perfection might only have been possible at the level of white noise. *Implements in Their Places*, courageously assuming that at least *that* minimal communication reached its audience, proceeds to supplement it with a question: what are we going to do about the increasingly rapid evaporation of meaning? It is as if the magician has turned into the animal-trainer, in several different senses: he wishes to train us in the use of his implements, but at the same time he wants to show us the limits of our own freedom, the extent to which we rely on the poet, depend on his strength to control language. Graham seems to feel that he has become a victim of trans-ference, that his strenuous negations have somehow made the reader dependent on him, and *Implements in Their Places* is a defining, and a partial shedding, of responsibility. There is no point, the book claims, in moving through the mazy thickets of language unless we become able to do it by ourselves, without a helpful guide at our elbow. Thus the emptying of the sign turns into an emptying of the writer's role: where the romantic conception of the poet ends in apotheosis, Graham's conception ends in absence and silence. We are, of course, constructing a fiction of endings: but *Implements in Their Places* is, for all that, a still point, part retreat and part stockade, in itself a constructed space for reflection; and, as an entire volume, a powerful image for refusals and strengths which are the keynotes of Graham's career, but also keys to the plight of the surveyed psyche.

9   Some cultural materials

But in fact the culture does not present itself to us in the neatly packaged ways beloved of literary criticism, and to remain at the level of the literary is to pass by in silence while the most effective of cultural implantations take place. In this last section, then, it seems appropriate to provide a collection of brief cultural snapshots, in such a way as to try to connect them to major preoccupations. The violently circular struggles of gender differentiation; the construction of illusory versions of the self; the specifically British plight of political and cultural supersession; the evolution of substitute models for the family; the obscuring of contemporary class co-ordinates; the ritualising and draining of meaning performed by linguistic formalism: each of these I hope briefly to take up again in a brief 'instance' of myth-making. I was tempted to add, after these instances, some form of 'conclusion' which would bring together the major themes attended to here; but this seems to me inappropriate, and another attempt to set up a convenient structure of global interpretation. The instances form their own discourse, replete as it is with hiatuses and contradictions, the hallmarks of the unconscious and its relation to materialisation.

Tommy

Just below the surface of Ken Russell's apparently heroic and celebratory film (1975), there is a homosexual mourning, as we might expect from the director and also from the film's birth in the music of an all-male rock group. Tommy, certainly, is subjected to the desires of a variety of figures, as they seek fulfilment in his blank eyes: but the central struggle is nonetheless between real father and false father, the lost airman and the present showman. It is natural that, in the hallucinated state which is Tommy's normalcy and the normalcy we are enjoined to share, both of these contestants are seen through the hall of mirrors: the airman as ghost and nostalgia, the showman through a succession of avatars (Cousin Kevin, Uncle Ernie, even the Acid Queen). Meanwhile the mother who is caught in the hollow of these two insanely clapping hands, applauding Tommy and egging him on, is objectified and reduced to a mere function of the scenes in which she happens to appear. For Tommy is the great male hope: a birth so sensorily immaculate that he may have escaped early feminine imprinting, and thus be ripe for transformation into the wholly masculine, free from any left-handed demands or urges.

The mother is never sure that the various rites of initiation through which Tommy is made to pass are good for him, but her new husband has no such doubts: the Acid Queen appears to proffer sexuality, but only in the form of the needle of death, of a penetration which will confirm the hardening of skin and soul against the soft and eroding affections. What Tommy is trained for is mechanical mastery: paradoxically liberated by early trauma into a world where sex and death are equivalent, and release means only the death of the inferior male, he is made to perfect a form of competitivity in which he does not even need to sully his hands. At the controls of the prone body of the feminine pin-table, he learns an extreme delicacy of touch which, he already knows, would be wasted or dangerous in connexion with a sexual partner. Therefore, when he begins to spread the word, it is among the symbolic representatives of abrasive and charismatic sexlessness, the Hell's Angels and the junkies, that he finds his converts. Tommy is the apotheosis of macho culture, a role in no way lessened by the fact that the game he plays is played not to win but merely for the demonstration of skill. He defeats, certainly, the previous Pinball Wizard, but only so that a more effective symbol of male domination can replace one which is outmoded, one whose style betrays through exaggeration the fact that it has ceased to convince.

The crucial hiatus in *Tommy* concerns the lesson, or the nature of the sign: we are brought to follow in detail the (familial) process which produces Tommy as exceptional, and to analyse the symbiotic father/son relationship which propels him into the public world, but thereafter meaning is suspended. It is as though the process of development turns back on itself: the game of pin-ball is not in itself the sign (and the final revolt of the disciples makes this clear), so the game must be either the procedure which will lead to revelation, or, alternatively, the procedure which will absorb enough of our energies to make us forget that revelation was ever imminent. In this perfection of manipulation, the distinction between ends and means is lost, but so too is the nature of pleasure: it is easy to lose sight of the multiplicity of paradoxes inherent in the relations depicted between sensory deprivation and gratification, easy to forget, in the glowing and noisy world of the film, that what is portrayed at its heart is absolute absence, a void in which touch, the only remaining sense, is not developed (since no evidence of perform-ance is available) but neatly severed like the other senses, the hands resting uselessly on the controls of a machine which can return nothing.

Thus the film is itself a developing absence, devoted to a demon-stration that precisely the aesthetic values it embodies are to be rejected and transcended on the path to an equally paradoxical 'enlightenment'. The trajectory is complex: the dead airman, amalgam of flying (infantile visions of sexuality) and an inescapable grounding, is replaced by the showman, for whom everything is based in a metaphysic of presence, whose world is one of tawdry surfaces and whizzing wheels.[1] But Tommy in effect reverses the process, drops the world of the holiday camp into the abyss. His journey is suicidal, although there again there is an ambiguity, about the murderous role of the (partly surrogate) parents.

What gets suppressed in the obsessively 'contemporary' trappings of the film is that this is a relived post-war fantasy, rooted in admiration for the lost father, the heroic individual who found, by the luck of history, a way of publicly demonstrating that heroism. The generation for which Tommy (silently) speaks does not have that chance: thus the final line-up of pin-ball machines, each with a silent, helmeted figure at its controls, forms a parallel with the night-flights of the fighters, but there is no external enemy. Then, typically, the organisational beauty of a latter-day militarism breaks down into pointless violence, and the 'army' Tommy's mentors appear to be trying to form degenerates into thug-gery, their victims their own self-professed officer class. The routines of Butlins form a thin skin over the wish for destruction: Tommy's supremacy derives from his possession of a vulnerability so intense and complete that he can temporarily hallucinate his followers into believing that he must have a reserve of unspoken strength which they might be able to tap. Tuned in at last to his silent and absent world, they see that even their destructiveness has not the will to proceed with this path towards utter negation: frenzied, they reassert the relative humanity of their inefficient brutality. Thus again, as so often in the Western canon, the vice of violence is posited as forgiveable in the face of the supposedly greater threat of total organisation:[2] although the earlier Pinball Wizard, with his soccer hooligan's boots, has been defeated, it is his shadow which returns as Tommy's little group of controllers (controllers of him, and/or of his followers) is hacked and kicked to death.

It is in the late 1970s and 1980s that the elision of heroic forms which characterised the 1960s is beginning to come into focus: rock star, messiah, junkie were lifted above and beyond the world, switched into a different metabolism, multiple symbols for a masculine consciousness which was perhaps already presaging a troubling fate. For the sexual 'liberationism' of that decade was important only really as an early stage in the liberation of women: already it was clear that, for men, the outcome could only be an erosion of the old, privileged certainties. Kerouac had already made his run, but simply fleeing mother is too distant from more complex psychological needs and from economic demands to become a way of life.[3] By setting up figures of the residually admirable male, and simultaneously converting these icons into the substance of commercial transaction, several problems can be overcome in fantasy at once, but the synthesis is unstable (instability – unto death – is one of its repertoire of proffered pleasures). Tommy adds to the heroic battery another source of transcendence, his imperviousness to the deathly effects of commercially manipulated adulation, and this is perhaps at least enough to save him, but only alone and in impotence, obliterated, in the final frame, by the sun. Or, perhaps, it is enough at least to gain a revenge on behalf of the teenage audience, who see the manipulators themselves gunned down while Tommy preserves his effortless and useless superiority, see the impresarios and businessmen they have read about in the papers themselves becoming victims while the lone star survives.

J. R. R. Tolkien and the legendary

Tolkien's books made the difficult transition from text to cult, from a version of the world to a magical principle according to which versions of the world might be ordered.[4] The assumption must be that they caught and held within themselves the desires of part of Western society: a specific group, but also an area of feeling within the society itself, a wish to see the world laid out in *this* way. Mapping, obviously, was very important: amid burgeoning complexities, the map of Middle Earth reflects large empty spaces and clearly defined ethnic boundaries, a system which is not ruined by cross-fertilisation, a dream of harmless juxtaposition (or, militarily, stand-off) without pollution. Mordor is safely confined within its ring of mountains, not an active force despite its outriders but chiefly a lurking threat which can be dealt with according to our own time-scale.

And this mapping is not only spatial but also temporal: words are derived from clear antecedents, no awkward parts of history are lost for all survive in the neat family trees. Etymology holds the secrets of the world, and is perfectly prepared to yield up to curiosity and a modicum of technical expertise. Not that Tolkien's own expertise is anything but generous: but we can expect to be led by the hand through the mazes, safe from the Gollums of the underworld, knowing that the ring of knowledge and power is ours by right. As hobbits, we are treated to a tour of the modes of production and control, the nostalgically decaying aristocratic order of the elves, the co-operative labour of the dwarves, even the mysterious 'Asiatic mode of production' in Harad and other remote corners.[5] This is not at all a vindication of the status quo, not a defence of capitalism, but then the best trick of the bourgeoisie, from the romantics through William Morris to Lawrence and Leavis, has been to defend not their own order, the realm of surplus labour and the profit motive, but an older tradition of which, somehow, they are the guardians; an order of cottage industry which, it is claimed, lies at the roots of later development, even though the contrary historical facts are plain to see.[6] In this respect, the country of the hobbits fits into a long sequence of shadow-realms, of versions of 'the real England' which, we are called upon to believe, continues to exist (in rural communities, in childhood) and is protected (rather than savaged) by the benevolence of industry. Capitalism, according to this long-lived myth, is thus the price we have to pay for the continuation of this other England, which cannot, of course, be pinpointed on maps: merely the outward form within which the legendary can survive, the outer defences which preserve and succour the national spirit.

In fact, we know what happens to the Meriden Co-operative when it tries to fit itself into the wider system of exchange and labour; like an unsuccessful transplant, it fails to 'take'. On Middle Earth, no such experiment is necessary: each heartland is decently separated from its peers, free from the exigencies of the global system, radiating its own independent power which will, in turn, protect its emissaries when they move out from the group according to their deservingness on a scale of virtue. Thus Frodo moves in a cocoon, as we should like to move: protected from the predatory, whether external or arising from the psychic depths. In *Lord of the Rings* (1954–5), this protection has, however, a double face: Frodo is safe because he is a member of a decent and integrated community, but also because he has on his side the relics of older forms of sovereignty (Gandalf, Aragorn) and thus the assurance that he is himself an as-yet-undiscovered sovereign. His heroism lies partly in his willing apprenticeship, in his acceptance of wisdom and his unfailing ability to discriminate between the good and the bad advice which is proffered. As psychodrama, the book enacts a wide-ranging control and subjugation of the more vicious instincts, but also an acceptance of superego functions: in this battle, Frodo is at once protagonist and the unwitting representative of greater forces, the vehicle which carries the message of submission and sovereignty. What sets Frodo apart from his countrymen is that, on his path to power, he actually moves beyond cottage industry and self-sufficiency and is able to construct, and insert himself into, a small model of specialisation, with each of his travelling companions owning a specific responsibility, pooling resources although their individual goals may be divergent – or even, on occasion, unintelligible.

The conjunction of classical, exemplary narrative structure with an absolute restriction of authorial irony denotes an unchallengeable heroism, and thus facilitates the transition into cult: Frodo despises no knowledges, but neither does he probe them; instead he regards them as parts of a seamless whole, and thus enacts the remaking of the united meanings of the world.[7] What is excluded is Mordor, but this does not imply an untenably complete rejection of the unconscious: rather, Mordor becomes progressively superfluous as Frodo discovers (with us) more malleable images of Other-ness. In encountering the languages of other races and species, he encounters also a more acceptable version of the instincts: Mordor's single-minded encapsulation of threat becomes redundant as we meet with and become habituated to a number of separate minor threats. So long as the unconscious presents itself in the form of sequential lesser monsters, we can mobilise ourselves to overcome them: the lesser images of evil are the essential stages on the quest, as a little knowledge of psychoanalysis and mysticism can inoculate us against the more dangerous signs in the system. Thus the condensation (behind barricades) and displacement (into the farthest corner of the map) of Mordor are progressively renaturalised on the journey into an intelligible discourse of measurable and counterable powers, the language of the lower depths is brought within the purview of the conscious self's sequential rules, and a metonymic chain is unfolded which reveals that the uncanny is after all not the visible sign of an utter difference but evidence of gaps in knowledge which can be remedied piece by piece.

So as Frodo travels, he is recasting the unknown into the form of a jigsaw puzzle, the solution to which is already prefigured by his more powerful companions. The fate of the alternative (an actual journey through the darkness) is continuously exemplified by Gollum, and shown to be of no avail: plunging into the water only transforms you into a creature of mud, whereas if you hold your head high the beings of the depths will be gradually drawn up, one by one, to attack you on your own terms. This, certainly, would be one palatable version of warfare, as it would be a palatable version of the 'journey to self-knowledge', the very spirit of California. Yet self-knowledge is not, it appears, what Frodo is after: rather, he attains to a kind of forgetting, where his encounters with the difficulties and recalcitrances of the world prove sufficient for him to retreat into domesticity, the hobbit ideology fully justified, the draw-bridge of the island safely raised, the roads into the conservative shires closed, the terrors of language safely accounted for, arranged in neat chains, and no longer in need of attention. Although it is known that the hobbits are only one element in a relational field, once this is checked out it can be ignored, and the dangerous revelations of structuralism left outside the intellectual fold. The kind of investigation portrayed is not the continuous ground of change and fear, but a once-for-all trip, after which we can settle happily down again to the quieter pleasures of etymology and home brewing.

That Tolkien tapped a rich vein of regression is obvious; but he also proposed a way of dealing with knowledge, at a time when some kinds of knowledge appear to inspire terror. *Lord of the Rings* is a triumph of map-making and planning, in itself an encircling and barricading of the realm of fear, the realm which might otherwise be uncharted and unpredictable. For the kind of knowledge which the map offers pre-cedes all other kinds of knowledge. From the moment of outset, Mordor is the land to be reached, as we already know: thus the assertion is that, however far-flung and given to illusion, there is no realm which cannot be brought within the purview of the secure nation, or self. There are no imperial ambitions at stake for the hobbits: by regressing, they have settled happily into a situation of no growth, and their excursion into the outer world is to ensure that this stability is thoroughly understood and shared by everybody else. We no longer have the power to colonise the unconscious: but we can render it comprehensible, simple, light-ful, and this is effective in producing a fantasy of total intersubjectivity, a dream-world where, despite different languages, everybody really utters the same discourse, and difference can be plotted on a single master-chart.

The Englishness of Philip Larkin

The poetry of Larkin, and its insertion as a specific discourse, and as the *name* of a discourse, within the complex of literary discourses is central to the construction of the contemporary English 'literary'. Other poets who conventionally appear alongside are judged extreme and, in one way or another, foreign. Gunn is 'American', homosexual, ec-centric. Hughes is strident, un-gentlemanly, and practises a mythic inter-nationalism; he also writes for children (constructs a punishable child-reader). Plath is American, female, thanatic. There are, of course, the regions (R.S. Thomas/Wales; Causley/Cornwall; and so on).

Larkin is taken to convey a specifically English experience. Its com-ponents appear to include asexuality, which does not forbid adolescent nostalgia, as in *Jill* (1946), but exiles present desire. It allows a 'strong' sense of place, but also a strong assimilation of spaces. 'From Hell, Hull and Halifax', the old saying goes, 'Good Lord deliver us'; Larkin is eternal Hull to Blake's eternal Hell. In some ways, the literary in Larkin is extensive: it includes the old men in public libraries, and it has a relation to the civic (but compare Larkin's civic buildings with Roy Fisher's).[8] But it supposes that civic space serves to punctuate empti-ness; that the 'joining and parting' railway lines are two-dimensional boundaries, lines without substance. They mark a dissipation of content.

What is foregrounded as English is negativity, and this is manifested in an everyday encompassing of death. The deepening of experience through the literary is allowed; but with the provision that, for *us* (the English, the repressed, the marginal), that deepening is a familiar path, and can happen partly through sheer fatigue. Individual poems may separate small portions of life off from the general decline; but only temporarily, so that we can stare briefly at them before they too slide away into the night. It may be that Larkin's nights are intense, but this doesn't matter, because his self-appointed task is to give us only the days, the endless suburban afternoons; the reader of Larkin is badly in need of filling his (not, I think, her) time. We read him when, short of work and shorter of conviction, a space looms between *The Times* and a brief walk in the park.

Larkin, a man of the university, is aware of his work as a material to be *taught*; and his lesson is a preparation for an inevitable solitude. His discourse posits a devaluation of emotional experience; that to which the young may look forward will not come to pass, although it may remain unprofitably lodged in the present, and stand as a sign for the un-achieved. Thus with English history: the grand gestures have passed away and we stand at the end of time, although God, with a predictable perversity, has neglected to wind up the long day's proceedings. Larkin prefigures mass unemployment; in his experiential library, past events are reduced to quantity and shuffled around, covers peeling, dust settling.[9]

His poetry is less well-crafted than well-dressed, in an English way; his versification bears the traces of elegance, but is slightly, and decently, shabby. It does not do in Larkin's world to go on too long about things, because if we were to do so we might conjure up a terrifying rememoration, might suspect the possibility of recapture, and thus set off on a journey. Larkin's poetry does not indulge in journeys; he has no passport. By staying where we are, we might at least be able to hallucinate the cold light coming through the high windows (image of an oppressive schooling) into stained glass, into the dead beauty of the Arundel tomb; but we must hold on to the knowledge that we are only cheering ourselves up.

What is posited is a particular version of the suicidal, not as act but as rejection; a preference not to participate.[10] What may lie under this is a sense of England as having priced itself out of the market; if we cannot dominate the world, why should we have to do with it at all? Our only experience is administrative, and this can be exercised in only two ways: on a no longer existent empire, or in our own privacy, our half-jokey management of ourselves, which serves to fill up the dead spaces of which time is comprised.[11] Most of the time we are adrift from the world; our perception is patchy, but the blame lies not in us but in the world, which has ceased to acknowledge the unspeakable power of being English and has thereby ceased to deserve us.

Since we have parented for so long, and our children (America, India) are now being so predictably nasty to us, we can solace ourselves by saying that we had guessed they would be, all along; and we may as well use the consequent isolation to indulge in – only a little, of course – the childlike. We may also allow ourselves to feel some sympathy, but only for those, symbolised in the travelling salesman, who carry more obviously the burden of our general plight. There are those, says Larkin, who come appearing to proffer help or insight; but we know of old that this is unreal, for what can upstarts have to offer a culture freighted with wisdom?

The impact of this discourse is complex. There is an ironic valorisation of the 'English', which actually appears as the incommensurability of English and foreign experience. Thus Larkin's 'sense of place' is a harbouring of those places (town halls, churches) which might retain immunity from pollution (although they probably won't). And thus also Larkin's poetry resists comparison; the intrusion of the conversational is a reminder of the resistance inherent in cultural uniqueness. The image of the literary which is proffered has to do with a particular kind and level of permissible symbolism: symbols are not to be jammed together but to be inserted in various explicit relations to the category of narrative. Symbols are allowed so long as they stay half-formed; fully-fledged they might suggest transcendence rather than reinforcing the memory of defeat.

Remembering again Foucault's discourse of the 'spirals' of power and pleasure which characterise relationships, we might say that in the relationship between Larkin and reader, the charge of desire which is accommodated in these spirals is constantly punctured, as though the effort of the poetry is to expel power, to make us share in ineffectuality. The pleasure is nonetheless supposed to come from a communing of wise minds; yet even in this post-temporal Britain hierarchy, of course, survives. It is not at all that Larkin wishes to obliterate hierarchy; the project is to save it unchanged by claiming that, in any case, it has no purchase on the real, the levers of action have fallen off. By this useful fiction we are supposed to participate in absolution. Absolution will not eradicate anxiety, but it will disperse it, spread it infinitesimally thinly around us and around the landscape, so that at no point may we gather enough of it together to fuel efforts at interpretation.

'Dallas': modes of social identification

The sprawling soap opera flourishes not on interlocking narrative, but on the sheer variety of subject positions on offer. The variety itself is crucial: fast intercutting, predictable changes of scene and action mean that we can sample without being bound down, move among the presented stereotypes trying on roles, stereotypical sonhood, daughter-hood, the lineaments of the erring wife, the unreliable business colleague; knowing that soon these will pass away and we will be able to move on with the queue. The strength of *Dallas* lies in its combination of proffered variousness and strict control: after the expeditions into the world of oil trading, or of archaic ranching, or of seduction and attempted murder, there will always be the next family gathering, regular as clockwork, over breakfast or early evening drinks, where the versions of the truth developed by individual characters, and thus by ourselves, can be subjected to an apparent testing. Although the texture of the whole may be fantasy, it is a fantasy conducted according to strict rules, and there is no danger that we might encounter the void. On the contrary, what we are likely to encounter at the farthest end of our tether is only another surprising manifestation of the all-encompassing family; the apparently unexpected always leads us back into the safety of South Fork, and the routes which might appear to lead us towards discoveries about the wider history of the world turn back and reveal to us only further reticulations in the history of the family.[12]

Since the supreme power of the family is thus vindicated, and it becomes coterminous with the effective world, we are allowed to experience a rare connexion: between the roles we experience domestically and the wider realm in which, for most of us, those roles are ineffectual and being the son of a famous father, or the husband of a notorious wife, does not coincide with the exigencies of labour and survival. Although there is a clear line from the aristocratic family, the 'house', 'oikos', the differences are significant: the type of power at stake here is not demonstrated in the arbitrary manipulation and oppression of serfs, but in the ability to exercise such power through surveillance as will render other, non-family, persons of the *same* class serf-like. What the family here aspires to is a step beyond feudal power, with its apparatus of feuding among equals, of a network of parallel families secured by intermarriage and a balance of strength; it is rather the formation of a complete state within a state, such that the full range of state apparatus, repressive and ideological (police, hired thugs, lawyers, bureaucrats), can be brought into the service of the family. The inversion, and the compensatory gratification it promises, are obvious: the family as a social unit exacts a vengeance for the decades of subservience, for being continually the observed scene around which the agents of state power congregate, measuring, evaluating, surveying, judging. Where the family in the contemporary West, if it is to make a public appearance as a statistic, has to bend itself into the shapes which will fit the forms (and other shapes – one-parent families, community patterns – will be punished, socially and economically, for their resistance), here we are shown a world in which the surrounding apparatus bends according to the shape of the family:[13] the temporary alliances, estrangements, convolutions, the inner stuff of relationships for which there is no room in the anterooms of the state, produce gigantic shadows in the wider world, and the professional agencies scuttle to reflect these forms, to change their modes of work in accordance with the momentary redistributions of family power.

It is, of course, vital that the material sources of this power be inexplicit: the discourse of commerce enacted in JR's office is a shadow discourse, denoting nothing, moving in a world of pre-established signs. We are invited to deal not in oil and real estate but in fantasies of collaboration and coercion, to savour the words of power which we will never otherwise hear, to fondle them like talismans. Up here, at the top of the building, we maintain a decent distance from the world of labour and of direct communication, speaking instead from house-top to house-top, encountering only a series of rituals, reversals or advances of fortune drained of disturbing content. Thus we can come painlessly at the reading roles, at their clearest in the series of conjunctions in which the fate of commerce unexpectedly matches the fate of 'private' life, the moments when success and re-established love, or failure and marital collapse, coincide and we feel the vicarious pleasure of a world where the pressures to be felt, the decisions to be made, are truly enormous, and where our next move may shatter the universe, or ourselves.

Dallas, like pantomime, starts from the premise that the ways in which the ego may choose to identify have nothing to do with realistic representation of background, everything to do with conjuring a world in which the vicissitudes of the subject will be widely effective, in which, whatever action we may perform or refuse, there will be an apparatus to transmit these operations into the effects of power. The essential contradiction is that catastrophe and continuity coexist: the self-as-individual hovers, shuddering with excitement, on the brink of dissolution while the self-as-family-member experiences no doubt that cocktails will still be served at a quarter to six, even if most of the family happen at that time to be hospitalised/imprisoned/fomenting Third World revolutions. When this is the case, the family meeting simply acquires a further function, and mobilises its own state-like forces to disentangle the muddled portion of the web.

But there is a further self here, the self-as-many-possible-individuals, achieving a specific satisfaction from oscillation, from moving ceaselessly between different models of relationships: violence and tenderness multiplied by juxtaposition, permission to indulge in brutality sanctified by the knowledge that, shortly, we can recover our submerged affections in a different scene, another location. Thus we do not have to succumb to an overarching morality, we judge action in terms of its specific appropriateness to a character (part of the self), and can live fully each separate version of desire, remote from the world where we struggle within ourselves to allow our various desires to coexist. What is on display is also an instructive variety of methods for controlling the female: through a token distribution of power (Miss Ellie), through brutality and misrepresentation (Sue Ellen), through a conditional and distanced independence (Pam), through caricature (Lucy). If, in this catalogue, attributions to male character and to the makers of the programme have become confused, this reflects the fact: for in this family, the blood-related males are co-participants in the 'writing', the women doubly actors, scripted by their husbands/lovers. The male viewer, therefore, enjoys a spectacle of free agency, within which the female emerges in the guise of a 'problem', of the same order as commercial uncertainty, and to be dealt with according to the same principles of maximisation of profit and minimisation of trouble.

In *Coronation Street*, everything can be 'coped with', for expectations are low and there is no recourse against the actions of the state: even the Rovers' Return is a socially flimsy meeting ground. In *Dallas*, everything can be 'dealt with'; there are no spatial bounds which cannot be crossed, for on this new frontier there is no source of higher power which is not already bought. A corrupt grandeur is offered as solace for the struggling self, a land purged of mere operatives as compensation for the limitations of mass society. The bloodline flows smoothly, revealing the glory that could have been Lear's if only he had had sons, that could have

been ours if our birthright had not already been stolen before we were
born and before the family, seemingly guaranteed a role at the base of
society, was disabled and whipped into shape despite the promises.

The naming of cigarette brands

A principal stream of this imagery relates to the West End of London (Piccadilly, Pall Mall), but not the gaudy, commercial West End:
Embassy gives the game away, reveals this London as an archaically-
conceived diplomatic capital, insubstantial as smoke, a receiver and
transmitter of half-hidden messages. Not quite 'secret service', but
Senior Service: England as nobility and privilege, and still as imperial
power. Trade is wished away, and replaced by diplomatic and naval
superiority, the means of establishing and securing the empire which
yields tobacco, but which also provides the ground on which the suave-
ness of the successful smoker can be tested: smoking in this fantasy
world has nothing to do with anxiety, but is a function of a leisured
assurance.

To be sure, a navy must also have ratings, and there is a grittier side to
the fantasy: Navy Cut is a harsher matter altogether, but even there 'cut'
remains to remind us of a principle of selection, of clubby gentlemen
deciding on the precise strength required – to narcotise, or to bring the
natives to heel. Players No. 6 and No. 10 participate in this function,
contributing an image of an endless range of exactly defined and
arranged tobaccos, naturally all but indistinguishable to all but the
wealthy initiate.

With Silk Cut, an ambivalence rises closer to the surface: for 'cut' is
also the pleasurable pain of smoking, the incisiveness of toxin on tissue
and the incisiveness of the decision-maker, his faculties concentrated by
nicotine, but 'silk' is the smooth diplomatic cloak over the dagger. We
are here in the world of the Third Man, of pausing on street corners to
assess the direction of a nameless urban enemy, which might after all be
none other than carbon monoxide.

The idea of the fine, the silken, the filigree reappears in Gold Leaf,
which seeks to blend the natural and the artificial, the tobacco leaf with
the coin of exchange: Gold Flake introduces us to an even finer world,
wherein the least touch of value is appreciated, our senses become
refined to the appreciation of the smallest detail, the tiniest beauty. Gold
and silk represent the soft and acceptable face of capitalism; perhaps

Rothmans would not have survived within the collective fantasy were it not for the fruitful confusion with Rothschild, or Players but for the assured presence of the gentlemen.

So all is transformed into gold, and the empire is geared towards home supply: the oriental imagery represented by Abdullah disappears, except in the docile form of the Camel, as transport and as caricature. In America, the insistence on heritage and the referring back to a past point in history are reinforced in Marlboro and Chesterfield, general and adviser, power and diplomacy.

What is happening in this pedigree galaxy is the presentation of a world:[14] it is only within the accepted parameters of this world that competition can occur, and it is the widespread validation of that world which provides the base on which a structure of competitivity can be built. In that world, cigarettes are not products to be bought on the supermarket shelf; they are articles of taste, about which you commune with your gentlemanly elderly tobacconist, who will occasionally provide you with tips about a new shipment.

Thus every action of buying cigarettes takes place within a 'displaced' universe. It is as though, in some other world which is so similar to this yet not quite the same, there would be no supermarkets, and no pollution: cigarettes are thus inverted into a nostalgic purity, clean wisps of smoke rising through clear air, and each separate act of buying becomes a shadow of what it might be, just as the self-conscious consumption of junk food is contained with a perennial 'temporary'.

Marlboro is conjoined with the 'wide open spaces', and there is a tension: on the one side, the Dickensian urban kitsch of the smoke-filled tobacco shop, on the other the frontier and a place where a man might be free. At one level, as well as representing national difference, there is an economic contradiction here, home market/foreign conquest, but below that lurks a doubt about maturation. There is the womb, the safe harbour, the primal scene to which all goods are brought and which provides the last refuge of 'personal service' (that gentlemanly old tobacconist is also the endless valet of P.G. Wodehouse, Phileas Fogg's club servant, all of them guardians against the feared intrusion of the feminine) clothed in male tweeds: the tobacconist is both the Other as non-threatening, too old to compete, too male to frighten, and at the same time the Self as unthreatened, a Self which can never emerge into the external world. In the myth, like a hermit-crab the shopkeeper is perpetually emerging from an invisible back room, yet there is a doubt: if we were ever to see his back, would he be complete, fully able to separate and identify himself as a being in the world, or would there be a web, an arrangement, perhaps, of pulleys and wires, running back into that small back room, an unbroken umbilical cord?

And so it has to be 'out there' that a man can be a man, but only in splendid isolation, surrounded by cattle and horses, opening up fantasy frontiers whose existence will never be validated but which may, actually, turn out to be the vast image of the redcurrant bushes at the bottom of the garden. And, of course, it is not hard to see why, at the root of this constructed world, there lies a double structure of regression, for all this vaunted independence (inward and outward) is a cover for a double dependence, chemical and mythic. For cigarettes represent, not only dependence on *an* image, but dependence on *the* image: the very notion of self as Other, of self as observable, is bound up with the reflective moment, and it is this moment which is invaded by the insecurity of Craven A.

Somehow, the naming says, it is possible to gain purchase on all this confusion, either through retreat into the cosy warmth, or through removal to the shadow-line represented in the Old West: it is possible to stop history, to secure a pocket for the self, either in a club, like the Carlton, or in the open-air riches of BelAir. Or, indeed, in the privileged transnational space of the Consulate, where discreet figures move quietly about their work unhampered by the ties of belonging; thus the adolescent sees himself moving into a 'free space', using cigarettes to break the closed circle of domesticity and to aspire to a purported freedom of male action in a world where that freedom is economically unavailable.

For women too, there is the prospect of escape and simultaneous inclusion as equals; and for both sexes the prospect of reunion in some less urban world of Woodbines, sweet scents and unhurried activity. The conflict between the primitive and the sophisticated is mysteriously removed, and a personal exemption is granted: the minutest slowing of time is proffered as a gift, and growing up rendered unnecessary. Input from the world can be filtered, a moment of stopping and choosing established, a cool slim cleanliness and potency held against haste and muddle.

Memorials to death

JOHNSON – Treasured memories of
GLADYS MAY, a dear wife and mother,
called to rest January 1975.
> A silent thought, a secret tear,
> Keeps your memory ever dear.
>> – Loving husband Ernest.

JOHNSON – GLADYS. Chosen January 1975.
> You were called away so suddenly,
> No time to say goodbye,
> You had so much to live for,
> And yet you had to die.
> Last time we saw you smiling,
> You looked so fit and well,
> Little did we know,
> It was your last farewell.
>> – Loving son Philip, daughter-in-law Janet

Gentle Jesus up above,
Give nannie Johnson all our love.
> – Lynn and Julie

JOHNSON – Loving memories of a
dear mother, mother-in-law and
nannie, GLADYS MAY, taken from us
January 1975.
> Three little words forget me not.
> To say dear mum we haven't forgot.
>> Sadly missed.
>> – John, Christine and Clair.[15]

The mediation of death here, in the pages of a regional British news-paper, naturally entails a submission to form: the verses neatly rendered, the undistinguished surname advanced. There is a deliberate unclarity around the mode of production: as readers, we are not supposed to think that these offerings have been the spontaneous compositions of the members of the family, although equally they must have had some part in the process. Different lengths and patterns of verse can obviously be cut off a roll: the sentiments are pre-existing, a set of variations in a repertoire of petrified feelings, whereby a limited number of data (familial relationship, age of deceased, perhaps warmth of affection) can be fed in and produce the correct decor. There is even room here for a final competition, a closing battle between ostentation and reserve.

The discursive status of the 'treasured' and 'loving' memories is shadowy and complex: initially a hope for the future, they also become an admonition to the survivors, reminding the individual or familial subgroup of their future duty but also serving to remind the other subgroups of the past and continuing place in the hierarchy of recollection which they hope to enjoy. These memories are also, in some sense, an offering to Gladys Johnson, a collecting up and returning of gifts made in life; and also, again, a thanksgiving for those same gifts, an assurance that they were not wasted but will continue to resonate through time. Thus the family is rebonded, deriving not weakness but further strength from the memory of sudden absence: reaffirming, through the already given discourse of formality, the family's renewed pledge to those forms which Gladys herself, we presume, sanctioned. Thus the wording becomes an echo, an afterlife, for the values she herself embodied; around the dead body, a new replication of her discourse is set to ward off corruption and the dreaded failing of memory.

Here relationship is all, and what is celebrated is Gladys's able filling out (fleshing) in the past of the necessary roles: and the roles themselves shift, her maternal qualities becoming an index of the implied web of qualities required among the survivors. Gladys is herself elevated into a new station as the primary, modelling instance of these types (wife, mother), and is reassured of the adherence of her descendants, in a cancelling out of whatever marks of difference, rebellion, geographical distancing, may have marred the symbolic equations in the previous year. Thus God's 'choice' of her death is paralleled by the enactment of a choice by the family: to rededicate itself to Gladys as model for the future. This is necessary, of course, because death is persistently seen as having been 'in media res': there is a lurking thought that, by some process of magic, Gladys can be reincarnated by the appropriate word, so that she will be able to complete the business to which she was prevented from attending.

Yet there is also here some resentment, typically in the ambiguous phrase, 'And yet you had to die': alongside, and intertwined with, the overt reluctant acquiescence in the superior purposes of divinity is a restatement of the age-old annoyance of the living with the dying and the recently dead for upsetting their plans. Whenever death occurs, a brittleness in the social formation emerges, and the formality of the death greeting is hastily papered over the crack, reasserting continuity in the face of imminent disaster – imminent, because this disaster is not death itself but the irrecoverable posture of incomprehension which might, without swift action, result from it. It is this, we are led to believe, that Gladys herself would not have wanted: we are invited as readers to collude in the supposition that the dead would like us to carry on as before, to bury that disruption as rapidly as we have buried the body.

But then, as readers we are in the nexus of a very peculiar set of subject-positions. The first two addressees are Gladys herself, the third Jesus: it is only with the fourth, where the syntax becomes entangled, that the actual reader of the newspaper might be visible within the addressed audience. But this is to simplify: for these addressees might indeed be the intended recipients of the message, but insofar as the form is itself addressed, we need to think not lineally but in terms of concentric circles, whereby the form firstly cements the identity of each familial subgroup; thus it firms up the overall identity of the punctured family; and thus it provides us with a model of 'bricolage' from which we can go on to construct a model of the whole society, conveniently perceived as a mechanical linkage of familial units, the whole rendered homogeneous by the implied subscription to a limited and classifiable range of emotions, the simpler discursive equivalent of the graveyard as guarantor of community identity. It is thus that, for instance, a specific date is of no use here: what is wanted instead is identification by month, by that temporal unit which most effectively replicates our memory of past settings, which therefore most closely reconnects Gladys back into the cycle of nature.

Nothing here is arbitrary, and much is condensed: the multiple meanings, for instance, at stake in the repetition of 'called', wherein the valorisation of 'God's chosen' is linked to a necessary subservience on the part of the victim. We are thus enjoined precisely to pride ourselves on humility, with the added assumption that if we do God will play one of his benevolent tricks on us, calling us, apparently sternly, but in fact requiring us merely to 'rest', a twinkle in the divine eye. Again, the 'silent thought' and the 'secret tear' condense two operations: it is not enough for the fulfilment of this particular ideological necessity that such private manifestations of grief should act as *evidence*, they must also be seen as *agential* in keeping our duty of memory before us. They thus become, in the simple coupling of the couplet, the elements in a predicted ritual, a ritual which will have moved beyond the verbal; thus again, the inadequacy of the word is allowed and the crippled verses of these very greetings already excused – seen, indeed, as the very evidence of depth of feeling rather than as the sign of a powerful and purposive conformity.

The last lines of the longest verse virtually enact both this crippling and the sob at its heart, in the brevity of 'Little did we know' and the accepted inaccuracy of 'last farewell', within which again is condensed a double attitude to religious ideology: for this act of bonding to work, it must be multivalent, must allow both for the finality of death and for the possibility of an afterlife, although in the words of the children the latter can be permitted its full charge of comfort.

The year which has intervened between the death and this act of remembrance is virtually telescoped out of existence: it is important only insofar as it provides the evidence that Gladys's absence has been filled in by a shadow of Gladys which has continued to inform familial events. In the last couplet the process of rememoration flows in both directions; there is a hope that the survivors are themselves not forgotten, that somewhere an act of Gladys's will is sustaining them, and that it is necessary to reinvoke that will – necessary, also, to reinvoke the name, for it can be assumed that Johnson is not only Gladys's name but the name which stands for the entire, male-linear family. Indeed, the common patriarchal assumption conceals from view Gladys's own original name, and seals the woman into the fate of the name-of-the-father.

But this is perhaps to stay too close to the literal surface: further down, something else stirs, the shape of an apology, of a wish for this procedure to efface memory while it apparently sustains it. The vision of the deathbed is slid again under the 'fit and well' vision which serves as the frozen memory to be carried in the mind, the individual reduced to a (death-) still photograph. This is a family portrait, with ghost,[16] and like all portraiture it aims to defeat time and change, to hold within rigid boundaries. The question of authenticity thus takes on the contours of a paradox: it is precisely by willingly succumbing to formalism that emotion is sealed and avoided, reduced to a cipher, while the real nature of those emotions is sequestered away: like net curtains, the purpose is to conceal while giving the impression that there is that which could be revealed. Feeling is withheld – as, we are supposed to think, Gladys would have wished; instead we have these stilled gestures, the shapes of prayer and supplication, tiny models for those behaviours which will guarantee an ineradicable societal continuity.

Notes

Introduction: fantasies and the future

1   *The Guardian* (5 Aug. 1983); from a review of Gilly Fraser, *Somewhere Else*, Radio 4.

2   I am thinking here of the 'tradition' of criticism around Robert Scholes, *The Fabulators* (New York, 1967).

3   See Jacques Derrida, *Of Grammatology*, trans. G. C. Spivak (Baltimore, Md., 1976), pp. 74–93.

4   See my 'Politics, Pedagogy, Work: Reflections on the "Project" of the Last Six Years', in *The Politics of Theory*, ed. F. Barker et al. (Colchester, 1983), pp. 79–93.

5   I am thinking particularly of J. G. Ballard and the strangulation of language: see below, pp. 9–12.

6   See in this connexion Christopher Norris, *Deconstruction: Theory and Practice* (London, 1982), pp. 78–89.

7   See also my 'Blake/Hegel/Derrida', *Blake: An Illustrated Quarterly* (1984).

Chapter 1   J. G. Ballard: alone among the murder machines

1   The title, like the 'terminal beach' and the 'drowned world' mentioned below, of one of Ballard's earlier books.

2   On the psychological force of name-changing, see Freud, *The Psychopathology of Everyday Life* (1901), in the *Standard Edition of the Complete Psychological Works*, ed. James Strachey (23 vols, London, 1953–73), vol. VI.

3   The references here to Shelley, and to Count Volney, *Les Ruines, ou méditations sur les révolutions des empires* (1791), are not accidental: what is shared is a preoccupation with a terminal breakdown of power, and also an imagistic concentration on petrifaction: cf. Jung, *Alchemical Studies*, in *The Collected Works of C. G. Jung*, ed. W. McGuire et al. (20 vols, London, 1957–79), vol. XIII, pp. 94–101.

4   These remarks relate to my previous work on *The Atrocity Exhibition* in *The Literature of Terror: A History of Gothic Fictions from 1765 to the Present Day* (London, 1980), pp. 392–4.

5   Ballard, *The Atrocity Exhibition* (London, 1970), p. 65.

6   This should be compared with the rememorative force of the 'ancient cities' in Michael Moorcock's trilogy *The Dancers at the End of Time: An Alien Heat*

(1972), *The Hollow Lands* (1975) and *The End of All Songs* (1976).

7   On this effective shattering of the body, see Jacques Lacan, 'The mirror stage as formative of the function of the I' and 'Aggressivity in Psychoanalysis', in *Écrits*, trans. A. Sheridan (London, 1977), pp. 1–7, 8–29.

8   Cf. Ballard, 'Sixty Minute Zoom', *Bananas*, No. 5 (Summer, 1976), pp. 18–20.

9   Ballard, *Concrete Island* (London, 1974), sleeve-note.

10   The allusions in this paragraph are to Michel Foucault on global knowledge and strategies for surveillance: see, e.g., Foucault, 'Two Lectures', in *Power/Knowledge*, ed. Colin Gordon (Brighton, 1980), pp. 78–108.

11   Ballard, *Concrete Island*, pp. 175–6.

12   Ballard, *Concrete Island*, p. 176.

13   Ballard, *Concrete Island*, p.74.

14   Philip Larkin's words in 'Dockery and Son', in *The Whitsun Weddings* (London, 1964), p. 37; thus the phrase of another topographer of decline. See below, pp. 161–3.

15   There are resonances here of Hegel; see, e.g., *Phenomenology of Spirit*, trans. A. V. Miller (Oxford, 1977), p.245; J. Glenn Gray, *Hegel and Greek Thought* (New York, 1968), p.50.

16   Blake, 'The Mental Traveller' (c.1803), in *The Poetry and Prose of William Blake*, ed. D. V. Erdman (Garden City, N.Y., 1970), p.476.

17   Ballard, *High-Rise* (London, 1975), pp. 172–3.

18   Ballard, *High-Rise*, p. 173.

19   I have in mind the difference between these emptinesses and the frenetic decomposition of works like Thomas Pynchon's 'Mortality and Mercy in Vienna', *Epoch*, IX: 4 (1959), 195–213, and 'Entropy', *Kenyon Review*, XXII: 2 (1960), 169–85.

20   Ballard, *High-Rise*, p. 172.

21   See Ballard, *The Unlimited Dream Company* (London, 1979), p. 164.

22   Connexions, here and elsewhere in Ballard, can obviously be made with Foucault, *The Birth of the Clinic: an Archaeology of Medical Perception*, trans. A. Sheridan Smith (London, 1973).

23   Cf. the possibility in Ray Bradbury, *Fahrenheit 451* (London, 1954), that the books saved through memory might 'make every future dawn glow with a purer light' (p. 148); Blake re-*writes* (through rememoration) the world. See also below, pp. 100–2.

24   See Blake, *Milton* (1804–8), 23:49–24:9, and *Jerusalem* (1804–20), 55: 30–32, in *Poetry and Prose*, pp. 118, 202.

25   See Blake, *Milton*, 15:1–7, and *Jerusalem*, 55:33–46, in *Poetry and Prose*, pp. 108, 202–3.

26   Ballard, *The Unlimited Dream Company*, p.105.

27   Ballard, *The Unlimited Dream Company*, p.177.

28   Ballard, *The Unlimited Dream Company*, p. 222; cf. Blake, *Jerusalem*, 98:24–99:5, in *Poetry and Prose*, pp.255–6.

29   Ballard, *Hello America* (London, 1981), p. 127.

30   Ballard, *Hello America*, p. 152.

31   Ballard, *Hello America*, p.191.

32 There are parallels here with the birth process; especially as described by
    Frédérick Leboyer in, for instance, *Birth without Violence* (London, 1975),
    pp. 18–19.
33 As defined in Barthes, *S/Z*, trans. Richard Miller (London, 1975), p.19.
34 The allusion is to Theodor Adorno, 'Cultural Criticism and Society', in
    Prisms, trans. S. and S. Weber (London, 1967), pp.17–34.

Chapter 2   Angela Carter: supersessions of the masculine

1   This essay follows on from the analysis of some of Carter's earlier work in
    my *Literature of Terror*, pp. 396–400.
2   For the theory here, see Lacan, *The Four Fundamental Concepts of Psycho-
    analysis*, ed. J.-A. Miller (London, 1977), pp.67–119.
3   See, e.g., Rosalind Coward and John Ellis, *Language and Materialism:
    Developments in Semiology and the Theory of the Subject* (London, 1977), pp.
    10, 112–20.
4   Carter, *The Infernal Desire Machines of Doctor Hoffman* (London, 1972),
    p.190.
5   See, e.g., Flann O'Brien, *The Third Policeman* (London, 1967).
6   Carter, *Doctor Hoffman*, p.126.
7   See Gilles Deleuze and Félix Guattari, *Anti-Oedipus: Capitalism and
    Schizophrenia*, trans. R. Hurley et al. (New York, 1977).
8   Carter, *Doctor Hoffman*, p.268.
9   Carter, *Doctor Hoffman*, p.27.
10 I shall be returning at several points to this subtext: that there is a clear
    relation between the anxieties of the 1970s and the ambivalent heritage of
    the 1960s. See also my 'The Moral Majority', in *For Life on Earth: Writings
    against War*, ed. Maggie Gee (Norwich, 1982), pp.55–6.
11 Carter, *Doctor Hoffman*, p.128.
12 I am assuming that Desiderio's foreign name and location are displace-
    ments of a type familiar in Gothic and neo-Gothic fiction.
13 Carter, *Doctor Hoffman*, pp.249–50.
14 Carter, *Doctor Hoffman*, p.186.
15 See Freud, *The Psychopathology of Everyday Life*, pp.269–79.
16 See O'Brien, *Third Policeman*, e.g., pp.74–9.
17 Carter, *Doctor Hoffman*, p.239.
18 Carter, *The Passion of New Eve* (London, 1977), p.16.
19 I am using, of course, Lacan's discoveries about the formation of the
    psyche, although in a way which, I hope, does not involve too many
    phallocentric assumptions: see again Lacan, 'The mirror stage as formative
    of the function of the I'.
20 Carter, *New Eve*, p.39.
21 Carter, *New Eve*, p.54.
22 Carter, *New Eve*, p.74.
23 Cf. Jung on the 'glass-house': see *The Practice of Psychotherapy: Essays on the
    Psychology of the Transference and Other Subjects*, in *Collected Works*, vol. XVI,
    pp. 241, 245.

24 Carter, *New Eve*, p.181.
25 Carter, *New Eve*, p.101.
26 Carter, *New Eve*, p.51.
27 Calvino, *Invisible Cities*, trans. W. Weaver (London, 1974), p.101.
28 Carter, *New Eve*, pp. 49, 56.
29 Cf., e.g., the Editorial Collective of *Questions féministes*, 'Variations on Common Themes', in *New French Feminisms*, ed. E. Marks and I. de Courtivron (Amherst, Mass., 1980), p.221.
30 Carter, *New Eve*, p.104.
31 I am aware that this formulation runs counter to Lacanian theory; that, indeed, is the point. Cf. Lacan, 'On a question preliminary to any possible treatment of psychosis', in *Écrits*, pp. 179–225.
32 See, e.g., Andrea Dworkin, *Pornography: Men Possessing Women* (New York, 1981), pp.84–5.
33 See Carter, *The Sadeian Woman: An Exercise in Cultural History* (London, 1979), pp.9–17.
34 This, it seems to me, is part of the answer which needs to be made to Terry Lovell's critique of 'conventionalism': see Lovell, *Pictures of Reality: Aesthetics, Politics and Pleasure* (London, 1980), pp.14–17, 79–84.
35 See Carter, *Sadeian Woman*, e.g., p.146.

Chapter 3 Doris Lessing: moving through space and time

1 For criticism of Lessing see Barbara K. Rigney, *Madness and Sexual Politics in the Feminist Novel: Studies in Brontë, Woolf, Lessing and Atwood* (Madison, Wisc., 1978); *Notebooks, Memoirs, Archives: Reading and Rereading Doris Lessing*, ed. Jenny Taylor (London, 1982); Lorna Sage, *Doris Lessing* (London, 1983).
2 I have limited myself here to these books, and not included comments on the later volumes of *Canopus in Argos* (*The Making of the Representative for Planet Eight* (1982) and *The Sentimental Agents in the Volyen Empire* (1983)), because of the specific transitions on which I want to concentrate.
3 See Beckett, *Murphy* (London, 1973), e.g., pp. 63–6.
4 Lessing, *The Memoirs of a Survivor* (London, 1976), p.8.
5 There is an interesting parallel here with the 'egg of light' in Roy Fisher, 'City', in *Poems 1955—1980* (Oxford, 1980), p.28.
6 Lessing, *Memoirs of a Survivor*, p.49.
7 Lessing, *Memoirs of a Survivor*, p.54.
8 Cf. below, pp. 74–5.
9 Lessing, *Memoirs of a Survivor*, p.173.
10 Lessing, *Memoirs of a Survivor*, p.74.
11 See Freud, *Three Essays on the Theory of Sexuality* (1905), in *Standard Edition*, vol. VII, pp.125–243.
12 Lessing, *Shikasta* (London, 1979), p.56.
13 Lessing, *Shikasta*, pp.77–8.
14 Cf. Blake's meditation on the Selfhood in *Milton*, 14, in *Poetry and Prose*, pp. 107–8.

15   Lessing, *Shikasta*, p.136.
16   Lessing, *Shikasta*, p.178.
17   Cf. the bracketing of such films within the coupling 'exoticism and psychosis' in David Pirie, *A Heritage of Horror: The English Gothic Cinema 1946—1972* (London, 1973), pp.138–44.
18   Lessing, *The Marriages between Zones Three, Four and Five* (London, 1980), p.39.
19   Lessing, *Marriages*, p.242.
20   Lessing, *Marriages*, p.249.
21   Lessing, *Marriages*, p.243.
22   Lessing, *The Sirian Experiments* (London, 1981), p. 179.
23   Lessing, *Sirian Experiments*, p.317.
24   See Wells, *The Island of Doctor Moreau* (London, 1975), e.g., pp.80–1.
25   Lessing, *Sirian Experiments*, p.316.
26   Lessing, *Sirian Experiments*, p.182.
27   See Lessing, *Memoirs of a Survivor*, e.g., pp.123–4.

Chapter 4   Beryl Bainbridge: the new psychopathia

1   Richard von Krafft-Ebing was 'the great clinician of sexual inversion, rather than . . . its psychologist' according to Havelock Ellis, *Studies in the Psychology of Sex* (2 vols, London, 1897–1900), vol. I, p.30; see, of course, Krafft-Ebing, *Psychopathia Sexualis*, trans. F.S. Klaf (London, 1965).
2   It seems to me that Bainbridge's fictions are in fact directed towards the male reader, and that the tacitness of the text thus becomes a silence and a reserve in the presence of the masculine: as a male reader, I am forced to enact my own responsibility for this silence, and to experience, as an object, the grimace of contempt.
3   Cf. Freud, *Notes upon a Case of Obsessional Neurosis* (1909) (the Rat Man case history), in *Standard Edition*, vol. X, pp.241, 244. The most relevant development in Freudian discourse, and one which is, naturally, radically undermining is Juliet Mitchell, *Psychoanalysis and Feminism* (London, 1974).
4   I use the term 'Other' throughout in the strong sense, often thought of now as the property of psychoanalysis but in fact reaching back into older Hegelian traditions. The depiction of historical and interpersonal process in Alexandre Kojève, *Introduction to the Reading of Hegel*, ed. A. Bloom (New York, 1969), at, e.g., pp.45–60 and elsewhere still remains a relevant model for dialectical interpretation.
5   Cf. Freud, *The Claims of Psycho-analysis to Scientific Interest* (1913), in *Standard Edition*, vol. XIII, p.173; *Introductory Lectures on Psycho-analysis* (1916–1917), in *Standard Edition*, vol. XVI, pp.264–70; and the continuing discussion of the 'primal scene' in *From the History of an Infantile Neurosis* (1918) (the Wolf Man case history), in *Standard Edition*, vol. XVII, pp.7–122.
6   Bainbridge, *Harriet Said . . .* (London, 1972), p.154.
7   Freud's arguments in this area, as in, for instance, *An Outline of Psycho-*

analysis (1940), in *Standard Edition*, vol. XXIII, pp. 193–4, are of course problematically phallocentric. See, for instance, 'Women's Exile: Interview with Luce Irigaray', *Ideology and Consciousness*, No. 1, (May 1977), pp. 62–76.

8 Bainbridge, *Harriet Said* . . ., p. 134.

9 Bainbridge, *Harriet Said* . . ., p. 135.

10 Cf. Freud, 'Some Psychical Consequences of the Anatomical Distinction between the Sexes' (1925), in *Standard Edition* vol. XIX, pp. 243–58; clearly what is suppressed in this brief text has to do with the power of women *together*. There is no entry under 'sister' in the Index volume to the *Standard Edition*.

11 I have in mind, of course, Lacan's comments on mirroring:

> The *mirror stage* is a drama whose internal thrust is precipitated from insufficiency to anticipation – and which manufactures for the subject, caught up in the lure of spatial identification, the succession of phantasies that extends from a fragmented body-image to a form of its totality . . . and, lastly to the assumption of the armour of an alienating identity, which will mark with its rigid structure the subject's entire mental development.

('The mirror stage as formative of the function of the I', p.4). But the relation between 'armouring' and the substitution of an Other for the evacuated self remains unclear.

12 Bainbridge, *Harriet Said* . . ., p.105.

13 See Hélène Cixous, 'The Character of "Character" ', *New Literary History*, V (1973–4), 383–414.

14 Bainbridge, *Harriet Said* . . ., p.99.

15 Bainbridge, *The Dressmaker* (London, 1973), p.5.

16 Bainbridge, *The Dressmaker*, p.28.

17 Cf. the parapraxes concerning names cited by Freud in *The Psychopathology of Everyday Life*, pp. 224–5 (also pp. 83–4, 240–2).

18 Bainbridge, *The Bottle Factory Outing* (London, 1974), p. 146.

19 I mean 'erasures' in the sense used by Derrida in *Of Grammatology* and elsewhere; but there is also a connexion here with the Freudian erasure of women's specificity (and its frequent historical return in the ghostly).

20 Cf. Breuer and Freud, *Studies on Hysteria* (1893–5), in *Standard Edition*, vol. II; and particularly Breuer's case history of Fräulein Anna O. (21–47). For instance, the characteristics of her illness are said to have comprised:

> the existence of a second state of consciousness which first emerged as a temporary *absence* and later became organised into a '*double conscience*'; an inhibition of speech, determined by the affect of anxiety, which found a chance discharge in . . . English verses; later on, paraphrasia and loss of her mother-tongue, which was replaced by excellent English; and lastly the accidental paralysis of her right arm. (42)

Each of these symptoms appears imagistically in Bainbridge's writing.

21 See again Cixous, 'The Character of "Character" ', where this history is connected with Freud on the primal horde.

22 Bainbridge, *A Quiet Life* (London, 1976), p. 41.

23 Bainbridge, *Quiet Life*, p. 42.
24 Bainbridge, *Quiet Life*, pp. 7–8.
25 Bainbridge, *Quiet Life*, p. 156.
26 There is a complex further mirroring going on here, because each of the groups is searching symbolically for a way of (sexual) relating which will give birth to the future: the pram which is present throughout contains only money and a doll. Binny is pulled out of her group to occupy a space in the middle, between two groups of four: whereupon much of the puzzling seems to be around the question of whether the group symbol, or totem, into which she is thus fashioned represents hope or despair.
27 Bainbridge, *Injury Time* (London, 1977), p.134.
28 It is only when the hysteric renounces being what men fight over – we will have to precede her there – that she will be ready to conquer the truth. . . .
    It is then that we learn from her, from this mother in sufferance, that there is only one pertinent trauma: that of birth.
    (Moustapha Safouan, 'In Praise of Hysteria', in *Returning to Freud: Clinical Psychoanalysis in the School of Lacan*, ed. S. Schneiderman (New Haven and London, 1980), p. 59.) The paternalistic tone matches precisely the Bainbridge response, in the discursive hall of mirrors: thus the frozenness of trauma is re-enacted, not only within the unconscious but also in the conflicts of discourse *around* the unconscious.
29 Bainbridge, *Young Adolf* (London, 1978), p.134.
30 In any case, man cannot aim at being whole . . ., while ever the play of displacement and condensation to which he is doomed in the exercise of his functions marks his relation as a subject to the signifier.
    (Lacan, 'The signification of the phallus', in *Écrits*, p.287.) Cf. also Lacan on the 'Name-of-the-Father' in, e.g., 'On a question preliminary to any possible treatment of psychosis'.
31 See, for instance, Colin MacCabe, 'Theory and Film: Principles of Realism and Pleasure', *Screen*, XVII, 3 (Autumn 1976), 7–27, as one introduction to the politics of 'the point of view and the look'; and, in more detail, Lacan, *The Four Fundamental Concepts*, pp.67–119.

Chapter 5   Kurt Vonnegut: the cheerfully demented

1 For criticism of Vonnegut, see Tony Tanner, *City of Words: American Fiction 1950—1970* (London, 1971), pp.181–201; Stanley Schatt, *Kurt Vonnegut, Jr.* (Boston, Mass., 1976); *Vonnegut in America: An Introduction to the Life and Work of Kurt Vonnegut*, ed. J. Klinkowitz and D.L. Lawler (New York, 1977).
2 See Vonnegut, *Palm Sunday: An Autobiographical Collage* (London, 1981), p.13.
3 Vonnegut, *Breakfast of Champions* (London, 1973), pp. 187–8.
4 Vonnegut, *Breakfast of Champions*, p.204.
5 Vonnegut, *Breakfast of Champions*, p.136.
6 Vonnegut, *Breakfast of Champions*, p.105.
7 See Vonnegut, *Breakfast of Champions*, pp. 27–8.

8   Vonnegut, *Breakfast of Champions*, pp.215–16.
9   Vonnegut, *Breakfast of Champions*, p.25.
10   Vonnegut, *Breakfast of Champions*, p.195.
11   Vonnegut, *Breakfast of Champions*, p.76.
12   Vonnegut, 'Playboy Interview', in *Wampeters Foma and Granfalloons* (London, 1975), p.221.
13   Vonnegut, 'Why They Read Hesse', in *Wampeters Foma and Granfalloons*, p.117.
14   See Freud, 'The Dynamics of Transference' (1912), in *Standard Edition*, vol. XII, pp.97–108.
15   Vonnegut, 'Playboy Interview', in *Wampeters Foma and Granfalloons*, p.254.
16   See Vonnegut, 'Address to the American Physical Society', in *Wampeters Foma and Granfalloons*, p.100.
17   Vonnegut, 'Playboy Interview', in *Wampeters Foma and Granfalloons*, p.244.
18   See, e.g., Vonnegut, *Breakfast of Champions*, pp.126–41. Cf. Jung, *The Psychogenesis of Mental Disease*, in *Collected Works*, vol. III, pp. 78–9.
19   Vonnegut, 'Address to Graduating Class at Bennington College, 1970', in *Wampeters Foma and Granfalloons*, p.156.
20   Vonnegut, *Slapstick, or, Lonesome No More!* (London, 1976), p.24.
21   Vonnegut, *Slapstick*, p.182.
22   Vonnegut, *Slapstick*, p.41.
23   Vonnegut, *Slapstick*, p.113.
24   Vonnegut, *Slapstick*, p.148.
25   Vonnegut, *Slapstick*, p.171.
26   Vonnegut, *Slapstick*, p.185.
27   Cf. Jung, *The Structure and Dynamics of the Psyche*, in *Collected Works*, vol. VIII, pp.155–6.
28   Vonnegut, *Jailbird* (London, 1979), p.11.
29   Vonnegut, *Jailbird*, p.167.
30   Vonnegut, *Jailbird*, p.42.
31   Vonnegut, *Jailbird*, p.233.

Chapter 6   Fears of surveillance/strategies for the future

1   Foucault, 'Questions on Geography', in *Power/Knowledge*, p. 77; most of the thinking on Foucault in this chapter arises from the metacommentary on method contained in these interviews and writings.
2   See Foucault, 'Questions on Geography', p.69.
3   See, e.g., Foucault, 'Two Lectures'.
4   Foucault, 'Truth and Power', in *Power/Knowledge*, p.119.
5   See Foucault, *The History of Sexuality*, Vol. I: *An Introduction*, trans. Hurley (New York, 1978), p.45.
6   I.F. Clarke, *The Pattern of Expectation 1644—2001* (London, 1979), p.129; I have kept Clarke's 'history of the future' very much in mind, since it seems to me the best, but this chapter can also be read as a critique of the empiricist assumptions of the genre.
7   Foucault, 'Questions on Geography', p.71.

8   The obvious transmitters of this change are John Wyndham and Nigel Kneale; but it is caught up also in the mode of cultural production itself and the emergence of televisual habits.

9   Clarke, *Pattern of Expectation*, p. 313; this is itself a shadow discourse, an ironic proffering of empty signs.

10 Bradbury, *Fahrenheit 451*, p. 149.

11 Bradbury, *Fahrenheit 451*, p. 148.

12 Bradbury, *Fahrenheit 451*, p. 82.

13 Cf. Clarke, *Pattern of Expectation*, pp. 215–16.

14 Foucault, 'Two Lectures', p. 104.

15 Bradbury, *Fahrenheit 451*, p. 155.

16 There is clearly here a set of allusions to trauma: cf. my 'Blake, Trauma and the Female', *New Literary History*.

17 Vonnegut, *The Sirens of Titan* (London, 1967), p. 210.

18 Vonnegut, *Sirens of Titan*, p. 140.

19 Vonnegut, *Sirens of Titan*, p. 76.

20 Coover, 'Morris in Chains', in *Pricksongs and Descants* (London, 1971), pp. 36–47.

21 Coover, 'Morris in Chains', p. 38.

22 Coover, 'Morris in Chains', p. 47.

23 Coover, 'Morris in Chains', p. 37.

24 Cf. my *Literature of Terror*, pp. 249–55.

25 Coover, 'Morris in Chains', p. 41.

26 Coover, 'Morris in Chains', p. 43.

27 See Eugene Zamiatin, *We*, trans. G. Zilboorg (New York, 1924); also cf. Clarke, *Pattern of Expectation*, p. 233.

28 Coover, 'Morris in Chains', p. 47.

29 Clarke, *Pattern of Expectation*, p. 40.

30 Barthelme, 'The Balloon', *The New Yorker* (16 April 1966), pp. 46–8.

31 Cf. H. G. Wells, *The Shape of Things to Come: The Ultimate Revolution* (London, 1935), pp. 218–19.

32 It thus also reverses the Hegelian version of the history of civilisation, in accordance with Foucault's view (and those of, say, Deleuze and Guattari) on the problems of totalising knowledge.

33 Foucault, 'Questions on Geography', p. 69.

34 Foucault, 'Two Lectures', p. 81.

35 Dostoevsky, *The Brothers Karamazov*, trans. D. Magarshack (London, 1958), I, 304; also quoted in Clarke, *Pattern of Expectation*, p. 232.

36 See Foucault, 'Truth and Power', p. 126.

Chapter 7   The politics of fear

1   See my *Literature of Terror*, pp. 121–7, 256–63; and Franco Moretti, 'The Dialectic of Fear', *New Left Review*, 136 (Nov. – Dec. 1982), 67–85.

2   Cf. the deployment of 'adjuvancy' in Tzvetan Todorov, *The Fantastic: A Structural Approach to a Literary Genre*, trans. Richard Howard (London, 1973).

3   See D. R. Hofstadter, *Gödel, Escher, Bach: An Eternal Golden Braid* (Brighton, 1979).

4   It is not necessary to return to Marcuse for substantiation here; see Deleuze and Guattari, *Anti-Oedipus*, pp. 345–65.

5   See Foucault, 'Two Lectures', pp. 103–8.

6   This structure, which is the structure of trauma, is best explicated in J. Laplanche and J.–B. Pontalis, *The Language of Psycho-Analysis*, trans. D. Nicholson-Smith (London, 1980), pp. 465–9.

7   Cf. my *Blake, Hegel and Dialectic* (Amsterdam, 1982), pp. 224–40.

8   See, e.g., Nick Roddick, 'The Strong shall Inherit the Earth: Disaster Movies in the Seventies, (paper delivered at 'Image, Idiom and Ideology in Popular Theatre, Film and Television' conference, University of Kent, 1977).

9   I am relying here on the theory of fascination developed in Thomas Elsasser, 'Narrative, Acceleration, History: Towards a Theory of Fascination' (unpublished paper, University of East Anglia, 1983); crucially, that as we learn under specific historical conditions 'to project and articulate our experiences and our subjectivity in forms and modes that dispense with temporally stable categories . . . fantasy [becomes] the central mode of experience, but no longer constituted in opposition to the temporal modes ('reality', history, psychic or sexual identity) but as their substitute and surrogate' (p. 1).

10   See my *Literature of Terror*, pp. 352–3.

11   Yeats, 'Meditations in Time of Civil War', in *Collected Poems* (London, 1950), pp. 230–1.

12   Thomas, *The White Hotel* (London, 1981), p. 116.

13   See, e.g., Foucault, *The Archaeology of Knowledge*, trans. Sheridan Smith (London, 1972), pp. 50–5; and Lacan, *The Four Fundamental Concepts*, pp. 203–15.

14   Cf., e.g., Raymond Williams, 'Marxism, Structuralism and Literary Analysis', *New Left Review*, 129 (Sept. – Oct. 1981), 51–66.

15   I am referring here particularly to the wider argument in Dworkin, *Pornography*.

16   See my *Literature of Terror*, pp.240–5, 249–55.

17   See Freud, *The Interpretation of Dreams* (1900), in *Standard Edition*, vol. IV, pp.122–33.

18   See, e.g., Gramsci, *The Modern Prince and Other Writings*, trans. L. Marks (New York, 1957), pp. 72–5, 121–5, 186–7; and Foucault, *Archaeology of Knowledge*, pp.64–70.

19   We might make, for instance, a comparison between Bruno's dismissals of the transcendental and insistence on the discursive structure of the real in the Introductory Epistle to *On the Infinite Universe and Worlds* (1584), reprinted in D. W. Singer, *Giordano Bruno: His Life and Thought* (New York, 1968), pp. 229–49, and Foucault's statements on method in, e.g., *The Birth of the Clinic*, pp. xii–xix.

20   See, of course, Fredric Jameson, *The Prison-House of Language* (Princeton, N. J., 1972), e.g., p. 195.

21   Blake, 'London' (c.1794), in *Poetry and Prose*, pp. 26–7.
22   See Lucien Goldmann, 'Criticism and Dogmatism in Literature', in *The Dialectics of Liberation*, ed. D. Cooper (Harmondsworth, Middx., 1968), p. 146.
23   See Adorno, 'The Sociology of Knowledge and its Consciousness', in *Prisms*, pp. 37–9.
24   See Adorno, 'Freudian Theory and the Pattern of Fascist Propaganda', in, e.g., *The Essential Frankfurt School Reader*, ed. A. Arato and E. Gebhardt (New York, 1978), pp. 118–37.
25   See, e.g., Ian McEwan, 'Butterflies', in *First Love, Last Rites* (London, 1975), pp. 61–74; and Adam Mars-Jones, *Lantern Lecture* (London, 1981).

Chapter 8   W. S. Graham: constructing a white space

1   See, e.g., Michael Schmidt, *A Reader's Guide to Fifty Modern British Poets* (London, 1979), pp. 297–304.
2   Cf. Barthes, *Writing Degree Zero*, trans. A. Lavers and Colin Smith (London, 1967), e.g., pp. 80–4.
3   Thomas Blackburn, *The Price of an Eye* (London, 1961), p. 131.
4   Coover, 'The Hat Act', in *Pricksongs and Descants*, pp. 194–206.
5   'The Narrator', in Graham, *Collected Poems, 1942—1977* (London, 1979), p. 38.
6   Graham, 'The Narrator', in *Collected Poems*, p. 39.
7   Graham, 'Over the Apparatus of the Spring is Drawn', in *Collected Poems*, p. 15.
8   Graham, 'There was when Morning Fell', in *Collected Poems*, p. 20.
9   Graham, 'I, No More Real than Evil in My Roof', in *Collected Poems*, p. 24. A relevant comparison would be, of course, with Ted Hughes, 'Hawk Roosting', in *Lupercal* (London, 1960), p. 26.
10   Graham, 'His Companions Buried Him', in *Collected Poems*, pp. 32–3.
11   Calvin Bedient, *Eight Contemporary Poets* (London, 1974), p. 162.
12   Graham, 'The White Threshold', in *Collected Poems*, p. 77.
13   Graham, 'The Children of Lanarkshire', in *Collected Poems*, p. 57.
14   Graham, 'The Search by a Town', in *Collected Poems*, pp. 51–2; cf. Blake, 'The Mental Traveller'.
15   Graham, 'Three Poems of Drowning', in *Collected Poems*, p. 73.
16   Graham, 'Two Love Poems', I, in *Collected Poems*, p. 65.
17   See Freud, *The Ego and the Id* (1923), in *Standard Edition*, vol. XIX, p. 57.
18   Graham, 'The Nightfishing', in *Collected Poems*, p. 105.
19   Bedient, *Eight Contemporary Poets*, p. 168.
20   See John Jones, *John Keats's Dream of Truth* (London, 1969), e.g., pp. 225–6.
21   Which is, of course, one aspect of the processes of supplementarity which Derrida describes: see, e.g., *Of Grammatology*, pp. 111 ff., 144 ff.
22   Graham, 'Letter II', in *Collected Poems*, p. 111.
23   Graham, 'Letter V', in *Collected Poems*, pp. 120–1.
24   Graham, 'Baldy Bane', in *Collected Poems*, p. 137. The relevant comparison

for this mode of mythologisation is with the sadistic Glaswegian porn-ography of a book like Alexander Trocchi, *Thongs* (London, 1971).

25   Graham, 'Malcolm Mooney's Land', in *Collected Poems*, p. 143.
26   Graham, 'The Beast in the Space', in *Collected Poems*, p. 147.
27   The allusion is perhaps not as unlikely as it sounds; one of the messages the 'Great Beast' Aleister Crowley tries to convey in *Diary of a Drug Fiend* (London, 1922) and elsewhere is that magic has to do with the mastery and manipulation of linguistic and quasi-linguistic codes.
28   'The Terror of Blue John Gap', in *The Conan Doyle Stories* (London, 1929), pp. 506–25.
29   Graham, 'The Beast in the Space', in *Collected Poems*, p. 148.
30   Graham, 'The Lying Dear', in *Collected Poems*, p. 149.
31   Graham, 'Dear Who I Mean', in *Collected Poems*, p. 151.
32   Graham, 'The Constructed Space', in *Collected Poems*, p. 152.
33   Graham, 'Malcolm Mooney's Land', in *Collected Poems*, p. 145.
34   Graham, 'The Dark Dialogues', in *Collected Poems*, p. 158.
35   Graham, 'Approaches to How They Behave', in *Collected Poems*, pp. 170–1.
36   Graham, 'Clusters Travelling Out', in *Collected Poems*, pp. 185–6.
37   Jameson's brilliant account of the problems of structuralism in *The Prison-House of Language* is deeply relevant to the nature of Graham's enterprise.
38   Douglas Dunn, 'For the Love of Lumb: New Poetry', *Encounter*, L, 1 (Jan. 1978), 82.
39   Graham, 'What is the Language Using Us for?', in *Collected Poems*, pp. 195–6.
40   Graham, 'Imagine a Forest', in *Collected Poems*, p. 196.
41   Graham, 'A Note to the Difficult One', in *Collected Poems*, p. 199.
42   Graham, 'Language Ah Now You Have Me', in *Collected Poems*, p. 200.
43   Graham, 'Ten Shots of Mister Simpson', in *Collected Poems*, p. 203.
44   See below, pp. 161–3.
45   Graham, 'Enter a Cloud', in *Collected Poems*, p. 212.
46   See *Contemporary Poets of the English Language*, ed. Rosalie Murphy (Chicago, 1970), p. 436.
47   The films which spring to mind most immediately are Fassbinder, *Fear Eats the Soul* (1973) and Herzog, *The Enigma of Caspar Hauser* (1974).
48   Graham, 'The Third Lesson', in *Collected Poems*, p. 223.
49   Graham, 'Implements in Their Places', in *Collected Poems*, p. 236.
50   Graham, 'Implements in Their Places', in *Collected Poems*, p. 246.
51   Graham, 'Implements in Their Places', in *Collected Poems*, p. 251.

Chapter 9   Some cultural materials

1   See Freud, *Interpretation of Dreams*, pp. 370, 392–4.
2   I am thinking here of the peculiar manipulations of pleasure in Anthony Burgess, *A Clockwork Orange* (1962).
3   Cf., e.g., Robert A. Hipkiss, *Jack Kerouac: Prophet of the New Romanticism* (Kansas, 1976), pp. 15–28.
4   As is evident from the 'magical' status *as writing* of texts such as Robert

Foster, *The Complete Guide to Middle-Earth* (London, 1978); *Tolkien and the Critics*, ed. N. D. Isaacs and R. A. Zimbardo (Notre Dame, Ind., 1968).

5 Ernest Mandel, *Marxist Economic Theory*, trans. B. Pearce (London, 1968) is the standard work; see also Stephen P. Dunn, *The Fall and Rise of the Asiatic Mode of Production* (London, 1982) for the recent history of the concept.

6 Analyses of this phenomenon have mainly followed the lines set out in Perry Anderson, 'Origins of the Present Crisis', *New Left Review*, 23 (Jan. – Feb., 1964), pp. 26–53.

7 Cf. Derrida, 'From Restricted to General Economy: A Hegelianism without Reserve', in *Writing and Difference*, trans. A. Bass (London, 1978), pp. 251–77.

8 See, e.g., Fisher, 'In the Wall', in *Poems 1955—1980*, pp. 107–9.

9 The relevant contrast is with Borges, 'The Library of Babel', in *Labyrinths*, ed. D. A. Yates and J. E. Irby (Harmondsworth, Middx., 1970), pp. 78–86.

10 The world, of course, of Melville's Bartleby: see Melville, *Billy Budd, Sailor, and Other Stories* (Harmondsworth, Middx., 1970), pp. 57–99.

11 These topics clearly connect back to the issues Lessing is addressing in *Sirian Experiments*.

12 Cf. the transformations in Bainbridge, *Dressmaker* and *A Quiet Life*.

13 There is a large literature on this topic; one of the more recent contributions is Wally Seccombe, 'Marxism and Demography', *New Left Review*, 137 (Jan. – Feb., 1983), 22–47.

14 See Barthes, *Mythologies*, trans. Lavers (London, 1973), pp. 111–21.

15 *Eastern Evening News* (January, 1976).

16 There are connexions here with perceptions in Barthes, *Camera Lucida: Reflections on Photography*, trans. Howard (London, 1982).

Index

adolescence, 59, 61, 70, 72, 150, 160, 169
Adorno, Theodor, 127-8, 177
advertising, 1, 5, 41
alienation, 31, 43, 46, 83, 93, 108, 145, 180; generational, 46, 83, 156
Ananke, 119
Anderson, Perry, 187
Armageddon, 11
authorities, the, 75, 100, 104, 117, 120
authority, 45-8, 53, 62-3, 92, 100, 102, 116; anxiety about, 4, 92

Bach, Johann Sebastian, 114
Bainbridge, Beryl, 2, 59-77, 179, 181, 187
Ballard, J.G., 2, 9-27, 41, 133, 175
Barth, John, 1, 2, 59
Barthelme, Donald, 2, 107-10
Barthes, Roland, 4, 126, 177, 187
Beckett, Samuel, 45, 52, 151, 153
Bedient, Calvin, 134, 137
Blake, William, 20, 21, 23, 39-40, 118, 136, 161, 178
Blavatsky, Madame, 85
Bleasdale, Alan, 113
Borges, Jorge Luis, 187
Bradbury, Ray, 100-2, 176
Brecht, Berthold, 153
Breuer, Joseph, 180
brothers, 21
Bruno, Giordano, 127, 184
Burgess, Anthony, 186

Calvino, Italo, 39
capitalism, 4, 21, 78, 92, 114, 115, 158, 167
Carpenter, John, 121
Carter, Angela, 2, 28-42, 59, 177
castration, 11, 64, 105, 107
Causley, Charles, 161
Chaffey, Don, 52

chaos, 34, 103
childhood, 50, 57, 61, 70, 72, 114
childing, 51
children, 39, 46, 47, 57, 66, 71, 72, 73, 84, 87, 89, 90, 91, 115, 118, 119, 126, 163
child-worship, 118
chimerisation, 13, 67
China, the Chinese, 34, 48, 86, 92
Christianity, 85, 87
cinema, 40, 41, 67, 152
city, the, 12, 13, 33, 34, 39, 46, 48, 50, 52, 53, 86, 99, 102, 105, 106, 108-9, 112, 175
Cixous, Hélène, 64
Clarke, I.F., 182
class, 48, 72, 75, 78, 92, 114, 116, 120, 125, 127-8, 154
claustrophobia, 31, 52, 70, 117
coherence, see holistic fictions
computers, 12, 25, 99, 105, 107, 111
Conan Doyle, Arthur, 144
condensation, 105, 131, 159, 172, 181
conservatism, 33, 65, 70, 119, 126-7, 160
Coover, Robert, 105-7, 132
Crowley, Aleister, 186
Crusoe, Robinson, 17

Dalek, 11
daughters, 66, 73, 164
death-wish, 24, 47, 87, 125
deconstruction, 4, 132
Defoe, Daniel, 126
Deleuze and Guattari, 183
dependence, 52, 87, 88, 169
deprivation, 2, 32, 54, 59, 61, 65, 75, 76, 78; sensory, 156; sexual, 108
Derrida, Jacques, 2, 4, 180, 185
desexualising, 73
desire, 10, 13, 25, 29, 31, 33-4, 40, 41-2, 45, 51, 57, 60, 62, 64, 66, 67, 70, 93, 97,

188

109, 110, 131, 154, 157, 161, 163, 166;
acrobats of, 30; discourses of, 108; manipulation of, 117; object of, 30, 32
desire for supersession, 22
desire for transcendence, 58
determinism, 10, 30, 44, 123, 124, 133
Dickens, Charles, 168
disaster movies, 17, 120
displacement, 42, 65, 74, 75, 92, 103, 107, 114, 118, 123, 159, 168, 181; textual, 60, 106, 177
divided self, 42, 93
Donne, John, 137
double, the, 86-7
'double conscience', 180
double image, double symbol, 40, 100
doubling, 36-7, 53, 66, 72, 74, 87, 110, 169
dream, culture of, 116
dream of power, 89
dreams, 10, 15, 22, 24, 25, 46, 67, 87, 88, 103, 106, 116, 125, 138-9
dream-time, 10
dream-world, 161
Dresden, 89
Dunn, Douglas, 148
Dworkin, Andrea, 184

echolalia, 85
ecology, 19, 25
education, 1, 4, 47, 54, 100
ego, 15-16, 18, 56, 58, 83, 107, 113, 114, 116, 133, 135, 137, 141, 146, 165; male, 26, 106
Einstein, Albert, 91
Eliot, T.S., 43
Elsasser, Thomas, 184
empire, see imperialism
entropy, 19
envy, 46, 74, 91, 102
erasure, 9, 17, 55, 68, 180
Eros, 40, 106, 117
Escher, M.C., 114
evolution, 10, 48, 51, 124
exchange, 120, 158, 167
exchange value, see exchange

familial conditioning, 75
familial decay, 50
familial text, the, 63
familial violence, 24

family, the, 21, 23, 30-1, 46, 47, 57, 61, 66, 71, 76, 81, 84, 88, 90, 102, 103, 107, 118-19, 154, 164-7, 170-3; extended, 83
family entrapment, 2
fascination, 184
Fassbinder, Rainer Werner, 152, 186
father: interdictions of the, 40; name-of-the-, 173
fathers, 21-2, 25, 62-3, 68, 70, 75-6, 77, 81, 82, 90, 92, 107, 119, 154, 156, 164; absent, 63, 156; substitute, 66, 154
female, the, 26, 36, 38, 40, 51, 57, 64, 65, 69, 73, 92, 102, 105-6, 114-15, 161, 166
female homosexuality, 40
female subject, 65, 69
female superego, 64
femininity, 20, 36, 38, 41, 63-5, 67-9, 114, 155
feminism, 41, 52
film, 3, 46, 113, 114-22, 123, 127, 154-7
Fisher, Roy, 161, 178
Foucault, Michel, 3, 4, 97-8, 101, 109, 110-11, 117, 123, 124, 125, 126-7, 163, 176, 182, 183, 184
freedom, 37, 43-4, 53, 57, 71, 76, 78, 101, 105, 106, 123, 134, 153, 168, 169
free will, 10
freezing, 15, 16, 22, 40, 61, 66, 76, 81, 143, 151, 173, 181
Freud, Sigmund, 4, 24, 28, 33, 43, 44, 59, 92, 119, 122-4, 125, 127, 128, 175, 179-80
frozen forms, see freezing
future, the, 1-2, 5, 9, 13, 17, 21, 34, 44-5, 53, 60, 62, 66, 86, 97-9, 100-2, 104-5, 107, 108, 110, 111-12, 114, 117, 121, 123, 125, 131, 171, 181, 182

gaze, the, 23, 28, 36, 77, 119
gender, 19, 27, 28-9, 34, 35, 41, 42, 51, 57-8, 59, 69, 72, 102, 114, 122, 124-5
gender differentiation, 76, 154
gendered narrative, 37
generational conflict, 21, 50, 57, 72, 88, 90
Genet, Jean, 17
glass, 12, 36, 37, 177
global constructions, see holistic fictions
Gödel, Kurt, 114
Goldmann, Lucien, 127
Graham, W.S., 3, 131-53

Gramsci, Antonio, 125
Greenham Common, 125
group behaviour, 50, 53-4, 61, 72, 85, 89, 107, 120, 159, 181
group consciousness, group mind, 49, 53, 55, 56, 58, 86
group dreams, 88
group fantasies, 110
groups, ideal, 49
guilt, 19, 56, 61, 84, 123, 139, 147, 150
Gunn, Thom, 161

Hawkes, John, 2
Hegel, G.W.F., 118, 176, 179, 183
Hemingway, Ernest, 102
hermaphroditism, 28, 90
hero, the, 26, 83, 99, 104, 111, 114-17
heroic, the, 12, 17, 18, 31, 39, 72, 113, 127, 154, 156-7, 159
Herzog, Werner, 152, 186
Hesse, Hermann, 83-4
Hiss, Alger, 89
Hitler, Adolf, 60, 74
holistic fictions, 2, 3, 4, 14, 15, 29, 33, 138, 154, 183
holocaust, 19, 47, 85, 126, 128
homesickness, 83-5, 88
homosexuality, 37, 40, 154, 160
Hopkins, Gerard Manley, 136, 139, 151
Hughes, Ted, 133, 161, 185
Hurt, John, 120

imperialism, 25, 47, 54-5, 91, 106, 108, 124, 160-1, 167, 168
incest, 32, 86
information technology, 9, 99, 111
instincts, the, 10, 15, 24, 53, 118, 159
interpretation, 17, 19, 41, 46, 58, 61, 62, 63, 66, 69, 76, 83, 86, 109, 110, 124-5, 163
intolerable, the, 5, 26, 83, 85, 89, 92
invasion, fears of, 11, 72-3, 114, 117, 125

Jameson, Fredric, 127, 186
Jesus, 172
Johnson family, 170-4
Joyce, James, 43, 90
Jung, C.G., 175, 177

Kafka, Franz, 30
Keats, John, 139
Kennedy, John F., 13

Kerouac, Jack, 157
Khan, Kubla, 39
King, Stephen, 117-19
Kneale, Nigel, 183
Kojève, Alexandre, 179
Krafft-Ebing, Richard von, 59, 179
Kubrick, Stanley, 117-19, 121

labour, 4, 39, 80, 92, 118, 127, 158, 164, 165
Lacan, Jacques, 2, 3, 123, 124, 176, 177, 178, 180, 181
language, 3-4, 10, 13, 30, 33, 42, 49, 62, 81, 92, 118, 131-3, 135-7, 139-41, 144, 146-51, 153, 159-60, 175
language of power, 66
languages of commerce, 78
Lanyon, Peter, 142
Larkin, Philip, 131, 151, 161-3, 176
Laurel and Hardy, 88
Lawrence, D.H., 158
leadership, 18, 48, 72, 120
Leavis, F.R., 158
Leboyer, Frédéric, 177
Lessing, Doris, 2, 43-58, 59, 82, 86, 134, 187
Lincoln, Abraham, 88
literary, the, 1-2, 45, 97, 99, 100, 107, 113, 122, 151, 154, 163
'locomotor ataxia', 80
love, 12, 13, 76-7, 78, 84, 103, 146
Lovell, Terry, 178

McCarthy, Joseph, 89
McEwan, Ian, 128
male, subjugation of the, 63
male domination, 44, 64, 125, 155
male ego, 26, 106
male fantasies, 35-6
male psyche, 38
Mansfield, Jayne, 13
Manson, Charles, 24, 82-3, 85
Marcuse, Herbert, 31
marriage, 51-3, 68, 72, 74, 115, 117-19, 165
Mars-Jones, Adam, 128
Marx, Karl, 43, 44
masculine aspiration, 18
masculine narrative, 38
masculine power-structures, 36, 102
masculinisation, 27
masculinity, 18, 38-40, 51-3, 59-60, 65-6,

69, 70-1, 73, 105-7, 114-15, 120, 124-5, 126, 154-5, 157, 166, 168-9, 173, 179
matriarchy, 40
maturation, 27, 64, 65, 77, 119, 168
maturity, 46, 47, 64, 65, 87, 114, 116
Melville, Herman, 187
men, 19, 51, 53, 66, 67, 76, 80, 102, 157, 181
Meriden, 158
militarism, 25, 51-2, 156
military, the, 12, 18, 19, 35, 53, 79, 97, 103, 115, 120, 158
military intelligence, 104
mirroring, 12, 17, 32, 35-7, 38, 40, 57, 63, 72, 79, 81, 101, 109, 119, 154, 180, 181
Mitchell, Juliet, 179
monetarism, 113, 120
Monroe, Marilyn, 13, 25
Moorcock, Michael, 176
'moral majority', the, 40
Morris, William, 52, 158
motherhood, 74
mother-murder, 63
mothers, 21, 37, 38, 40, 62, 66, 67, 68, 76-7, 81, 93, 107, 119, 155, 157, 171, 181
music, 39, 102, 114
mysticism, 45, 56, 63, 159
myth, 1, 20, 25, 39-40, 47, 49, 51, 60, 91, 107, 121, 122, 168, 186; Freudian, 119
myth-making, 154
myth of the Fall, 50
myths of heroism, 39
myths of new beginnings, of origins, 48, 91
myths of solitude, 17

Nabokov, Vladimir, 59
name, the, 11, 26, 30, 37, 102, 103, 104, 123, 173
name-changing, 66, 175
nameless, the, 13, 38, 41, 62, 69, 75, 82
naming, 92, 126, 145, 169
narcissism, 125
narcotics, 35, 167
Neame, Ronald, 120
Nemo, Captain, 32
Nixon, Richard, 89, 90
nostalgia, 49-50, 102, 155, 158, 168
nuclear catastrophe, 1, 10, 24, 121-2
nuclear fusion, 27
nuclear war, 11, 51, 122

Nuremberg, 90

objectification, 23, 69-70, 76, 155, 179
O'Brien, Flann, 29, 33
Oedipus, 29, 44, 88, 143
onanism, 27
order: forces of, 32; wish for, 2, 34, 140
Other, the, 11, 17, 30, 35, 52, 60, 63-4, 69, 71, 76-7, 79, 111, 140, 151, 159, 168, 169, 179, 180
overpopulation, 15, 24, 47, 55, 103
Ozymandias, 12

'panoptism', 98, 111
paranoia, 37-8, 79, 89, 108
parapraxis, 33, 180
parental absence, 61
parental conditioning, 88
parents, 47, 59, 70, 71, 84, 107, 114, 118, 156, 163; substitute, 75, 156
patriarchy, 44, 89, 125, 126, 173
Paul, Saint, 115
Pearl Harbour, 116
Pentagon, the, 12, 85
phallic, the, 22, 51, 64, 65, 66, 106, 125
phallocentrism, 177, 180
phallomorphism, 26, 35
phallus, 25, 31, 36, 42, 89
photography, 14, 77, 173
Pinter, Harold, 52, 69
Pirie, David, 179
pity, 78
Plath, Sylvia, 161
Plato, 41
pleasure, 5, 11, 33, 41, 42, 53, 60, 68, 73, 98, 101, 102, 104, 106, 111-12, 117, 119, 126, 156, 157, 163, 167, 186; textual, 98, 101, 111
Polo, Marco, 39
pornography, 64, 76, 81, 124
postmodernism, 1, 78
poverty, see deprivation
Powell, Michael, 22
prefiguration, 122, 124
primal scene, the, 60, 87, 119, 168, 179
projection, 30, 41, 97, 108
psychosis, 59, 60, 179
Pynchon, Thomas, 1, 2, 99, 176

racism, 75, 84, 116
radioactivity, 12, 14
redundancy, see unemployment

Reich, Wilhelm, 28, 31
resource greed, 24
resource starvation, 15, 91
resources, 21, 48, 61, 77, 87, 120, 159;
    search for, 12; technology of, 11
Rigney, Barbara K., 178
ritualism, 88, 118
robots, 25, 79
romanticism, 43, 75, 107, 111, 118, 153,
    158
Russell, Ken, 154-7

Sade, Marquis de, 42
Safouan, Moustapha, 181
Sage, Lorna, 178
scarcity, 76, 119, 127
Schatt, Stanley, 181
schizophrenia, 85
Scholes, Robert, 175
science, 26, 54, 98, 106, 108, 116
science fiction, 9, 79
scientists, 10, 13, 16, 106
scopophilia, 64
Scott, Ridley, 119-21
search for origins, *see* teleological fictions
Sekely, Steven, 122
sexlessness, asexuality, 155, 161
sexual curiosity, 19
sexuality, 4, 12, 26-7, 28-9, 41-2, 51, 53,
    57, 64, 66-7, 80, 92, 115, 117-19, 122-
    3, 145, 155-6, 179, 181
sexual liberation, 157
sexual objects, 76
sexual violence, 75
Shelley, P.B., 175
sibling rivalry, 22
siblings, 71, 76, 107
Siegel, Don, 121
silence, 4, 49, 61, 71, 92, 116, 131, 145,
    153, 156, 179
sisters, 21, 63, 70, 93, 180
social democracy, 56
socialism, 56, 92
sons, 114, 155, 164, 166
sovereignty, 17, 97, 101, 106, 107, 111,
    159
Spielberg, Steven, 114-17
splitting, 69, 72, 75, 76
subject, the, 3, 15, 17-18, 28-9, 32, 36, 58,
    65, 75, 77, 99, 103, 106, 107, 110-12,
    123-4, 164, 165, 180; deconstruction of
    the, 132

subject-formation, 123
subjectivism, 150
subjectivity, 9, 24, 34, 41, 75, 105, 108,
    148
subject-positions, 5, 164, 172
substitute gratification, 5, 165
suburb, the, 19, 20, 162
Sue, Eugène, 113
superego, 64, 159
surveillance, 15, 20, 55, 97-112, 117, 119,
    153, 164-5, 176
survival, 15, 46, 77, 116, 120-1, 126-8,
    164, 171
sword-and-sorcery, 30

Tanner, Tony, 181
Taylor, Jenny, 178
technicians, 18, 54, 111, 134, 144
technological change, 3, 120
technology, 10, 11, 12, 15, 24-5, 30, 40,
    52, 55, 78, 103, 113, 114, 116, 121
teleological fictions, 3-4, 30, 74, 84
television drama, 113
terrorism, 50
Thanatos, 32, 40, 67, 128, 160
theosophy, 85
Thomas, D.M., 122-5, 127, 128
Thomas, Dylan, 131, 136-7, 151
Thomas, R.S., 161
Titan, 25
Todorov, Tzvetan, 183
Tolkien, J.R.R., 157-61
totalitarianism, 32, 34
totem, 85, 119, 181
transference, the, 84, 118, 153
trauma, 26, 48, 59, 60, 64, 70, 85, 92, 114,
    115, 126, 155, 181, 183, 184
trauma, birth, 74, 181
Trocchi, Alexander, 186
Truffaut, François, 116

uncanny, the, 160
unconscious, the, unconscious process, 2-
    5, 13, 28, 30, 34, 36, 45-6, 48, 56-8, 62,
    66, 69, 71, 100, 102, 131, 154, 159, 161,
    181; structure of the, 3, 47, 62
unconscious fears, 117
unconscious of the text, 31
unconscious wishes, 1, 3, 73, 110
undifferentiation, wish for, 4, 17, 19, 27,
    42, 73, 90
unemployment, 53, 107, 125, 162

unnaming, 150
urban, the, *see* city, the
use-value, 15, 19

vampirism, 20, 30, 47, 141
Verne, Jules, 99
Vietnam, 84, 116
Volney, Count, 175
Vonnegut, Kurt, 2, 78-93, 102-5, 133

Wall of Death, 14
Watergate, 89
Wayne, John, 24
Wells, H.G., 55, 108

Wilson, Harold, 56
Wodehouse, P.G., 168
womb, 17, 37, 38, 42, 168
womb envy, 102
women, 1, 18, 19, 35-6, 38, 41, 42, 43,
    51-4, 60, 64, 67, 69-70, 72-3, 76, 102,
    106-7, 115, 120, 124, 126, 157, 166,
    169, 173, 180
Wyndham, John, 183

Yeats, W.B., 122

Zamiatin, Eugene, 106